MW00426196

the new

West Highland White Terrier

The West Highland White Terrier is naturally endowed with an abundance of charm and good humor. These qualities, combined with convenient size, appealing looks, intelligence and the desire to please, have made the breed universally loved. The model here is Ch. Whitehaus Double Trouble, owned by Nancy Spelke and bred by Shirley Jean Niehaus and Shirley Goldman. *Missy Yuhl*

the new

West Highland
White Terrier

Daphne S. Gentry

HOWELL
BOOK
HOUSE

Howell Book House

A Simon & Schuster Macmillan Company
1633 Broadway
New York, NY 10019

Macmillan Publishing books may be purchased for business or sales or promo-
tional use. For information please write: Special Markets Department, Macmillan
Publishing USA, 1633 Broadway, New York, NY 10019.

Library of Congress Cataloging-in-Publication Data
Gentry, Daphne S.
    The new West Highland white terrier / by Daphne S. Gentry.
        p.   cm.
    Includes bibliographical references (p. 243).
    ISBN 0-87605-356-8
    1. West Highland white terrier.   I. Title.
SF429.W4G46   1998
636.755--dc21   98-12606
                                             CIP

10 9 8 7 6 5 4 3 2 1

Book Design: George McKeon
Cover Design: Michele Laseau

To Mrs. John T. Marvin
One of the West Highland White Terrier's longest-standing friends
and an ongoing inspiration to all who love the breed.

A Westie always knows the right mood for the right moment. *Richard P. Mason*

Contents

A zest for living is proverbial with Westies. Here Allison Platt's "Sprite" pauses just long enough during her TDX training to flash her winning smile for the photographer. *Sue Ammerman*

This handsome group consists of (from left) Am., Can. Ch. Dawn's Up 'N Adam, Am., Can. CDX, CG, with his daughters Ch. Dawn's Vivacious Vivia'N, Country Girl Up 'N At It and Ch. Country Girl Up 'N Arrogant. They are all owned by Dawn Martin. *Chet Jezierski*

Foreword

The West Highland White Terrier and Howell Book House share a long history. In May 1961, we published the first edition of *The Complete West Highland White Terrier* by John T. Marvin, truly a household name wherever this endearing breed is known. That landmark book went through four editions, the last appearing in September 1977, and during that period Westie enthusiasts came to rely on the "Marvin book" as both a reference and a teaching tool of the highest integrity.

Time, like any good Westie, never stands still, and there has been a long-standing need for an in-depth book on this popular breed. That need has now been satisfied with the publication of *The New West Highland White Terrier*. This new book brings the breed's story to the present, introducing a host of outstanding dogs and the people who have raised the Westie to new heights. There are two new grooming chapters that will help any owner make the most of his or her own dog. There are chapters on Westies in Obedience, Agility, Tracking and Earthdog activities that prove any member of this breed can become a couch potato only if allowed to get away with it.

In sum, we respectfully offer *The New West Highland White Terrier* to friends of the breed as the book for today, with the expectation that it will prove a worthy successor of what has gone before.

In this Foreword it is appropriate to make mention of the author in the context of what she would not say about herself. To know Daphne Gentry is to know a true scholar. A historian by training and profession, she applies her enthusiasm for recording events to the other great love of her life—the West Highland White Terrier. Anyone who becomes actively involved in the Westie fancy comes to know Daphne Gentry. She is always there for her breed, and nothing she is ever asked to do for the breed is too much. Her list of achievements is given under her profile, but it is her personal love of the breed that truly sets her apart. She has successfully infused that feeling into every page of this book, and this will particularly endear the result of Daphne's labors to all who share their lives with "Colonel Malcolm's favorite."

As I did in 1977 for the final edition of *The Complete West Highland White Terrier*, I wholeheartedly recommend the first edition of *The New West Highland White Terrier* to every fellow Westie enthusiast, prospective owner and student of the breed. You are sure to enjoy owning and learning from it as much as Daphne Gentry has enjoyed writing it.

Seymour N. Weiss
WHWTCA Columnist
AKC Gazette

The author, Daphne S. Gentry. *Missy Yuhl*

The Author

Daphne Gentry, a North Carolinian who has lived in Richmond, Virginia, since 1964, purchased her first West Highland White Terrier as a companion in 1972; her first champion came in 1976 and her first litter arrived a year later. She has bred or co-bred about twenty-five Westies who have successfully completed their championships; of these, several have also had Sweepstakes and Specialty wins. Daphne has judged Sweepstakes for a number of regional clubs, the Canadian national Specialty and the West Highland White Terrier Club of America roving Specialty Sweepstakes, and has been elected to judge the 1999 national WHWTCA annual Sweepstakes in 1999, a most coveted honor.

Daphne Gentry has been a member of the WHWTCA since October 1973 and has been editor of the Club's quarterly publication, *Westie Imprint,* since 1991; she served as president 1989–1990, and is currently a member of the Board of Directors. She is a three-time recipient of the WHWTCA President's Award. Daphne is also a member of the WHWTC of Greater Washington, of which she is secretary and Specialty coordinator, and the WHWTC of Indiana. She serves on the Board of Directors of the Westie Foundation of America, is a member of her local all-breed and Obedience clubs and has held various offices and committee positions in each.

Daphne Gentry holds a Master's degree in history from the University of North Carolina at Greensboro. She has been employed at the Library of Virginia since 1964, either as an archivist or historian, and is now assistant editor of *The Dictionary of Virginia Biography*. She is the author of *Dog Art: A Selection from the Dog Museum* and is editor of *Sirius*, the Museum's newsletter.

A gathering of Westies in the ring at the West Highland
White Terrier Club of America national Specialty is the
focus of rapt attention.

To the delight of all who know and love the breed,
today's Westie is a dog of many talents. It comes from a
long tradition as a working terrier and manages to fit perfectly into our supercharged lifestyle.

chapter 1

Profile of the West Highland White Terrier

The West Highland White Terrier, affectionately known as the Westie, is a small, game, well-balanced, hardy-looking terrier native to the Scottish Highlands. There, and in the Western Islands, where jagged, bare rocks stand out on challenging hillsides forming rough terrain wherein fox and badger are a constant threat to game, was the perfect climate for the development of a dog able to go to ground and drive vermin into the open. Such a dog needed to be relatively small yet robust, to have a thick, wiry and almost waterproof double coat, short strong legs and feet, powerful jaws and, most importantly, a bottomless reservoir of courage. Such is the description of that dog we to-day know as the West Highland White Terrier.

While the origins of some breeds are easily traced, that of the Westie is not. There are, of course, many and varying claims, ranging from the Westie descending from those legendary Spanish white terriers that were kept aboard ships to kill rats and who swam ashore following the defeat of the Spanish Armada in 1588 to being simply the white variation of the Cairn or Scottish Terriers. Those who follow the story line that the Westie descends from those dogs surviving the Armada defeat claim that the *terrieres* or *earthe dogges* James I (1566–1625) requested be sent to a friend in France from Argyll were in truth the forerunners of the Westie. Truthfully, however, the origins of the breed are cloaked in the clouds that hang over the Highlands from which it came.

While it is unlikely that the actual origin of the West Highland White Terrier will ever be determined, the breed was well on its way to being strongly defined by the mid-Victorian period. The art of Sir Edwin Landseer (1802–1873) depicted dogs that resemble the Westie on at least two occasions: his *Dignity and Impudence*, painted in 1839, includes a head study of a small white dog with prick ears, dark eyes and nose and an alert, inquisitive expression, while his *Waiting*, sometimes called *Highland Dogs* (about 1839),

The West Highland White Terrier was developed as an earth dog and still maintains an instinctive keenness for the work, as demonstrated by this pair owned by Ann Budge.

McIvor of Springmeade (Ch. Conejo Barone ex Nancy of Springmeade), owned and bred by Marguerite Van Schaick, strikes a rugged pose in this rare photo, circa 1915.

These no-nonsense Highland workers circa 1905 make up a *Scottish Eleven*. Note the wide variation in types and carriage of ears and the four couples chained together.

Dignity and Impudence by Sir Edwin Henry Landseer (1839) is loved by Westie fans the world over. The model for the Westie here, "Scratch," was a friend of the artist.

shows a small dog with a light-colored coat, prick ears, black nose and slightly bowed-out left front leg in the foreground. Gourlay Steele, in his *Dandie Dinmont and His Terriers*, painted in 1865, portrays three white dogs with Westie characteristics, and John Emms' *The Warrener's Pony and Terrier and Puppy*, painted in 1876, depicts a bitch and young puppy obviously of the West Highland stamp.

In literature as in art, breed patrons find support for early origins. As early as 1774, Oliver Goldsmith described the terrier as "a small kind of

In *Dandie Dinmont* (1865), artist Gourlay Steele includes three white terriers of the Westie stamp in the group.

"The Warrener's Pony and Terrier and Puppy" (1876), *by John Emms.*

hound, with rough hair, made use of to force the fox and badger out of their holes; or rather to give notice by their barking, in what part of their kennel the fox or badger resides." In 1800, Sydenham Edwards in *Cynographia* noted that terriers occurred in several varieties, with the "most distinct [being] the crooked-legged and the straight-legged; their colors generally black . . . though they are sometimes reddish-fallow or white or pied. The white kind have been in request of late years." In 1829, another writer, speaking of the rough-haired Scotch terrier as opposed to the smooth English terrier, noted that the Scotch "is generally low in stature, seldom more than twelve or fourteen inches in height with a strong muscular head rather large in proportion to the size of his body, and the muzzle somewhat pointed; . . . he is generally of a sandy color or black . . . when white or pied, it is a sure mark of impurity of the breed."

Other writers have not viewed the white dog with as much disdain, witness one report that the Scotch terrier had rough harsh hair and was "generally dirty white" and another that the Scotch variety of terrier was short of limb and had a wire-haired coat "of a white or sandy color." In the final decade of the nineteenth century, the oft-quoted Captain Mackie described the Poltalloch terriers, those that would soon be called Westies, as being of a "linty white color, cream in an otherwise white dog and the skin of the body is generally pigmented." The same writer noted a "dorsal line of cream or fawn" in the dogs he saw.

Development of the Modern Westie

In the Scottish Highlands, terriers were strictly utilitarian dogs; they never were intended for lap-sitting. While the dogs did not tend livestock, they did help entrap the fox and badger that were a constant threat to that livestock as well as the rats that invaded the farm yards and grain supplies. These dogs routinely accompanied their masters on hunts for those same vermin and made a great difference in the sanitation of home and homestead. The Westie had its loyal adherents among several nineteenth-century Highland families, each of which had its own name for the breed.

Among the earliest proponents of the breed, if not the earliest, were the Malcolms of Poltalloch. Modern breed literature tends to credit Colonel Edward Donald Malcolm (1837–1930) with developing the breed, although Malcolm himself gave credit to his father, John Malcolm (1805–1893), and grandfather, Neill Malcolm (1769–1837). Ian Zachary Malcolm (1868–1944), son of Colonel E.D. Malcolm, stated that the dogs were kept on the family's Argyllshire estate as early as the 1830s. According to one oft-told story, in the 1860s, while hunting, Colonel Malcolm accidentally shot to death one of his favorite reddish-brown terriers when he mistook it for the rabbit he sought; from that point, he vowed to breed for the white-tinged coat only. Another story relates that it was not until 1906, when the English Westie Club adopted the breed Standard that called for white coats, that Malcolm ordered

Colonel E.D. Malcolm with a Poltalloch group in the early 1900s.

his kennel manager to breed for pure white, eliminating the creamy tint in his dogs' coats. The truth probably lies somewhere in between, as photographs taken in the 1890s show the white dogs on the estate grounds.

Among the rivals to the Malcolms was one Dr. Americ Flaxman of Fifeshire, who owned a Scottish Terrier bitch whose litters included white pups. At first these white pups were destroyed, but eventually Flaxman decided to breed them. Within several generations, after about ten years, Flaxman had developed a strain of white dogs with dark pigment. Flaxman's contributions to the breed, however, are seldom recognized today. Another whose contributions are many but whose name is itself little noted was George Clarke, a man employed as head keeper at several Scottish estates. Eventually Clarke ended up at Roseneath, the seat of the Duke of Argyll; there the dogs Clarke brought with him were bred with care and crossed with local terriers to develop the strain named after the Duke's estate.

These two strains, Poltalloch and Roseneath, evidently were similar in appearance, as the names were used interchangeably around the turn of the twentieth century. Partly in an effort to foster good will about the dogs, Colonel Malcolm championed the adoption of a name that credited the area in which the dogs were developed rather than those who developed them. Recognition of the area came in the name adopted when the Kennel Club of

England accepted the Standard of the breed in 1906: The name was fixed upon as the West Highland White Terrier. In 1907 the breed was recognized as being purebred and the first registrations were accepted. The next year, the first breed champion was recognized in a 2-year-old dog named Morven.

The Westie Comes to the New World

The breed found its way across the Atlantic early in the twentieth century, even before it had been recognized under its current name in England. The individual who imported the first Westie may, like the origins of the breed itself, be cloaked in anonymity, but certainly a case can be made for that person to be Mrs. H.M. Harriman, although Mrs. Robert Low Bacon and Robert Goelet each laid claims to having been the first to import a Westie to the United States. At the Westminster Kennel Club's 1906 show, Mrs. Harriman exhibited three dogs under the breed classification of Roseneath Terriers; one had been whelped in 1903 in England and the other two, of which Mrs. Harriman was the breeder, were born in January 1905. Thus Mrs. Harriman clearly had the breed on these shores by 1904. The other two Roseneath Terriers exhibited at the 1906 Westminster were owned by Mrs. Archibald S. Alexander and had been whelped in England. Mrs. Bacon based her claim on having imported a dog called "White King" in 1907, clearly after the breed was present in this country but well before the date of 1913 that Mr. Goelet stated he imported his first West Highland. Many of the first Westies to come to the United States were never registered with The American Kennel Club; in fact, none of the five entered at that 1906 Westminster show were!

The American Kennel Club accepted the first registrations for its stud book in 1908 under the Roseneath Terrier designation, with the first dog so registered being Mrs. Clinton E. Bell's English-bred "Talloch." Within a year, however, the breed's name in both the stud book and show catalogs was the one we know it by to this day: West Highland White Terrier; the first actually to be registered under that breed designation was the bitch "Sky Lady," who along with her son and another bitch were imported by R.D. Humphreys and Philip Boyer. The first Westie to be registered in Canada was named Calehaig and had been whelped in Scotland; he was brought to Canada the year following his 1908 birth. It was another three years before shows including classes for the breed were held in Canada.

Through the years, the Westie has enjoyed success in all elements of dog events. In the conformation ring, the breed won its first all-breed Best in Show with Ch. Clarke Hill's Snooker, a dog owned by Miss Claudia Phelps, who achieved that honor at the Ladies Dog Club (Massachusetts) in 1921. In 1942, the bitch Ch. Wolvey Pattern of Edgerstoune, owned by Mrs. John G. Winant, was the first of the breed to take top honors at the Westminster Kennel Club. Twenty years later, Ch. Elfinbrook Simon, under the banner of Wishing Well Kennels, captured Best honors at this same show and, with the rosette, the

Ch. Clarke's Hill Snooker, the first Westie to win a Best in Show in the United States.

attention of a country; the popularity of the breed rocketed with Simon's win. During the early 1970s, Mrs. B.G. Frame's Ch. Pinmoney Pedlar, under the guidance of handler George Ward, won fifty Bests, an achievement that stood for a quarter century. It was not surpassed until 1993, when Ch. Round Town Ivan the Terror, breeder-owned by Amelia Musser and handled—again—by George Ward, won magical number fifty-one. Ivan was retired early in 1996, having won a total of seventy-six all-breed Bests in Show.

The first Westie to obtain an Obedience degree was Mrs. A.S. Monroney's Robinridge Bimelick, who got his Companion Dog title in 1942, followed by his breed championship later the same year and his Companion Dog Excellent title the next. In 1956, Mrs. Margaret Barr's Katie McLeod became the first Westie to earn a Utility Degree. In recent years the breed has participated in the event for which it was originally bred, the working terrier events sponsored by The American Working Terrier Association and, more recently, The American Kennel Club's Earth Dog Trials; several Westies have already won advanced degrees in this event.

Today the West Highland White Terrier can be found as a standout in Conformation and Obedience competition, making the divots fly from the earth at den trials and successfully following the message of a scent in the tracking field. It is also to be found in nursing homes in the role of therapy dog and as a companion to families of one and families of a dozen; but wherever he is found, the dog exhibits that "no small amount of self-esteem" that sets him apart and endears it to all those who are privileged to know him.

Ch. Wolvey Pattern of Edgerstoune, owned by Mrs. J.G. Winant and bred by Mrs. C.C. Pacey, was the first Westie to win BIS at Westminster. The year was 1942.

Ch. Elfinbrook Simon, owned by Wishing Well Kennels and bred by Mr. and Mrs. A. Mitchell, followed Pattern's Westminster triumph in 1962.

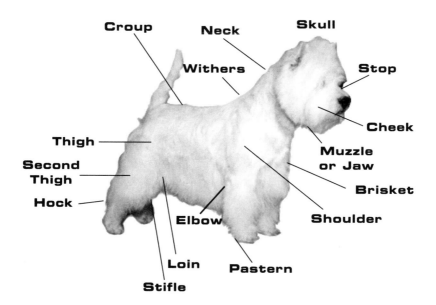

Blueprint of the West Highland White Terrier

chapter 2

The Standard of the West Highland White Terrier

When the West Highland White Terrier was recognized by the American Kennel Club in 1909, it was necessary to create a written Standard, or a word picture, by which dogs could be judged either in the show ring or in the breeder's mind. This Standard was written by the members of the West Highland White Terrier Club of America and was based on the Standard recognized by the Kennel Club in England. Indeed, the two Standards were almost identical, as can be seen below, where the English Standard is shown indented under the 1909 American document.

The breed Standard has been changed several times over the years: in 1948, 1950, 1968 and 1988; in 1995 the Standard was not so much changed as was the format in which it was contained. Few of the changes implemented were drastic; they served rather to clarify points and rectify ambiguities existing between practice and theory. Falling into this latter category is the treatment of grooming. The 1909 Standard stated that "the dog should be shown strictly in natural condition, no trimming being allowed," whereas the current Standard calls for the dog to "be neatly presented, the longer coat on the back and sides trimmed to blend into the shorter neck and shoulder coat." Nevertheless, the general type and conformation of the dog have not been altered through the changed Standards, as a comparison of the Standards of 1909 and 1988 demonstrates.

STANDARD OF POINTS OF THE WEST WHITE HIGHLAND TERRIER, 1909

[with the Standard as adopted by the West Highland White Terrier Club of England shown indented]

The Standard of the West Highland White Terrier describes a dog that has always been the sworn enemy of vermin and the faithful friend of man. In appearance and demeanor, the breed should look like both. An example is Ch. Cruben Melphis Chloe, a well-known winner of the 1950s, owned by Wishing Well Kennels. *Tauskey*

The general appearance of the West Highland White Terrier is that of a small, game, hardy-looking terrier, possessed with no small amount of self-esteem, with a varminty appearance, strongly built, deep in chest and back ribs, straight back, and powerful quarters on muscular legs, and exhibiting in a marked degree a great combination of strength and activity. The coat should be about 2½ inches long, white in color, hard, with plenty of soft undercoat, and no tendency to wave or curl, and the dog should be shown strictly in natural condition, no trimming being allowed. The tail should be as straight as possible and carried gaily, and covered with hard hair, but not bushy. The skull should not be too narrow, being in proportion to the terribly powerful jaw, but must be narrow between the ears. The ears should be as small and sharp pointed as possible, and carried tightly up, but must be either erect or semi-erect and both ears must be exactly alike. The eyes of moderate size, dark hazel in color, widely placed rather sunk or deep set, with a sharp, bright, intelligent expression. The muzzle should be proportionately long and powerful, gradually tapering towards the nose. The nose, roof of mouth, and pads of feet distinctly black in color.

No. 1. The general appearance of the West Highland White Terrier is that of a small, game, hardy-looking terrier, possessed with no small amount of self-esteem, with a varminty appearance, strongly built, deep in chest and back ribs, straight back, and powerful quarters on muscular legs, and exhibiting in a marked degree a great combination of strength and activity. The coat should be about 2¼ inches long, white in colour, hard, with plenty of soft undercoat with no tendency to wave or curl. The tail should be as straight as possible and carried not too gaily, and covered with hard hair, but not bushy. The skull should not be too broad, being in proportion to the powerful jaws. The ears shall be as small and sharp-pointed as possible, and carried tightly up, and must be absolutely erect. The eyes of moderate size, dark hazel in colour, widely placed, with a sharp, bright, intelligent expression. The muzzle should not be too long, powerful, and gradually tapering towards the nose. The nose, roof of mouth, and pads of feet distinctly black in color.

The White West Highland Terrier has come down built on what may be called the "fox lines", a straight limbed, rather low, active-bodied dog, with a broad forehead, light muzzle and underjaw, bright and intelligent eye, and a remarkable look of interest. There is a very unfortunate tendency to judge by what is called the "Scottish" Terrier Standard. The judges have their eyes filled with the Scottish Terrier type with its heavy long face and so-called strong jaw, and prefer mongrels that show it to the real "Simon Pure" West Highland type.

COLOUR—White
   No. 2. Colour.—Pure white; any other colour objectionable.

COAT—Very important, and seldom seen to perfection. Must be double coated. The outer coat consists of hard hair, about 2½ in. long, and free from any curl. The under coat, which resembles fur, is short, soft, and close. Open coats are objectionable.

No. 3. COAT—Very important, and seldom seen to perfection; must be double coated. The outer coat consists of hard hair, about 2 inches long, and free from any curl. The under coat, which resembles fur, is short, soft, and close. Open coats are objectionable.

SIZE—Dogs to weigh from 14 lb. to 18 lb., and bitches from 12 lb. to 16 lb., and measure from 8 in. to 12 in. at the shoulder.

No. 4. SIZE—Dogs to weigh from 14 to 18 lbs., and bitches from 12 to 16 lbs., and measure from 8 to 12 inches at the shoulder.

SKULL—Should not be too narrow, being in proportion to his powerful jaw, proportionately long, slight domed, and gradually tapering to the eyes, between which there should be a slight indentation or stop, eyebrows heavy. The hair on the skull should be from ³/₄ in. to 1 in. long, fairly hard.

No. 5. SKULL—Should not be too narrow, being in proportion to his powerful jaw, not too long, slightly domed, and gradually tapering to the eyes, between which there should be a slight indentation or stop, eyebrows heavy, head and beck thickly coated with hair.

EYES—Widely set apart, medium in size, dark hazel in colour, slightly sunk in the head, sharp and intelligent, which, looking from under the heavy eyebrows, give a piercing look. Full eyes and also light-colored eyes are very objectionable.

No. 6. EYES—Widely set apart, medium in size, dark hazel in colour, slightly sunk in the head, sharp and intelligent, which looking from under the heavy eyebrows give a piercing look. Full eyes and also light-colored eyes are very objectionable.

MUZZLE—Should be powerful. The jaws level and powerful, and teeth square or evenly met, well set and large for the size of the dog. Black in colour.

No. 7. MUZZLE—Should be nearly equal in length to the rest of the skull, powerful and gradually tapering towards the nose, which should be fairly wide. The jaws level and powerful, the teeth square or evenly met, well set and large for the size of the dog. The nose should be distinctly black in colour.

EARS—Small, carried erect or semi-erect, but never drop, and should be carried tightly up. The semi-erect ear should drop nicely over the tips, the break being about three-quarters up the ear, and both forms of ears should terminate in a sharp point. The hair on them should be short, smooth (velvety), and they should not be cut. The ears should be free from fringe at the top. Round-pointed, broad, and large ears are objectionable, also ears too heavily covered with hair.

No. 8. EARS—Small, erect, carried lightly up, and terminating in a sharp point. The hair on them should be short, smooth (velvety), and they should not be cut. The ears should be free from any fringe at the top. Round pointed, broad, and large ears are objectionable, also ears too heavily covered with hair.

NECK—Muscular, and nicely set on sloping shoulders.
No. 9. NECK—Muscular and nicely set on sloping shoulders.

CHEST—Very deep, with breadth in comparison to the size of the dog.
No. 10. CHEST—Very deep, with breadth in porportion to the size of the dog.

BODY—Compact, straight back, ribs deep and well arched in the upper half of rib, presenting a flattish side appearance. Loins broad and strong. Hind quarters strong, muscular, and wide across the top.
No. 11. BODY—Compact, straight back, ribs deep and well arched in the upper half of ribs, presenting a flattish side appearance, loins broad and strong, hind quarters strong, muscular and wide across the top.

LEGS AND FEET— Both fore and hind legs should be short and muscular. The shoulder blades should be comparatively broad, and well sloped backward. The points of the shoulder blades should be closely knit into the backbone so that very little movement of them should be noticeable when the dog is walking. The elbow should be close into the body, both when moving or standing, thus causing the fore leg to be well placed in under the shoulder. The fore legs should be straight and thickly covered with short, hard hair. The hind legs should be short and sinewy. The thighs very muscular, and not too wide apart. The hocks bent and well set in under the body, so as to be fairly close to each other, either when standing, walking, or running (trotting), and when standing, the hind legs, from the point of hock down to fetlock joint, should be straight or perpendicular, and not far apart. The fore feet are larger than the hind ones, are round, and covered with short hard hair. The foot must point straight forward. The hind feet are smaller, not quite as round as fore feet, and thickly padded. The under surface of the pads of feet and all the nails should be distinctly black in colour. Hocks too much bent (cow hocks) detract from the general appearance. Straight hocks are weak; both kinds are undesirable, and should be guarded against.
No. 12. LEGS AND FEET—Both fore and hind legs should be short and muscular. The shoulder-blades should be comparatively broad, and well sloped backwards. The points of the shoulder-blades should be closely knitted into the backbone, so that very little movement of them should be noticeable when the dog is walking. The elbow should be close in to the body both when moving or standing, thus causing the fore leg to be well placed in under the shoulder. The fore legs should be straight and thickly covered with short hard hair. The hind legs should be short and sinewy.

The thighs very muscular, and not too wide apart. The hocks bent and well set in under the body, so as to be fairly close to each other either when standing, walking, or trotting. The fore feet are larger than the hind ones, are round, proportionate in size, strong, thickly padded, and covered with short hard hair. The hind feet are smaller and thickly padded. The under surface of the pads of feet and all the nails should be distinctly black in colour. Cow hocks detract from the general appearance. Straight or weak hocks, both kinds are undesirable, and should be guarded against.

TAIL—Six or seven inches long, covered with hard hair; no feather; as straight as possible, carried gaily, but not curled over back. A long tail is objectionable.

No. 13. TAIL—Five or six inches long, covered with hard hair, no feather; as straight as possible, carried gaily, but not curled over back. A long tail is objectionable. On no account should tails be docked, vide K.C. Rule VI.

MOVEMENT—Should be free, straight, and easy all round. In front the leg should be freely extended forward by the shoulder. The hind movement should be free, strong and close. The hocks should be freely flexed and drawn in close under the body, so that, when moving off the foot, the body is thrown or pushed forward with some force. Stiff, stilty movement is very objectionable.

No. 14. MOVEMENT—Should be free, straight, and easy all round. In front the leg should be freely extended forward by the shoulder. The hind movement should be free, strong and close. The hocks should be freely flexed and drawn close in under the body, so that when moving off the foot the body is thrown or pushed forward with some force. Stiff, stilty movement behind is very objectionable.

FAULTS

COAT—Any silkiness, wave or tendency to curl is a serious blemish, as is also an open coat.

No. 1. COAT—Any silkiness, wave, or tendency to curl is a serious blemish, as is also an open coat, and any black, grey, or wheaten hairs.

SIZE—Any specimens under the minimum weight or above the maximum weight are objectionable.

No. 2. SIZE—Any specimens under the minimum weight, or above the maximum weight are objectionable.

EYES—Full or light colored.
No. 3. EYES—Full or light coloured.

EARS—Round-pointed, drop, broad, and large ears, also ears too heavily covered with hair.

No. 4. EARS—Round-pointed, drop, semi-erect, also ears too heavily covered with hair.

MUZZLE—Either under or over shot, and defective teeth.
   No. 5. MUZZLE—Either under or over shot, and defective teeth.

SCALE OF POINTS

	Value
Skull	5
Muzzle	5
Eyes	$7^1/_2$
Ears	$7^1/_2$
Neck	5
Chest	5
Body	10
Legs and Feet	10
The Tail	5
The Coat	$12^1/_2$
Color	$12^1/_2$
General Appearance	15
	TOTAL 100

OFFICIAL AMERICAN STANDARD OF THE WEST HIGHLAND WHITE TERRIER AS REVISED, MARCH 1988

GENERAL APPEARANCE—The West Highland White Terrier is a small, game, well-balanced hardy-looking terrier, exhibiting good showmanship, possessed with no small amount of self-esteem, strongly built, deep in chest and back ribs with a straight back and powerful hindquarters on muscular legs, and exhibiting in marked degree a great combination of strength and activity. The coat is about two inches long, white in color, hard, with plenty of soft undercoat. The dog should be neatly presented, the longer coat on the back and sides trimmed to blend into the shorter neck and shoulder coat. Considerable hair is left around the head to act as a frame for the face to yield a typical Westie expression.

SIZE, PROPORTION, SUBSTANCE—The ideal size is eleven inches at the withers for dogs and ten inches for bitches. A slight deviation is acceptable. The Westie is a compact dog, with good balance and substance. The body between the withers and the root of the tail is slightly shorter than the height at the withers. Short-coupled and well boned.

Faults: Over or under height limits. Fine boned.

HEAD—Shaped to present a round appearance from the front. Should be in proportion to the body.

EXPRESSION—Piercing, inquisitive, pert.

EYES—Widely set apart, medium in size, almond shaped, dark brown in color, deep set, sharp and intelligent. Looking from under heavy eyebrows, they give a piercing look. Eye rims are black.

Faults: Small, full or light colored eyes.

EARS—Small, carried tightly erect, set wide apart, on the top outer edge of the skull. They terminate in a sharp point, and must never be cropped. The hair on the ears is trimmed short and is smooth and velvety, free of fringe at the tips. Black skin pigmentation is preferred.

Faults: Round-pointed, broad, large ears set closely together, not held tightly erect, or placed too low on the side of the head.

SKULL—Broad, slightly longer than the muzzle, not flat on top but slightly domed between the ears. It gradually tapers to the eyes. There is a defined stop, eyebrows are heavy.

Faults: Long or narrow skull.

MUZZLE—Blunt, slightly shorter than the skull, powerful and gradually tapering to the nose, which is large and black. The jaws are level and powerful. Lip pigment is black.

Faults: Muzzle longer than skull. Nose color other than black.

BITE—The teeth are large for the size of the dog. There must be six incisor teeth between the canines of both lower and upper jaws. An occasional missing pre-molar is acceptable. A tight scissors bite with upper incisors slightly overlapping the lower incisors or level mouth is equally acceptable.

Faults: Teeth defective or misaligned. Any incisors missing or several premolars missing. Teeth overshot or undershot.

NECK, TOPLINE, BODY

Neck—Muscular and well set on sloping shoulders. The length of neck should be in proportion to the remainder of the dog.

Faults: Neck too long or too short.

Topline—Flat and level, both standing and moving.
    Faults: High rear, any deviation from above.

Body—Compact and of good substance. Ribs deep and well arched in the upper half of rib, extending at least to the elbows, and presenting a flattish side appearance. Back ribs of considerable depth, and distance from last rib to upper thigh as short as compatible with free movement of the body. Chest very deep and extending to the elbows, with breadth in proportion to the size of the dog. Loin short, broad and strong.
    Faults: Back weak, either too long or too short. Barrel ribs, ribs above elbows.

TAIL—Relatively short, with good substance and shaped like a carrot. When standing erect it is never extended above the top of the skull. It is covered with hard hair without feather, as straight as possible, carried gaily but not curled over the back. The tail is set on high enough so that the spine does not slope down to it. The tail is never docked.
    Faults: Set too low, long, thin, carried at half-mast, or curled over back.

FOREQUARTERS

Angulation and Shoulders—Shoulder blades are well laid back and well knit at the backbone. The shoulder blade should attach to an upper arm of moderate length and sufficient angle to allow for definite body overhang.
    Faults: Steep or loaded shoulders. Upper arm too short or too straight.

Legs—Forelegs are muscular and well boned, relatively short but with sufficient length to set the dog up so as not to be too close to the ground. The legs are reasonably straight, and thickly covered with short hard hair. They are set in under the shoulder blades with definite body overhang before them. Height from elbow to withers and elbow to ground should be approximately the same.
    Faults: Out at elbows, light bone, fiddle-front.

Feet: Forefeet are larger than the hind ones, are round, proportionate in size, strong, thickly padded; they may properly be turned out slightly. Dewclaws may be removed. Black pigmentation is most desirable on pads of all feet and nails although nails may lose coloration in older dogs.

HINDQUARTERS

Angulation—Thighs are very muscular, well angulated, not set wide apart with hocks well bent, short and parallel when viewed from the rear.

Legs—Rear legs are muscular and relatively short and sinewy.
    Faults: Weak hocks, long hocks, lack of angulation, cowhocks.

Feet—Hind feet are smaller than front feet and are thickly padded. Dewclaws may be removed.

COAT—Very important and seldom seen to perfection. Must be double-coated. The head is shaped by plucking the hair to present the round appearance. The outer coat consists of straight hard white hair, about two inches long, with shorter coat on neck and shoulders, properly blended and trimmed to blend shorter areas into furnishings, which are longer on stomach and legs. The ideal coat is hard, straight and white, but a hard straight coat which may have some wheaten tipping is preferable to a white fluffy or soft coat. Furnishings may be somewhat softer and longer but should never give the appearance of fluff.
   Faults: Soft coat. Any silkiness or tendency to curl. Any open or single coat, or one which is too short.

COLOR—The color is white, as defined by the breed's name.
   Faults: Any coat color other than white. Heavy wheaten color.

GAIT—Free, straight and easy all around. It is a distinctive gait, not stilted, but powerful with reach and drive. In front the leg is freely extended forward by the shoulder. When seen from the front the legs do not move square, but tend to move toward the center of gravity. The hind movement is free, strong and fairly close. The hocks are freely flexed and drawn close under the body, so that when moving off the foot the body is thrown or pushed forward with some force. Overall ability to move is usually best evaluated from the side, and topline remains level.
   Faults: Lack of reach in front, and/or drive behind. Stiff, stilted or too wide movement.

TEMPERAMENT—Alert, gay, courageous and self-reliant, but friendly.
   Faults: Excess timidity or excess pugnacity.

Westie People and Their Dogs

Since the West Highland White Terrier was recognized by the American Kennel Club in 1909, there have been many persons involved with the breed—some for a short while and others for much longer. Many of the names that follow carry definite recognition, while others may be the subjects of trivia quizzes.

The Allbee family, of Houston, Texas, purchased their first Westie in 1977 as a Father's Day gift for Gene. Sons Shane and Scott decided it would be fun to show their dog, so off they went to their first show with their rather ungroomed specimen. The other exhibitors, members of the local Westie club, took the youngsters under their care, set up grooming sessions and offered advice on handling, and the dog was ready to be entered in the club's Specialty in March 1978.

Shane laughs that while Shasta never beat another Westie in the breed ring, he did receive a number of wins in Junior Showmanship and eventually earned a CDX title. The Allbees then acquired a bitch puppy from the Tom Wards, who became Ch. Donnybrook's Trudy and, bred to Ch. Ardenrun Andsome of Purston, had a litter of four, all of which finished. Over the next years, they had several generations through her. In 1982, Sophie Roberts offered Shane a young dog she and her late husband had bought from the Lays; their planned year's co-ownership became permanent. Midas was a multiple Specialty and Group winner in the mid-1980s; in 1984 he won the San Francisco Bay Specialty while his daughter, Ashscot Diana, was Winners Bitch. In the late 1980s, Shane got Am., Can. Ch. Sno-Bilt's Eliminator from Jodine Vertuno a full year after seeing him at age 6 months. "Armani" also was a multiple Specialty and Group winner and sired more than thirty champions.

Ch. Sno-Bilt's Eliminator, owned by Shane Allbee and bred by Jodine Vertuno. *Sosa*

Ch. MacLay's MacClare, owned by Shane Allbee. *Missy Yuhl*

Ch. Cedarfell Milk-N-Honey, CD, JE, CGC (Ch. Haweswalton Sportman ex Cedarfell Maple Leaf Rag), owned by Mrs. A. Fleming Austin and bred in England by Muriel Coy.

Vilma Amato, Glenmoor Westies, of Mount Airy, Maryland, became involved in the breed with the purchase of a pet male in 1968; falling in love with the Westie, she returned to the same breeder six months later for a show bitch and purchased one from a repeat breeding of her male at age 5 weeks. Although Vilma showed her for awhile and even bred her once to a champion male, she quickly realized the show bitch purchased at 5 weeks was not of show quality. She then started reading and studying pedigrees. She contacted Ida Weaver for a definite show-quality bitch. While Guinevere had excellent conformation, she was "soft" and did not like to show, but from her first breeding to Bettina King's Ch. Briarwood Blockbuster, Vilma got her first champion: Balan of Glenmoor, a dog that combined the bloodlines of Weaver with those of the old New England lines. To introduce some new blood, Vilma purchased a bitch in England, Ch. Trethmore Twopence-Off. In twenty-eight years with the breed, Vilma has bred twenty-one litters totaling sixty-three puppies, of which she took eleven to their championships; she has finished another eight, several of whom had Sweepstakes and Specialty wins, including Best of Breed. To Vilma, her Ch. Shadowmere of Glenmoor epitomized what she wants to see in a West Highland.

Judy Arenz, of Cincinnati, Ohio, had never been to a dog show when she purchased her first Westie in 1988; instead, she was looking for a companion and selected the breed because they were cute. The breeder of her Snickers made arrangements for a veteran breeder to see the puppy at 6 months old. The assessment was that he should be shown . . . and shown Snickers was. Another local breeder-exhibitor taught Judy the rudiments of grooming and showing. Am., Can. Ch. Lor-E-El's Snickers Bar None, in an extended campaign, achieved national rating and was a Specialty BB and a multi-Group winner, as well as a sire of champions. Judy also purchased a bitch who was finished, and now that she is showing Snickers' progeny, she has selected a kennel name based on Snickers' name: Bar One Westies.

Angeline Austin, Eastfield, of Princeton, New Jersey, has had Westies since early childhood. During the 1930s, when fewer than 100 of the breed registered yearly, her grandmother bought a dog called "Jock" from Edgerstoune Kennels. Angie owned American Cocker Spaniels in the 1950s and 1960s. Never forgetting her childhood companion, however, she contacted terrier handler Clifford Hallmark in the late 1960s and through him acquired Millburn Misty Bern, a character to end all characters. Another Westie, a male named Ashley, by Ch. Braidholme White Tornado of Binate, soon joined Eastfield; when the bitch passed away at age 12, Ashley grieved so badly that Angie knew another dog must join the household. She called Muriel Coy in England and acquired "Emma," Cedarfell Milk-N-Honey, a future champion, dam of two champions including a Canadian BIS winner, dam of three Obedience titlists, and, at age 11, the recipient of both a Companion Dog degree and a Junior Earthdog title, entitling her to a Versatile Dog Award from the WHWTCA. With Martha Black, she co-owned the multiple BIS winner, Ch. Ashgate Alistair of Trewen.

Mrs. Robert Low Bacon, the former Virginia Murray, registered her first Westie in 1909 before her marriage. The dog was "White King," bred in Scotland by C.F. Thompson and whelped in August 1907. She was one of the first to bring Westies to the United States. Her last champion was Edgerstoune Ronny O'Moneymusk, who finished in 1949. As the wife of a New York Congressman, she was able to get the breed favorable publicity. She died in February 1980.

Margaret Barr, of Menlo Park, California, got her first Westies in 1935, Glassary Lassie and Angus McLeod. She bred, owned and trained the first West Highland White Terrier to win the Utility Dog degree: Barr's Katie McLeod, who won her title in September 1956. Katie, whelped August 19, 1948, by Danny Boy ex Frosting Morning, was bred by Frank Radovich. Her program combined lines of Tyndrum, Roseneath, Humby, Huntinghouse, Petriburg and Glenhaven. Mrs. Barr died in January 1984 at age 85.

Barbara and Thomas H. Barrie, O'Peter Pan Westies, now of Rowlett, Texas, got their first Westie while living in New Mexico in 1964. After a move to California, they met Ron Davis at their first dog show. He invited them to a West Highland White Terrier Club of California match; there, their puppy was placed second in an entry of three in the novice class, and the Barries were hooked! Today, thirty-three years later, her trophy—a small tile with a Westie decal—occupies a place in their trophy case. They got their first show bitch from Florence Sherman; Kirk O'The Glen Winsome Wendy did not finish and was bred only once but produced their first champion, Pride O'Peter Pan, who finished in 1969. In 1968 the Barries bought a Simon granddaughter from Ron Davis, Jenessey Paradox O'Peter Pan. Bred to Ch. Elfinbrook Simon, she had four puppies, and three finished. "Penny," a champion herself, had nine puppies, and five finished their championships. Their second Penny—Penelope O'Peter Pan—also produced five champions, was herself a champion, completed her obedience title at 10 years of age and earned her Certificate of Gameness from the American Working Terrier Association, thereby becoming the first top producer to win the Versatile Dog award from the WHWTCA. The highlight of the Barries' Westie experience was the May 1994 day their Playboy O'Peter Pan had a BIS from the classes; Charlie has since had a Specialty BB and was nationally ranked. In thirty-two years of breeding, the Barries have finished twenty-two homebred champions.

Mrs. Clinton E. Bell, of Springfield, Massachusetts, owned the first AKC–registered West Highland White Terrier, though it was registered as a Roseneath Terrier. The dog was Talloch; whelped May 1, 1907, he was bred in England by Mrs. Nana S. Hunter, by Treach Bhan ex Kylach. Five Roseneath Terriers—four males and one bitch—were registered by the AKC in 1908. If Talloch sired a litter, none of the puppies were AKC–registered.

Mary and Vern Bell, Belvar Westies, of Durham, North Carolina, wanted a dog soon after moving into their new home. Vern, just having seen the movie *Patton,* leaned toward the White Bull Terrier, but Mary chose to differ.

Looking through a book, they saw another white terrier and so decided on a Westie. The price difference between a show-quality puppy and one from a pet store led to their purchase of the latter, Windermere of Rosewood, in June 1973. Since this was the first dog Mary had ever owned, she wanted to do things right. After a local groomer offered some advice about plucking, they took Windy to a match where she came in second in a class of two, but, as Mary says, "We were hooked!" Now, deciding they needed a hobby, the Bells looked for a show dog, which they thought they were purchasing later the same year. While Angel did not prove to be show quality, she did produce their first two homebred champions, Belvar's Theodore J. Bear, CDX, in 1976 and Belvar's Oopsey Daisy, CD, in 1978. In the meantime, they were showing Windy in Obedience, who got her CDX. Then Windermere Of Rosewood became the second Westie to get a Tracking Degree. She also had a Certificate of Gameness, and these accomplishments made her the second West Highland White Terrier to receive a Versatile Dog Award from the WHWTCA. By the time the Bells finished their second homebred, they were hooked for good! Breeding only when they want to keep a puppy, they have had a limited number of litters over the years but have finished ten champions, eight being homebreds.

Ruth Birmingham, Loch Crest, of Litchfield, Connecticut, obtained Mistfield Flora MacIvor in 1955 as her foundation and bred on Rachelwood and Rannoch-Dune lines. Flora survived into her teens, occupying the house with four generations of champions. Mrs. Birmingham died on February 27, 1985.

Martha W. and Robert D. Black of Washington Crossing, Pennsylvania, purchased a pet Westie from Polly Walters in 1968; in 1974 they obtained a dog of Polly's breeding, Tyndrum Dartmoor of Trefall, who was, except for his majors, owner-handled to his championship. The first litter bearing their Lockmede prefix was born in May 1982 from Brookline Pennyghael of Mull, who traced to Tyndrum bloodlines. In 1987 Martha obtained a Scottish import, Pilot of Keithhall, who finished his championship in seven shows that summer and, his first time in the ring as a champion, was Best of Breed at the WHWTCA annual Specialty show. Under her kennel prefix of Silvery Dee, Martha, in collaboration with Angeline Austin, Eastfield Westies, campaigned Ch. Ashgate Alistair of Trewen to multiple Bests in Show and Specialty wins during the 1990s.

Robert D. Black of Wrightstown, Pennsylvania, continues the Lockmede kennels, breeding an occasional litter and exhibiting dogs of his breeding. In 1987, his Ch. Jack the Lad of Jopeta from Purston was America's number-one Westie.

Mrs. S. Marge Blue, of Elkhart, Indiana, and later Scottsdale, Arizona, started her Klintilloch kennels in the early 1940s in collaboration with her daughter, Mrs. Marion DeLuzansky, later Marion Williams, with Edgerstoune Ripple, who was to complete her championship in 1946. Bred to Belmertle

Drummond, she produced Klintilloch's first litter on January 23, 1944. Klintilloch kennels produced two BIS winners, including the bitch Ch. Klintilloch Molly Dee, and at least thirty-seven champions bearing the Klintilloch prefix. It was involved as co-breeder or co-owner of at least another dozen champions and provided the foundation stock for several kennels still active today. Mrs. Blue died in April 1980.

James and Elizabeth Boso, Glengloamin, of San Carlos, California, got a bitch puppy as a pet in 1976 from Ann Marie Rose; soon thereafter, they bought a second bitch from the same breeder. While Malarkey's Wee Tiffany was not finished, she did produce the Bosos' first champion, Glengloamin's Jillian, who won the points at two regional specialties. In 1983 they bought Glenfinnan's Something Dandy from Mary Lowry. "Nicky" was a multiple Specialty winner, with a BB from the Veterans class at the 1991 annual WHWTCA Specialty. Nicky and Jillian together had four litters, with at least one Specialty winner in each. In 1988, when Nicky was seven months old, the Bosos bought Holyrood's Hootman O'Shelybay from breeders Marilyn Foster and Judy Francisco; "Manley" won the points at both the Roving and Annual Specialty shows in 1988 and went on to numerous Specialty and BIS wins, including the three Rovings—the last from the Veterans Class in 1997, to retire the Eng. Ch. Pillerton Peterman Memorial Trophy. He was twice BB at the Annual Specialty. Their Ch. Glengloamin's Rise N Shine, co-owned with Gail and Gene Miller, has won the breed at six regional Specialties, once from the classes, and multiple BIS wins. Most of the Bosos' more than twenty-five champions have been homebreds, many with Specialty wins and breed wins at the prestigious Westminster KC show; among the Specialty winners, Glengloamin's Syncopation, a Nicky daughter, had three Specialty wins. Their first home-bred, Jillian, produced seven champions, while Nicky and Manley have sired multiple champions, including many Specialty winners. Nicky is the sire or grandsire of six Westies who have, between them, won 150 all-breed Bests in Show.

Philip Boyer of Mt. Kisco, New York, was co-breeder with R.D. Humphreys of the first West Highland White Terrier litter born in the United States that was registered with the AKC. Again with Humphreys, he owned the first of the breed to become an American champion. Cream of the Skies, born in England on October 4, 1907, and registered there as Clonmel Cream of the Skies, finished his American championship in 1909.

Clare W. Lowe Brumby, Rannoch-Dune, began in 1942 under the single prefix of Rannoch when living in New York and married to Herbert Lowe. The breeding was based on Furzefield, Cruben and Cranbourne lines. Adding "Dune" to the prefix, she also introduced Springmeade and Klintilloch bloodlines. She later married handler and then judge Frank Brumby; after his death she joined S. Marge Blue, and the two grand dames of the Westie world moved to Scottsdale, Arizona. Clare was involved in Westies for more than forty-five years before her death in 1988 at the age of 86.

Mrs. Chester C. Caldwell owned the first Westie to finish its championship in Hawaii: Ch. Rannoch-Dune Dorris. She was by Ch. Mi Laddie of Sharon out of Ch. Rannoch-Dune Ditto, and finished in 1958. The Caldwells showed under the prefix of Piperport.

Sandy Campbell's start in Westies is not quite the normal story: A friend told her of a Washington puppy mill that was being closed down, and the inventory included Westies. Wanting a small dog for her daughter, Sandy "rescued" two bitches, ages five and six years. At the time, Sandy was showing Collies and eventually decided to show the Westies. Of the two bitches, one got an Obedience title and the other, Bluemarc's Heather, finished her championship in the summer of 1974 at age 8. Sandy then purchased Ch. Woodlawn's Rendition from Betsy Finley and bred her twice, first to Ch. Whitebriar Jofane and then to Ch. Merryhart's Honest John. From the Honest John litter came nationally ranked Ch. Woodlawn's Calamity Jane. A bitch from the Jofane litter was bred to Ch. Ardenrun Andsome of Purston, and a bitch from that litter was bred to Ch. Mac-Ken-Char's Irish Navigator; the bitch puppy kept from that breeding was Camcrest Andsomething Else. In 1992 she was bred to Ch. Liberty's Chairman of the Board; the only bitch in the litter, called "PuppyDo," was registered as Camcrest Andsurely Trouble. At 10 months of age she was Winners Bitch at the Specialty show of the WHWTC of Puget Sound; less than one week later, breeder Daphne Gentry placed her Best in Sweepstakes at the WHWHTCA 1993 Roving Specialty in Houston. Two months later she came from the Bred By Exhibitor class to go BB at the Annual Specialty of the WHWTCA. Taking time out for maternal duties, she returned to Montgomery County in 1996, where breeder-judge Tom Ward awarded her yet another WHWTCA Specialty BB, making her the third bitch in breed history to win two national Specialties (the others being White Cloud of Nishkenon, winning from the classes in 1926 and as a champion the following year, and Wolvey Privet of Edgerstoune, again taking her first win from the classes in 1938 and her second as a champion in 1940). PuppyDo is the dam of two champions to date and is a multiple Group winner at all-breed shows.

Janice Carkin, Stonecourt, of Cherry Valley, Massachusetts, got her first Westie in a pet store while Christmas shopping with her children in 1967. They went into the shop and there she was, one ear down, in a cage . . . so off to the Carkin home she went. Janice later took her to Bettina King, the mentor of so many in New England, and the bitch was bred to a Briarwood dog; Janice kept a male from that litter and trained him to his Companion Dog title. Bettina got Janice interested in conformation showing and sold her a male; Briarwood Laird Malcolm died of heartworm disease needing only a major to finish. In 1973 Janice bought a bitch, Dunemoor's Governess, from Ann Taylor, combining the bloodlines of Loch Ness and Twickenton. "Nanny" finished her championship, and in her first litter produced Stonecourt's Tuppence and Stonecourt's Beau Brummel. In the ensuing years, during which Janice has finished eleven champions, she has continued to breed on the lines of Loch Ness, Twickenton, Briarwood and Florentine Locke's Briarton. Once a Stonecourt dog has finished, Janice moves it into Obedience training to prepare for the Companion Dog title.

Monica Carlson, Celtic Westies, of Medina, Ohio, in 1963, while still in college, once saw a green convertible in which sat a white dog; she followed the car and asked the driver what kind of dog it was. Within a week she had located a local breeder with two male puppies and had selected the cute fluffy one over the hard-coated boy, and "Mac" was part of her life for more than fourteen years. Just before Mac's death, Monica decided she wanted a show-quality dog and located breeder Lois O'Brien, whose dogs carried the Loch O'Fee's prefix. This dog, Loch O'Fee's Pirate's Ransom, became her first champion; the bitch Loch O'Fee's Celie, purchased soon thereafter from Ms. O'Brien, finished in Canada and the United States and had a number of Group placements. Breeding the two resulted in a litter of four, two of which finished in both Canada and the United States: Celtic's Dirk and Celtic's Cory. Cory, campaigned in 1987 and 1988, won forty-two Group firsts, five all-breed BIS, and several Specialties. Cory was never bred, but Monica currently has grandchildren from Dirk. Both Cory and Dirk died in January 1996.

Perry Chadwick, Inverary Westies, of Winfield, Illinois, owned Ch. Highland Ursa Major, who won his first two BIS on consecutive weekends in 1947 as well as a Specialty BB the day before his second BIS.

Janis Chapman, Dalraida Westies, of Fairfax, Virginia, lived in England between 1968 and 1972; while there, she saw all these little white dogs everywhere and inquired as to what the breed was. So, having been in England about a year, she did the obvious: went to Harrod's pet shop and bought a bitch puppy, named Bonnie by her children. Shortly thereafter, she passed a pet store that had a litter in the window and bought a male, whom the children named Clyde. Just before coming home, Janis purchased a Melwyn bitch. Settling in northern Virginia, she joined the regional Westie club and was encouraged to show the male by a member who used to live on the West Coast. Thus, Janis' "doggie in the window" became Ch. Clyde of Creag Meagaidh in 1975. In 1981 she got Happiness Iss Rowdee from Kathleen Kurdziolek, and it was that bitch who became her foundation. The homebred Ch. Dalriada Sam I Am, who finished in February 1989, is a multiple Group and Specialty show winner and has sired eighteen champions. In the course of her involvement with the breed, Janis has finished thirteen champions, of which eight have come from the Bred By Exhibitor class. A number have received titles in Canada and/or Bermuda as well, including Sam.

Henry E.H. Chipman, of Madison, Connecticut, was the owner of Charan Kennels, based largely on the descendants of English Ch. Wolvey Poacher, a dog bred by Mrs. C.C. Pacey in 1931. Heavy Poacher blood came in through Eng., Am. Ch. Wolvey Poet of Charan and Eng., Am. Ch. Wolvey Pandora of Charan. Among the outstanding Charan homebreds was Ch. Charan Merry

Am., Can., Bda. Ch. Dalriada Sam I Am (Ch. Happiness Iss Harlee ex Happiness Iss Rowdee), owned by Janis Chapman and co-bred with her by Kathleen Kurdziolek, was a winner and sire of note. *Ashbey*

When Bergit Coady originally came to the United States she worked for an Indiana Scottish Terrier breeder and brought a Westie with her. She is shown in a 1969 photo with that Westie, Ch. Monsieur aus der Flerlage, and the Scottie Ch. Reanda Rocksand.

Whimsy. Although active into the 1950s, the Chipmans were most active during the 1920s and 1930s. Captain Chipman died in January 1955.

Bergit Zakchewski Coady emigrated from her native Germany to England in 1965 to work as the kennel maid for Elizabeth Meyer of Reanda Scottish Terriers; soon Mrs. Meyer suggested that Bergit also learn to trim Westies and sent her to study with Joan Kenney-Taylor of Sollershott. Bergit recalls that Mrs. Kenney-Taylor would groom one side of a dog; they would have lunch, and she would then be expected to groom the other side of the same dog. Attendees at Bergit's grooming seminars will recognize the same technique. In England, she had the opportunity to handle the Westie Monsieur Aus Der Flerlage ("Bobby") to his English championship in less than two months, an event practically unheard of either then or now. In 1968, Betty Malinka of Gary, Indiana, a Scottish Terrier breeder, brought Bergit to the States to work for her. Bergit was able to purchase Bobby before she came over, and he quickly added an American championship to his international titles. He won two all-breed BIS and ten Groups, among many other awards. Bergit bred Westies, finishing five of her own. In 1970, she married and began handling professionally; since then Bergit estimates she has finished almost 300 West Highland White Terriers and has successfully campaigned many top winners. Of her beloved Bobby, she recalls that he always gave 100 percent, never letting her down in the ring.

Crecia Closson, Crannog, of Holderness, New Hampshire, showed Boxers from 1966 until the 1970s. In 1986, for her twentieth wedding anniversary, she decided that, instead of jewelry, she wanted a dog and found herself attracted to Westies—little white dogs that were, in reality, large dogs in small bodies. Her Skaket's Nigel Saunders, bred by Nancy Gauthier, quickly obtained his American, Canadian and Bermudan championships. In the meantime, she got a bitch from Janice Carkin, Stonecourt Kendra of Farrway, who was bred on the English Famecheck lines. From "Kendra" came Ch. Crannog's Luce O' Stonecourt, and from "Luce" came the good producer Am., Can., Ber. Ch. Crannog's Mioscais Maigdean. In 1995 she became the co-owner of Ch. Wynecroft Wild at Heart with breeder Marcia Montgomery; "Gigi" was a multiple Specialty and BIS winner with top ranking in 1995 and 1996. Because of Crecia Closson's strong interest in the Famecheck lines, she became the co-owner, with Alice Shepard, of Ch. Famecheck Aviator.

Edward Danks, of Battison Kennels, Clifton, New Jersey, emigrated to the United States from his native Scotland in 1906 at the age of 25. Establishing his kennels with Taybank imports from England, he exhibited his first Highlander in 1926. Among his dogs was Ch. Battison Beacon, one of the great stud forces of the breed, siring more than a dozen well-known dogs. A judge for many years, Mr. Danks closed his kennels in 1958.

Darlene Cox Davis, Ridgmar Westies, of Porter, Oklahoma, grew up with Pekingese; when it came time to get her own dog, she remembered having been drawn to a picture of a cute little white dog in a book. She found a breeder

Ch. Gulliver of Guilliland, a Scottish import owned by Darlene Cox Davis, had a fruitful career both as a winner and a sire. *Ashbey*

and knowingly bought a puppy with a bad bite because her only interest was in having a companion. At her vet's suggestion she put Davenport's Jigger of Scotch into Obedience training and then competition, where she became the seventh of the breed to earn a Utility title. Attending shows as an Obedience competitor put her into contact with conformation, and she began a lengthy search for a show-quality male. Just before deciding she would not find a dog to her liking, she heard from Chuck and Peggy Lewis that they had a 2-year-old she might like; Darlene finished Lochinmar Laird of Nic Mac to both his championship and CDX. In 1984, after not being actively involved with the breed for almost ten years, she married; the honeymoon was a trip to England, complete with visits to a number of kennels on a quest for Westies. Darlene and Jim returned with two bitches, one of whom finished her championship, and a 2-year-old dog that was obtained from Jimmie Guthrie. Darlene worked a year to get Gulliver of Guilliland ready for competition and finished him at the Southeast Texas Specialty. Once he matured, he was shown during 1986–1988 by Georgia and Bill Harris and was consistently in the Top Ten ratings. "Gully" sired more than six-teen champions who have themselves produced both Sweepstakes and Group winners, including the WHWTCA Sweepstakes winner Ridgmar's Rock N Rye.

Sandy J. Davis, now of Renton, Washington, bought her first Westie in 1968 from Ida Weaver. While interested in showing, she had little initial success in the conformation ring, although she did put Obedience titles on her first Westie. Later, she bought a bitch from Patsy Gustin of Acreages kennel; the original purchase was followed with a half-brother and half-sister to establish her Lanarkstone Westies. Sandy considers the best dog she ever bred Am., Can. Ch. Lanarkstone Winter Witch, a product of a father-daughter breeding (Ch. Clacton's Acreages Coker ex Can. Ch. Acreages Teeter Tot). She is also proud to have owned Am., Can. Ch. Poolmist Philoralia of Valucis, a dog imported from Scotland at age 8½ years who, the month before his tenth birthday, was Best of Winners at the Greater New York Specialty and the next week, after winning the Veteran Dog class at the national Specialty, made the cut in BB competition. "The General," as he was called, was a dog with heart.

Dorinda Dew, now of West Newbury, Massachusetts, got her first Westie in 1965 while her husband was serving in the U.S. Navy. Amy, bred on Maxwelton, Famecheck and Klintilloch bloodlines, was actually bought as a companion for the family's mixed-breed dog. Finally settling in Massachusetts, and on the advice of Katharine Hayward, Dorinda purchased a bitch from Ida Weaver; Weaver's Highland Marrona was bred to Ch. Royal Tartan Glen O'Red Lodge, a Ch. Elfinbrook Simon son. Since then, her limited breeding program has resulted in thirteen champions, including Ch. Tacksman Pipit, who finished with a Group first; in addition, one of her dogs obtained an Obedience title and another a Tracking title.

Mrs. Claire Dixon had been a part of the dog fancy for over forty years in 1951 when she added Westies to the other breeds she maintained at her Long Island estate. Her imported Cruben Moray of Clairedale was BB at three WHWTCA Specialties, the first in 1955 from the classes and again in 1956 and 1958. Her sudden death in 1959 removed a vibrant force from the Westie scene, although a daughter did continue her kennel operations for another ten years.

Tom and Lois Drexler of North Huntington, Pennsylvania, purchased their first Westie from Claire Cardinali in 1970. Bonnie was bred to a Simon son, Ch. Jenessey Sir Scott, and gave the Drexlers their first champion, Taradink Lord Dunsinane. To improve his grooming skills, Tom, an engineer by profession, began sculpting, first in wood, then in ceramic, and finally in porcelain; his pieces were never mass produced— the most ever made of any one piece was ten. Today, Drexler porcelains are highly prized and keenly sought after. Tom Drexler was a WHWTCA President and died in office on March 12, 1984, at the age of 56.

Sue Durcan, Dur-Canty, of Cincinnati, Ohio, got her first Westie in 1974 from Peg Lammert, also of Cincinnati, as a pet. When the breeder saw Duffy at 6 months, she suggested that Sue might enjoy showing him, and soon Sue was hooked. Lammert's MacDuff, heavily bred on Mac-A-Dac, Klintilloch and Rannoch-Dune bloodlines, was the first of Sue's five champions, two of which were homebreds. Her Dur-Canty's Irish Mist was Best in Sweeps at the 1992 Northern Ohio Specialty.

The gorgeous porcelains of Tom Drexler are his permanent legacy to the breed. Collectors of Westie artwork
are quick to snap up these pieces on the rare occasions
they become available.

Neoma and James Eberhardt got their first Westie—the future Am., Can.,
Mex. Ch. Kirk O'the Glen Merryhart—from Florence Sherman in 1963. When
bred to the incomparable Simon, the litter included the Eberhardts' first homebred champion and Specialty winner, Am., Can., Mex. Ch. Merryhart
Pettipants. With an eye for the right dog from the first, the Eberhardts purchased an 8-week-old puppy from Ida Weaver; this dog became the BIS winner Am., Can., Mex. Ch. Weaver's Drummond and, like all their dogs, was
owner-handled to his titles and future accomplishments. Over the course of
time, they purchased three other males, which they used with their homebred females. During the 1960s and 1970s, Merryhart Westies made up more
than seventy-five champions and had innumerable Specialty wins, including
BB at the 1975 Roving Specialty and Sweepstake wins, and consistently made
the top producers lists.

Doris Eisenberg, of southern California, started her Kar-Ric kennels with
Ch. Wigtown Margene as her foundation. Margene produced five champions, who, in turn, produced another eight.

Harry and Eve Ellis, Argyle Westies, of Kansas City, Missouri, began their
long involvement in the breed in the mid-1950s. They owned, among other
winners, Ch. Ellis Bonnie Lady Argyle, a Specialty and Group winner and
dam of four champions, and her daughter Ch. Argyle Lady Macbeth, also a
Group winner.

Robert and Susan Ernst, Sweet Sounds Westies, originally from Weston,
Connecticut, and later Wilmington, North Carolina, began with Principal's
MacGyver, who combined Holyrood and Elsinore bloodlines. Purchased in
1986, he completed his championship with a Group first; during his specials
career, he won multiple Groups and BIS. Coming out of retirement in 1995,
"Mackie" became the oldest dog to win Veteran Sweepstakes at the
WHWTCA Annual Specialty. Following in the footsteps of MacGyver was
Biljonblue's Best of Times, bred by William Ferrara and John Price of
Biljonblue Kennels. "Timer" was shown to more than two hundred breed
wins, multiple Group and Specialty wins from late 1990 to early 1993. In

Ch. Principal's MacGyver, owned by Robert and Susan M. Ernst, was the first winner for his owners' Sweet Sounds Kennels.

Ch. Biljonblue's Best of Times, owned by Robert and Susan M. Ernst.

Ch. Sweet Sounds King O' Rock N Roll, Robert and Susan Ernst's first homebred top winner, has won strongly in Specialty and all-breed competition handled by Kathleen J. Ferris. *Tatham*

1991 the Ernsts obtained their foundation bitch, Sweet Sounds Song of Holyrood, from her breeder, Judy Francisco; once finished, Melody was bred to MacGyver. The three puppies resulting each obtained either Sweepstakes or Specialty victories en route to their championships. One, Sweet Sounds King O' Rock N Roll, a.k.a. "Elvis," finished easily, had multiple Group and Specialty wins and won his first Best in Show in June 1997.

Pam Evans and her sister Dianne Pritchard, of San Jose, California, began Padiwak Westies in 1982 when they sought a Westie pet; their first came from the Sanders' Rime's kennel on a co-ownership. This bitch, referred to lovingly as "Lumpy Louise," did not enjoy showing and as a result, despite her good conformation, did not finish her championship. She did, however, produce well. Her daughter, Padiwak-Rime's Amelia, bred to Ch. Glenfinnan's Something Dandy, produced Padiwak's Centerfold, who was Winners Bitch at the 1988 annual Specialty held in Montgomery County. Her first breeding to Ch. Holyrood's Hootman O'Shelly Bay produced Padiwak's Great Expectations, Winners Bitch at the 1990 annual Specialty. With occasional breeding, Padiwak has bred eight champions and finished three others. In 1990 Pam, especially, began working with her regional club's rescue program.

Maurice Evans, the stage actor and producer, in association with Emmett Rogers, bred and showed Westies under the Whipstick prefix between 1958 and 1966. His professional commitments caused him to cease his breed activity in 1966.

Ruth Faherty, Fairtee, of Hixson, Tennessee, was introduced to Westies in 1962 through television, with the incomparable Ch. Elfinbrook Simon's Westminster BIS win. It was, however, nine years later that her daughter presented her with a Westie as a birthday gift. While Duffy was not shown in Conformation, he was trained in Obedience; while working with Duffy and looking for a show-quality bitch, she was also learning to groom. From her first litter came the Group-winning Ch. Fairtee Simon Pure Pippin. She was the author of *Westies from Head to Tail* (Loveland, Colorado: Alpine Publishing, 1981), a standard reference for breeders and novices alike.

Clarence C. Fawcett, of Kirkwood, Missouri, was a breed enthusiast and illustrator whose drawings grace a trimming chart first appearing in the third edition of *The Complete West Highland White Terrier* (New York: Howell Book House, 1971). "Tex" did oil paintings of some of the top-winning Westies of the 1950s and 1960s, including those of the Marvins and B.G. Frame. He died on February 12, 1988 in his eighty-sixth year.

Jeanne Fawcett established her Forest Glen kennels with husband, Tex, in 1956. She handled her homebred Ch. Forest Glen Simon Sez Be Brisk to a 1966 BIS victory at Columbia, Missouri.

Marilyn Foster, O'Shelly Bay Westies, of Mystic, Connecticut, like many people bought her first Westie for a pet in 1979. Two years later she had decided on the kennel name of Saltcoats and gave that prefix to the bitch she purchased who was to become her first champion, Ch. Saltcoats Holly By

Ch. Forest Glen Simon Sez Be Brisk (Ch. Elfinbrook
Simon ex Ch. Brisk of Forest Glen), owned and bred by
Mrs. C.C. Fawcett. *Welgos of Denver*

Golly. After one litter, she retired to became a beloved pet. In the meantime,
Marilyn learned that another Westie breeder was using the same prefix and
so selected a new name, one that has evolved over time to its present spell-
ing. In 1985 she bought in co-ownership with their breeder, Judy Francisco,
littermates, Holyrood's Ms. Mayhem and Holyrood's Liza With A "Z." The
former, "Shelby," who resided with Marilyn, finished her championship and
was bred to Ch. Glenfinnan's Something Dandy, with a litter of three males
and two bitches resulting; four of those puppies completed their championships and one male, Holyrood's Hootman O'Shelly Bay, was campaigned
under James and Betty Boso's Glengloamin banner. Shelby's second and last
litter resulted in two male puppies, one of whom was Holyrood's Hotspur
O'Shellybay, better known to the fancy as "Ted." In February 1995, Ted won
his fifty-first all-breed BIS, topping the record of Ch. Purston Pinmoney Pedlar
and giving him the second highest BIS record; at the same time, he won his
156th Terrier Group. Ted had eight Specialty Bests, including the Roving
Specialty in 1992 and 1993; his Group and BIS wins have come at some of
the country's most prestigious shows. His champion get include Sweepstakes,
Specialty, Group and BIS winners, including the bitch Ch. Glengloamin's Rise
'N Shine.

 Mrs. Paul (Beulah G.) Frame, of Indianapolis, Indiana, established
Wigtown Kennels in 1942, with foundation stock obtained from Marguerite
Vance; she added Edgerstoune bitches in 1946. Her program continued until
her death in 1975. She joined with Ann McCarty to show under the Wigmac
prefix. The names of B.G.'s dogs read like a *Who's Who in Westiedom*,

Ch. Wigtown Talent Scout, owned and bred by Mrs. B.G. Frame. *Frasie*

Ch. Wigtown Talent Scout, Ch. Rannoch Dune Down Beat and Ch. Purston Pinmoney Pedlar being prominent among them.

Judy Johnson Francisco, after having shown and bred Westies for some years under the Puddintane prefix, obtained Whitemount Frolic TWA as the foundation for her Holyrood prefix in 1979. "Frolic," bred by Muriel Whitman from a Lonsdale-bred bitch by Ch. Jeremy of Windy Hill, finished in 1981, but it was in the whelping box that she made her contributions to breed history. Bred to three different dogs, Frolic produced eleven puppies, of which six daughters became champions. One of those daughters, Holyrood's Liza With A "Z," co-owned with Marilyn Foster but resident with Judy, finished her championship with four Specialty wins and achieved national ranking in 1987. Her progeny have won Sweepstakes and Specialties while their descendants have won Sweepstakes, Specialties, Groups and all-breed Bests in Show.

Virginia Frederick, along with her late husband, Don, Glen Shar, Louisville, Kentucky, got their first Westie from B.G. Frame about 1965. While they did not show Wigtown Nightrider Rebecca, she was bred once. B.G. then offered the Fredericks a dog out of Marge Blue's breeding; this dog, Wigtown Man-power, became their first champion. When active, the Fredericks bred only occasionally and Ginny is now no longer breeding, but she has always had at least one Westie in her home. In fact, she is often kidded about running a resort for senior citizens, including Am., Can. Ch. Lair O'Lyon's Killundine Chip, CD, who spent his final years in her care.

Gary R. Gabriel, L'Esprit Westies, Amboy, Washington, showed Old English Sheepdogs for a number of years before deciding he would like to have a Westie pet. A friend familiar with both breeds, Mona Berkowitz, referred him to a friend in England who had a dog available. Gary insisted he only wanted a companion and had no intention of showing. "Geoffrey" arrived early in 1982 and, because Gary had stopped showing, it was about two years before Mona happened to see the dog. Although he until then had only been clippered, Mona asked if she could start grooming Geoffrey. Gotten into coat, he was shown— straight into the Top Ten ranking for two years in a row; Nozomi's Rainbow Warrior died during the summer of 1997, still Gary's beloved pet. Next, Gary got Waterford of Wyndam and then Tweed Take By Storm, both imports and both multiple Specialty and BIS winners. For a while both Mac and Oliver were campaigned at the same time, but in different areas. Next Gary imported another Swedish-bred dog, Bushey's Mister O'Smash, called Robin. He won the points at the national Specialty and went on to a winning career. A number of bitches owned by Gary and his partner Florence MacMillan also finished and have produced well, but none have been campaigned.

Carolyn Gardner, of Closter, New Jersey, purchased her first Westie as a family pet. Since the bitch was well-bred, Carolyn decided to show her and attained her championship in June 1980. Ch. MacSkathill's Lady Harrison thus became the foundation for Gardner's Westies and was the dam of Carolyn's first homebred champion, Gardner's Morning Glory, a Roving Sweepstakes Best of Opposite Sex winner as a puppy. Her Ch. Gardner's Blk Eye Susan Orion had multiple Group placements and her most recent champion, Gardner's Golden Rod, also did well in the Specialty classes. Breeding on a limited scale, Carolyn has more than a dozen champions to her credit.

Berna and Peter Gaul, BryBern Westies, of Naperville, Illinois, purchased their first Westie from Jodine Vertuno in July 1986. Not planning on showing, they entered Bogie in puppy kindergarten classes and then in conformation classes. Bogie became Ch. Sno-Bilt's Bogart with a Group first, owner handled. In their first litter, born in September 1991, was BryBern's Errol Flynn, recipient of an Award of Merit at the 1993 national Specialty and the sire of multiple champions, and BryBern's White Diamonds, Reserve Winner at the 1993 national Specialty. There have been twenty-one champions, fifteen of which were homebred, including back-to-back Best of Winners at the 1995 and 1996 WHWTC national Specialties.

Nancy Gauthier, Skaket, of North Andover, Massachusetts, purchased her first Westie from a pet store in 1966. As it turned out, there were excellent bloodlines behind the bitch and, along with a second bitch purchased in 1970, she became the foundation for Nancy's breeding. Along with breeding and exhibiting those Westies, Nancy became involved in performance events— Obedience, Tracking and go-to-ground trials—and her dogs hold multiple titles. After finishing his championship in 1974 by taking the points at the club's Roving Specialty, her Ch. Skaket's Chunkies obtained his Utility degree and then his Certificate of Gameness. "Chucky" was the first recipient of the WHWTCA's Versatile Dog Award for achieving titles in three areas.

Ch. BryBern's Errol Flynn, owned by Peter C. and Berna Gaul, a dog that won nicely and went on to produce quality stock. *Booth*

Ch. The Lady Lorna Doon MacDuff, owned by Daphne Gentry and Betty Williams, was the dam of six champions, five from two litters by Ch. Round Town Duke J. Ellington.

Ch. Killundine Made in a Dandy Way (Ch. Glenfinnan's Something Dandy ex Ch. Killundine Shortbread Made), owned and bred by Daphne Gentry and Betty Williams, retired the Hal Aspy Memorial Challenge Trophy for Best of Opposite Sex at the WHWTC of Indiana. *Tim Omer*

He sired a number of champions, his last litter being whelped when he was 14 years old. Through his daughter, Ch. Skaket's Lady MacDuff, he is the grandsire of FCI, Int., Ber., Mex., Can., Am. Ch. Skaket's Candy Man, CDX, TD, CG, TT. "Buster" was BB at the 1981 annual Specialty show at age of 2½ years; returning as a veteran dog in 1988 at the age of 9½ years, he got the nod for the breed from Neoma Eberhardt and went on to a Group second. Although Nancy still has a hand in the Westies, daughter Mitzi Gauthier Beals now shows under the Skaket prefix.

Joan Giancola, Colonial Westies, of Louisville, Kentucky, bought her first Westie as a companion for her only child in May 1984. While purchased as a pet, Jenny proved to have an enthusiasm for the show ring and, being of excellent quality, she was shown by Joan to her single points and then finished by a handler. By the time Jenny was sent off, Joan had purchased a show-quality male from Betty Williams. This dog, Colonial Doon MacDuff Merlyn, finished and has sired a number of champions, including Maxamillion II, bred and owned by Edie Nixon and co-owned by Joan. "Max" earned his championship with three five-pointers, all won at Specialty shows, including the WHWTCA annual Specialty. Although Max was killed in an accident when only 4 years old, he sired a number of champions, including a Group winner. Since 1987, Joan has bred five champions and shown nine Westies in co-ownership to their titles.

April Gieseking, Rise N Shine, of Belton, Missouri, as a school child saved her allowance to buy a dog like the one she had seen in a book—Ch. Wolvey Peach. April's first Westie, acquired in 1963, was her constant companion until it died of cancer at age 11. Fifteen years later she got another Westie. In the spring of 1989 and with the help of the Bob Starkeys of Heartsome Westies, April obtained a 10-month-old bitch of Shari Novak's Whistlewood breeding. The puppy, called Revie, became Ch. Whistlewood's Rise and Shine and was the dam of April's first homebred champion, Rise N Shine Miss Merry Mac. This bitch, in turn, was bred three times: once line bred on her sire's line, once line bred on her dam's line and once outcrossed with each of the breedings, producing a champion. From the outcross breeding came Ch. Rise N Shine's Taylor Made, who has multiple Group placements and Specialty awards. His daughter, Ch.Mi Wee Perfect Impression co-owned by April and co-breeder Pam Johnston, has multiple Sweepstakes (including Montgomery County 1997 and Specialty wins.

Joanne Glodek started Mac-Ken-Char Kennels in Severn, Maryland, with the support of her husband, Joe, in the mid-1960s. In 1968, Ch. Battison's Good Friday, bred by Edward Danks, joined the kennel and from him they got the first champion to bear their prefix, Ch. Mac-Ken-Char's Friday's Child, who finished in 1972 and subsequently sired seventeen champions. In 1974 the Glodeks' import, Ch. Keithall Pilot, was shown to a BIS victory in Puerto Rico by preteen daughter Jaimi. Breeding Pilot to Mac-Ken-Char's Wild Irish produced, in 1980, Ch. Mac-Ken-Char's Irish Navigator, credited as the breed's top sire. Westies bearing the Mac-Ken-Char prefix have won innumerable Sweepstakes, Specialty shows, Groups, and, with Ch. Mac-Ken-Char's Ashscot Liberty's all-breed victory in August 1997 and his WHWTCA BB at Montgomery County in October 1997, their second home-bred BIS and annual national Specialty winner.

Robert Goelet, a British expatriate, ran Glenmere Kennels on his vast estate in Chester, New York. He registered his first Westies in 1910: two dogs and two bitches, all born in the British Isles and all bred by different persons. To Goelet belongs the honor of being the first person in the United States to breed a Westie litter from which an American champion resulted. This was Rumpus of Glenmere, whelped June 17, 1911, out of a dog registered in 1910 (Kiltie of Glenmere) and a bitch registered in 1911 (Rhuellen of Glenmere). For a long while, Goelet was credited with bringing the first Westie to the United States, but recent investigations have indicated that person was in all probability Mrs. H.M. Harriman. Goelet registered his last Westie litter in 1915.

Shirley Goldman, of Thousand Oaks, California, was introduced to Westies by a loaf of bread! In 1954, she found a trade card showing Ch. Inverary Charlemagne enclosed in a loaf of bread and asked for a puppy for her upcoming birthday; with considerable effort, her husband, Robert, found her a puppy from Margaret Jensen. While neither this dog nor their next were of show quality, an interest in and love of the breed flourished. In 1976, 2-month-old Happymac's Li'l Mandy, bred by Roberta Mocabee, was added to the Goldman home and became the foundation of Shirl's Westies; Mandy enjoyed success in the show ring and the whelping box as one of her sons, Ch. Shirl's Beach Boy, had Specialty wins and Group placements. Another bitch purchased from Bobbe Mocabee also produced well for Shirl's Westies: Happymac's Dancealong Dawn, added to the household in 1980, was bred three times to Beach Boy, with the Specialty winners resulting. One of those, Ch. Shirl's Highland Sprite, was the dam of Ch. Shirl's Proud Highlander, to whom the pedigrees of several top winners of the late 1990s trace. While Shirley's kennel closed on her death in December 1994, friends finished her last dog, Ch. Shirl's Fire and Ice, a Sweepstakes winner.

Joan Graber, of Middleton, Wisconsin, knew exactly what she wanted in a Westie: a bitch from the lines of Ch. Elfinbrook Simon. Thus she approached Barbara Keenan and bought a 7-week-old puppy in 1960. This young bitch, Wishing Well's Wee Winklot, finished in 1964 and won at least one Group—almost an unheard-of feat for a Westie bitch at the time. Joan considers her best Westie to have been Ch. Rudh'Re Fionn Sian, who was tightly line-bred on Simon; "Judy" won the Breed at the 1972 Northern Ohio Specialty and went on to take the Group at the all-breed show with which the Specialty was held. Judy had a number of Group placements, with at least five firsts. Her son, Ch. Rudh'Re Glendenning by Ch. Reanda Byline Pisces, is the only male to have won Best in Sweepstakes at both the Roving and

National Specialties of the WHWTCA, doing so at the Roving Specialty in June 1972 under Westie breeder Thelma Adams (Roseneath) in an entry of forty and again at Montgomery County in October 1972 under British breeder Sylvia J. Kearsey (Pillerton) in an entry of forty-seven. That same year, with noted Inez Hartley officiating, both Judy and Dennis were exhibited at Montgomery County, and both were pulled out for further consideration. Joan herself officiated at the breed's annual Specialty show in October 1986.

Nancy Guilfoil, of St. Louis, Missouri, got her first Westie in 1977. Admittedly not of show quality, T.J. MacGillies was shown to his CD title and was being trained in advanced work when an accident ended his career. Nancy then purchased a show-quality bitch from Janet Lindgren named Briarcliff Kiss Me Kate; she finished quickly and inspired Nancy's prefix, Katydid. Next came Biljonblue Belle of Katydid, called TiTi, from Bill Ferrara's and John Price's Biljonblue Kennels. Undefeated to her championship and as a veteran competitor, she produced Nancy's first Group and Sweepstakes winner, Ch. Katydid Krossfire, known as "Stevie." Other sweepstakes winners and some fifteen champions have come from her breeding.

Mrs. R.H. Gustin, Acreage's Westies, of Salt Lake City, Utah, began in Westies in 1960 with the purchase of an 8-month-old bitch bred on Shiningcliff lines from Robert Lowry of Maxwelton Westies; she later bought a male from the same breeder. Although neither dog finished its championship, the male sired Tamlor's Danny O'Dunoon, a 1965 owner-handled BIS winner from the classes. Just before this, Mrs. Gustin purchased an already finished Sweepstakes winner, Ch. Cranbourne Alyssa, from her owner, Barbara Sayres. Her interest extended to Obedience as well as Conformation and during the 1960s, her "Missy" was a High in Trial winner. Early in the 1970s, with children growing up, both Mrs. Gustin's breeding and showing activities slackened, but not her love for and interest in the breed, as she kept at least two Westies until she was able to resume her breeding and showing in 1986.

Joanne Hancock, Ashdown Westies, of San Diego, California, began showing Westies early in 1982; later that year she also acquired a rescue Westie who went on to win a Certificate of Gameness and was shown in Junior Showmanship by Joanne's oldest daughter. Her first champion was Shirl's Topper and Tails, who finished with all majors in March 1986, having been shown only six times. Later that year, she got her foundation bitch, Glengidge Lady Hawk, bred by the Seymour Weisses and selected at only 9 weeks old for Joanne by the experienced eye of Roberta Mocabee. "Tuppence," bred to Ch. Liberty's Chairman of the Board, resulted in Joanne's first homebred champion, Ashdown Willoughby ("Tugman"), while Tuppence's daughter, Ch. Ashdown Wild At Heart ("Chloe"), also bred to the same stud, produced four more homebred champions. In June 1995, at the first Great Western Terrier Association of Southern California Group event, Joanne's Ashdown All For Love won that event's first Group Sweepstakes; "Coco" later finished her championship.

Ch. Glengidge Lady Hawk (Ch. Mac-Ken-Char's Irish Navigator ex Am., Can. Ch. Glengidge Plum Candy). Owned by Joanne Hancock and bred by Helene and Seymour Weiss, was the foundation for her owner's Ashdown Westies.

Ch. Ashdown All for Love, owned and bred by Joanne Hancock, was Best in the first Group Sweepstakes of the Great Western Terrier Association of Southern California. She was shown by her owner to this nice win. *Mitchell*

Dorothy Hardcastle, of Egypt, Massachusetts, never bred Westies but had a lifelong association with the breed through her father, handler Harry Hardcastle. It was he who handled Ch. Clarke's Hill Snooker to the breed's first all-breed BIS. Dorothy was associated with Robinridge Kennels and in fact trained and showed Ch. Robinridge Bimelick to his Obedience titles in 1942 and 1943. She was recognized for her lovely Westie paintings.

Mrs. H.M. Harriman of Westbury, Long Island, was probably the first person to bring the breed now known as the West Highland White Terrier to the United States and to whelp the first litter, in January 1905. This litter was not registered with the AKC. Her Peter the Great, whelped in 1903 by Cheeky ex Ancrum Peach, won Best of Breed in the Roseneath Terrier classes at the 1906, 1907 and 1908 Westminster Kennel Club shows; the dog was never AKC registered.

Katharine Hayward, of North Scituate, Rhode Island, uses the prefix Huntinghouse. She was introduced to the breed by a picture of the 1934 Crufts BB winner, Ch. Edgerstoune Rowdy. Ms. Hayward bought her first Westie—a dog born on July 16, 1935—from Mrs. John G. Winant, from whom she later purchased Edgerstoune Trusty. The foundation of her line was Charan Adair, whom she purchased from Captain H.E. Chipman. Her first litter from this pair was born on December 9, 1950, thus founding Huntinghouse Westies. She owned Ch. Huntinghouse Starmist, for years the breed model in AKC's *The Complete Dog Book*. She bred and owned Ch. Huntinghouse Little Fella, a national Specialty sweepstakes winner and 1968 BIS dog. Katharine Hayward celebrated her hundredth birthday on August 24, 1997.

Jane Esther Henderson campaigned Ch. De-Go Hubert under the hand of Clifford Hallmark; "Hollis" won the parent Specialty, going on to BIS at Montgomery County in 1971 in a monumental downpour. His highly successful career in the ring and as a sire were cut short by his early death, the result of a bee sting.

Harold Heubel and wife, Maura, of Phoenix, Arizona, established the Bel-West prefix in 1977 with the purchase of an Andsome daughter who later finished. Hal imported several dogs from prominent British kennels, including Ch. Purston Primemover, whose daughter Bel-West Buttercup produced thirteen champions, and Ch. Olac Moonpenny of Bel-West, a top-winning bitch for 1988 and 1989, with several Group placements including at least one first, a Specialty BB and Best of Opposite Sex at the 1989 WHWTCA annual Specialty. The Heubels have also bred their own dogs, with Ch. Bel-West's Taco Belle being both a Group winner as well as achieving national ranking.

Florise Hogan, of Rockford, Indiana, established her Flogan kennels on Rannoch-Dune and Klintilloch bloodlines in 1961. Between 1964 and 1975 more than twenty-five Flogan Westies finished their conformation titles, but, as she entered the ranks of judging, she decreased her breeding activity.

Katharine Hayward's Huntinghouse Kennels are truly an institu-
tion in Westies. Shown here are two of Miss Hayward's most celebrated campaigners with their handler, Roberta Campbell: Ch.
Huntinghouse Telstar (left) and Ch. Huntinghouse Little Fella.
Evelyn Shafer

Emilou Hooven, White Watch Westies, of Anderson, Indiana, set out to
find a Sealyham Terrier; in the course of her quest, she contacted Ann
McCarty, who referred her to Westie breeder Marguerite Vance in Indianapolis. Emi got her first Westie, a male called "Dudley," in the fall of 1942. Soon
after, she had her first date with her future husband, George; Dudley met
George on the front porch and sat up on his haunches, and George was won
over . . . to the breed as well as to Emi. After the war, Emi got a young bitch
from Marguerite and had one litter, all of whom were sold. Later, the Hoovens
purchased littermates sired by Down Beat from B.G. Frame; one lived to age
16½ and, after her death, Emi spent two years looking for another, as she
had decided she would like to become more actively involved in competition.

In January 1988, the Hoovens got Dylan-Dale Crystal Edition—"Casey," who finished and was bred to Ch. Nor'Westie's Wee Mac. Emi kept a bitch, while two others were sold and finished by their new owners. Over a fifty-five-year period the Hoovens have owned nine different Westies. Now, that's longevity!

R.D. Humphreys of Mt. Kisco, New York, co-bred, with Philip Boyer, the first registered West Highland White Terrier litter born in the United States. Again with Boyer, he owned the first of the breed to become an American champion, Cream of the Skies, who finished in 1909.

Dr. Alvaro T. Hunt, Bayou Glen, of River Ridge, Louisiana, campaigned several Westies between 1973 and 1980. While his biggest winner, shown by Dora Lee Wilson, was the 1975 Westminster Group winner and 1976 Montgomery County BIS winner Am., Eng. Ch. Ardenrun Andsome of Purston, who had thirty-eight Bests between 1974 and 1976, other toppers were Ch. Highland's Angus (six BIS in 1973 and 1974), Ch. Purston Primate (nine BIS in 1978 and 1979) and Ch. Purston Merrymick (five BIS in 1980).

Margaret Jensen, of South Gate, California, established her Marjen kennels in the early 1960s with a combination of imports and American-breds. Her import Ch. Famecheck Viking was BB at the WHWTCA national Specialty and Westminster in 1963 when he was 9 1/2 years old. Mrs. Jensen died in 1971.

Barbara Worcester Keenan's Wishing Well kennels are truly a Westie legend. With her mother, Mrs. Florence Worcester, Barbara has been involved in the breed since her mother purchased Edgerstoune Cindy from Mrs. Winant in 1947; Cindy finished in 1950 to become the first of many Wishing Well Westie champions. Not long after being imported in 1954, English Ch. Cruben Dextor attained both American and Canadian championships; he has the distinction of winning the first back-to-back Bests in Show for the breed. The honors and the dogs that brought them home to Wishing Well are beyond recounting but include, in addition to Dextor, Ch. Symmetra Snip, the first Montgomery County BIS Westie, besting 416 in 1960; Ch. Elfinbrook Simon, Best at Westminster in 1962; and the following BIS winners: Can., Am. Ch. Cruben Flashback, Tri Int. Ch. Tulyar of Trenean, Ch. Whitebriar Journeyman, Ch. Lymehill's Birkfell Solstice, Ch. Pinmoney Puck and Ch. Glenncheck May Be.

Ida and Joe Keushgenian, of Dix Hills, New York, started in Westies with the 1976 purchase from a local breeder of a dog named Cynosure Orion the Hunter, who went back to Ch. De-Go Hubert, Prosswick and Illusion lines. "Sport," the Keushgenians' first champion, was the foundation stud for Orion Kennels, producing fourteen champions including Specialty winners and a Canadian BIS victor, and was among the Top Ten Westies in both 1978 and 1979. A Sport daughter, Ch. Cynosure Orion's Morning Star, took a Group first from the classes at her first show and followed up with Specialty wins herself and national ranking in 1980. Their Ch. Orion's Rising Sun, another

Ch. Cynosure's Orion the Hunter (Ch. Illusion's Sir Gaylord Scott ex Har-Tis Cynosure Ursa Major), owned by Ida and Joe Keushgenian and bred by Anthony Parrotta, was the foundation stud for his owners' well-regarded Westie family. *Gilbert*

Ch. Cynosure Orion's Morning Star, owned by Ida and Joe Keushgenian, was an owner-handled Specialty and Group winner.

Ch. Roslynde's Razzmatazz, owned and bred by Gwen Law, was ranked number-three Westie in the United States (all systems) in 1989.

Sport son, has brought to Orion Sweepstakes and Specialty wins. The Keushgenians' star as this book goes to press is Ch. Orion's Mercury, a Group winner shown and conditioned by daughter Debbie Keushgenian.

Bettina King, of Needham Heights, Massachusetts, joined Barbara Langdon of North Scituate, Rhode Island, to establish Briarwood Westies in 1962 with the purchase of Huntinghouse Heather, who finished in 1965. Like most breeder-exhibitors of the period, their show dogs were their house pets; from the occasional litter, the best was kept and shown to its championship. Having come under the tutelage of Katharine Hayward, winning was not their top priority but to have quality dogs that exhibited proper temperament and good health. Along the way, they had fun with their dogs and instilled that in others whom they mentored. Bettina was the guiding force behind the West Highland White Terrier Club of New England and its first president. Late in 1980, Betina and Barbara retired but kept at least one Westie as a member of their household until health required them to enter a retirement home. Barbara Landgon died in 1995 in her eighty-first year and Bettina King, now in her late eighties, still enjoys her memories.

Kathy and Wayne Kompare's Kilkerran Westies were based on the bitch Ch. Kortni of Windy Hill, bred by Ann M. Frinks, who is linebred on Eng., Can., Am. Ch. Cruben Dextor, a Westie they purchased late in the 1970s. While she produced only nine puppies, one, Am., Can. Ch. Kilkerran D'Artagnan, was a multiple BIS winner. From Kortni descends two other BIS Westies bearing the Kilkerran prefix: Ch. Kilkerran 'N Wicket a Kut Above and Ch. Kilkerran Quintessence, both co-owned with Nancy Spelke, who handled the dogs to their numerous achievements.

Barbara Krotts, Bar-Dan Westies, Bellbrook, Ohio, got her first Westie in 1970 as a family companion, without even knowing the name of the breed. She became interested in Conformation showing in 1985 and got a bitch of Marwood breeding. Her first champion, Bar-Dan's Showgirl, finished in 1987, and in the decade since, Barbara has finished twenty-one Westies to their American championships; several others have attained their Canadian, Mexican or International championships. Her dogs have included multiple Specialty and Group winners. A third-generation homebred, Ch. Bar-Dan's Naughty But Nice, has produced seven champion daughters, including the Specialty and Group winner, Ch. Gaelforce The Vicar's Wife.

Mary Kuhlman got her first Westie in 1983, almost as a rescue dog, as she purchased him from a person who had bought him from a pet store and quickly tired of him. Interested in Obedience, she started Wee Geordie MacPeg in that arena; he won his CDX, was the first Westie to earn a Junior Earthdog title and in April 1991 became the first dog—not just the first Westie— in the United States to pass the proposed Master Hunter Test. Geordie, who celebrated his fourteenth birthday in June 1997, has enjoyed considerable success in commercials, appearing for BMW™ and Mighty Dog™ among other companies. The second Westie in her household, Evermore's Miss

Gillian Marple, CD, CG, had a role in the HBO film *Barbarians at the Gates*. Her daughter Molly, a.k.a. Clanblairs Piper O'Peter Pan UD, NA, CG, has appeared in Diet Coke™ commercials and, in her spare time, won High in Trial at five Specialty trials and at one all-breed show—one of three Highlanders to attain that achievement.

George Laurer, Jr., of Greenwich, Connecticut, owned the first American-bred West Highland White Terrier litter registered with the AKC. The litter of four—three males and one bitch—were whelped July 29, 1909, by Tighnabruaich Glenailort ex Glenailort Fassie, incidentally the second and third of the breed registered with the American Kennel Club. The litter bore the prefix Glenailort and the names Brogach, Piper, Rascal and Alma. This was apparently Mr. Laurer's only litter.

Gwendolyn Law, Roselynde's Westies, of Severn, Maryland, saw her first Westie while she was working at the American Embassy in London in 1977. First inquiring into the name of the breed and then into its characteristics, she determined that was the dog for her. When she returned home in 1979, she brought with her a 12-week-old puppy bitch from Muriel Coy of Cedarfell Westies. She met Vilma Amato, who taught her to groom and introduced her to dog shows. Gwen purchased her foundation bitch from Vilma. When Lady MacBeth of Glenmoor was bred, both Gwen and Vilma kept their choice puppy; both became champions. Gwen's choice, Roselynde's Radiant Star, finished from the Bred By Exhibitor class, winning Specialty points en route. Bred to Ch. Mac-Ken-Char's Irish Navigator, "Dew Drop" produced a litter of seven, five of which finished. Westies carrying the Roselynde's prefix have had numerous Sweepstakes and Specialty wins, and Ch. Roselynde's Razzmatazz was nationally ranked in 1989. Gwen has bred a dozen champions herself and co-bred another twenty Westies that went on to finish.

Linda Leavelle Leidolph, Liberty Westies, now of Sacramento, California, bought her first Westie in 1974 from Mrs. Robert Gustin. Her first show dog, Happymac's Liberty Bill, came along in 1975 from Roberta Mocabee and was owner handled to his title. In 1984 Linda joined forces with Judy Hartwell, of Stag's Leap. Like many Westie breeders, Linda breeds sparingly, usually only when she wants a puppy to show. One such was Liberty's Chairman of the Board, "Hamilton," whose multiple champions include Ch. Camcrest's Andsurely Trouble, twice BB at the WHWTCA Specialty, once from the classes, multiple Specialty winners and BIS winners.

Karen Lindberg, of Duluth, Minnesota, started her Craggencroft kennels in 1960 with the purchase of Argyle McBeth, a dog with Maxwelton bloodlines, from Harry Ellis; she took this dog to championships and advanced Obedience degrees in both Canada and the United States. Interestingly, he had back-to-back Canadian HITs, with scores of 198 and 195. Her foundation bitch, Wolvey Paper Girl, came from May Pacey just before her death; Paper Girl finished in 1967. Am., Can. Ch. Craggencroft Impressario, CD, was a Sweepstakes and Specialty winner and a 1976 Top Ten Westie. In almost forty years with Westies, Karen has finished more than thirty champions, one-third of whom also earned Obedience titles.

Frances Loring, of Pasadena, California, was one of that state's earliest exhibitors, showing as early as 1914 with a string of imports including Walpole Waxey—a Morven son—and Charm of Childwick from C.C. Vicars' Childwick kennels in London, who finished that year.

Robert Lowry of Aurora, Missouri, obtained his first West Highlander in 1945, although he did not establish his Maxwelton Kennels until 1951, when he bred his first litter. His dogs were all strongly linebred on the Crufts BB winner, Eng. Ch. Shiningcliff Simon, through the imports Ch. Shiningcliff Sim, Ch. Shiningcliff So-So and the Simon daughter Shiningcliff Donark Dancer, who became twice an all-breed BIS winner and the dam of seven champions. Lowry was the final owner of Am., Can. Ch. Belmertle Imogene, dam of four American champions and the recipient of the Award for Canine Distinction, given to recognize her waking the Lowry family when their home filled with smoke from a defective furnace. There were more than twenty-five Maxwelton Westie champions when he disbanded his kennels in 1971.

Melinda Lyon, Lair O' Lyon, of Louisville, Kentucky, purchased her first Westie from a local hobby breeder. Six months later, she got from Betty Williams the dog that would become the first of her more than fifteen champions. Among the eight champions sired by Laird Doon MacDuff of Lyon was Lair O'Lyon's Killundine Chip, bred by Daphne Gentry out of her first homebred champion, Killundine Gentle As The Rain. Melinda, as co-owner, showed "Chip" to his championship and to back-to-back WHWTCA Roving Specialty bests in 1982 and 1983. He was also a multiple Group winner and a Canadian champion, had his CD title and sired multiple champions. Chip died in 1995 at age 15-plus.

John and Bertha (Bea) Marvin lived in Dayton, Ohio, in 1941 when they purchased a 10-week-old puppy from Marguerite Vance. The couple combined their talents, John conditioning their dogs while Bea handled them. In 1948 their homebred, Ch. Cranbourne Arial, won the first of his four BIS from the classes. Three homebreds bearing the Cranbourne prefix—Arial, Atomic and Alexandrite—won multiple all-breed BIS between 1948 and 1956, setting a record that still stands. The Marvins bred more than a dozen Westie champions. Following John's 1966 retirement from General Motors, they moved to Doylestown, Pennsylvania. Both were respected judges and frequently adjudicated Specialties. John wrote the standard reference work on the breed, *The Complete West Highland White Terrier* (New York: Howell Book House). The first edition was published in 1961 and was updated through four editions, the final being published in 1977. John Marvin died on July 21, 1988, in his eighty-second year. Bea Marvin is retired from judging, but maintains an active interest in the sport as she achieves nonagenarian status.

Margaret (Jean) McAndrews, Nor'Westie's, of Ridgeville, Washington, first became a Westie owner in 1942 when her mother bought her a puppy. When Jean left home it was necessary for her Westie to remain behind. In 1964, Jean and Paul McAndrews moved into a house and immediately began looking for a Westie puppy, which she got from Arleen Cooper of the Arlwyn prefix. When he was 3 years old, Jean enrolled him in Obedience classes, where she was encouraged to enter him in Conformation at an upcoming all-breed show. She took her first-place ribbon in the Novice class and went to sit in the bleachers, not realizing she was to return for Winners competition; she did get to the ring in time to go Reserve in a major entry. This dog bore the simple name of Wee Mac, to which he added the prefix Champion, becoming a Group winner and Nor'Westie's foundation dog. Jean then purchased a bitch from the same breeder; Ch. Miss Tilloch of Arlwyn, who was bred to Wee Mac and a bitch puppy kept from that breeding, Nor'Westie's Wee Dancer was bred to Ch. Merryhart Aspen Able. Nor' Westie's Wee Piper, one of five champions from that breeding, was a multiple BIS winner in Canada. A full sister, Nor'Westie's Wee Muff, bred to her great-grandsire, Dreamland's Cyclone, produced Nor'Westie's Wee Roderick, also a multiple BIS in Canada. After a move to California, Jean became the first Westie breeder-owner-handler to win a Group in that state, and her Ch. Nor'Westie's Wee Charger became the first of the breed to win both the California and San Francisco Bay Specialties. Jean has had several bitches to produce at least five champions, allowing her to have bred more than thirty champions over the years.

Mrs. Edwin P. (Ann) McCarty, of Indianapolis, Indiana, had the Mac-A-Dac Kennels. Two of her best-known winners were bitches Ch. Mac-A-Dac Mistletoe and Mac-A-Dac Highland Kilts, each shown by Florise Hogan. She joined with B.G. Frame to show under the Wigmac prefix as well. Ann McCarty died on July 8, 1994.

Linda McCutcheon and her "Country" Westies live in Pennsylvania's Pocono Mountains. Her dogs have been tightly line-bred on Stergo Debbie, a bitch who carried Whitebriar and Famecheck bloodlines, co-owned with Poodle fancier W. H. Sterg O'Dell. Her first champion out of Debbie was Country Girl Scooter Pie, whelped in April 1980, who had major wins at two Specialty shows and has proven herself in the whelping box as well by being the dam of five champions. Her homebred Ch. Country Boy Rootin Tootin, whelped in 1994, who traces back to Debbie through each of his four grandparents, has multiple Specialty wins.

Gale McDonald, showing under the Cloudcroft prefix, purchased her first Westie in 1981; two years later she obtained Glenfinnan's Proud As Punch from Mary Lowry and Geoff Charles. This bitch later finished and became the foundation of her breeding program, which boasts Specialty and Sweepstakes winners.

Ch. Hylan's Up and Coming, owned by Patti Marks. *Ritter*

Westies have always been a natural in brace competition. Here Ch. Dawn's Pride N' Joy and Ch. Dawn's Pard N' Me Boys pose with their co-owner/handler Jonathan Marks and Australian judge J.G.W. Head in a Montgomery Country Best Brace in Show presentation. *Ashbey*

Patti Marks, A'Hylan Westies, of Willow Grove, Pennsylvania, met Dawn Martin in 1983 when both were training Scottish Terriers in Obedience. Dawn, who also had Westies, introduced Patti to the breed, and in 1984 Patti got her first Westie, the future Ch. Dawn's Peaches N' Cream, JE. In 1996, at age 11, "Peach" was Best Veteran in Sweepstakes at the WHWTCA national Specialty, one year after earning her Junior Earthdog title. In 1989 young Jonathan Marks, at barely four feet tall, handled his own Dawn's Pride N'Joy and her half-sister, Dawn's Pard N' Me Boys, to Best Brace in Show at Montgomery County, the fifth time the breed had achieved this recognition. A number of Westies of Patti's breeding have had sweepstakes and Specialty wins, including Hylan's Up N' Coming, Winners Bitch at the annual Specialty.

Dawn Martin, Dawn's Highland Scots, of Saylorsburg, Pennsylvania, has enjoyed Westies in Conformation, Obedience, go-to-ground and, more recently, Agility, since 1979. Her foundation, Am., Can. Ch. Royal Scott's Lady Abigail, Am. Can. CD, CG, was bred by Roy Wuchter; her dam came from the last breeding of Dorothea Daniell-Jenkins. Abigail produced Am., Can. Ch. Dawn's Up N' Adam, Am., Can. CDX, CG. Dawn has taken twenty-eight Westies to their championships; of these, twenty-five were homebreds and ten have had Specialty and Sweepstakes wins, including Dawn's Moment N' Time, who was Winner at the WHWTCA 1991 annual Specialty show. Dawn's Free N' Easy has the distinction of being the first bitch to win Best in Sweepstakes at both Roving and National WHWTCA Specialty shows, this at Montgomery County 1996 and at the Roving in March 1997. Dawn's breeding program is in collaboration with Patti Marks, A'Hylan. Several dogs of their breeding have enjoyed modeling assignments for television and magazines, thus serving as excellent public relations examples. Dawn has been active in pet therapy with her Westies since 1983.

Wendell and Dee Marumoto, Deeside Westies, of Honolulu, Hawaii, got their first Westie in August 1984 by answering a newspaper ad and buying a 17-month-old neutered male who would be part of their family for over thirteen years. Later, they imported two more Westies—a male and a bitch—but never got a show dog. Encouraged to improve the quality of their dogs, they went to the 1988 Crufts, where they met Barbara Hands, whose Crinan prefix is world-famous. It happened that Barbara had a young litter at the time and, after seeing the litter, the Marumotos selected a dog they would call "Chester," after his birthplace. Chester arrived in Hawaii in October 1988 and entered the show ring in 1989; in four shows, he had two Group firsts. He was not shown again until 1990, when, in back-to-back events, he had two BIS, each worth five points, and his championship. Thus, Ch. Crinan Counterpoint had become a champion and a BIS winner without defeating another Westie. Later, Deeside Westies produced a number of champions both homebred and imported from the Whitebriar Kennels of Maureen Murphy in New Zealand.

Ch. Hayastan Highland King, CD, ME, owned by Lou Herczeg and Dawn Martin and bred by Dorothy Grocott, was the first of the breed to earn a Master Earthdog degree.

Ch. Dawn's Ace N' the Hole (Ch. Hayastan Magic Moment ex Ch. Dawn's Kop N' A Plea, SE), owned and bred by Dawn Martin and Patti Marks.

Ch. Dawn's Kop N' A Plea, SE (Am., Can. Ch. Dawn's Up N' Adam, Am., Can. CDX, CG ex Am., Can. Ch. Dawn's Kit N' Kaboodle, CD, ME), owned and bred by Dawn Martin and Patti Marks, has shown herself to be a successful show and performance dog and—obviously—a prolific producer.

Constance Prosser (Mrs. R.K.) Mellon, of Ligonier, Pennsylvania, owned Rachelwood Kennels, home to a number of imports and homebreds. Among her dogs were Eng., Am. Ch. Bannock of Branston and Ch. Hookwood Marquis. It was Mrs. Mellon who, in 1960, financed the production of the bronze medallion presented to the BB winner at each parent and local Specialty show; this medallion was designed by noted Afghan Hound fancier and artist Kay Finch.

Frederick Melville, WestPride Westies, of Miami, Florida, and Guatemala City, Guatemala, bought his first two Westies in the United States in 1984; neither proved to be of show quality. When he met Neoma Eberhardt, who was vacationing in his home country, the conversation turned to Westies and . . . the rest, as they say, is history. Fred purchased a young bitch from Shane Allbee and then litter sisters, Aberglen On Top of the World and Aberglen Westpride Is Showing, from Mark and Sally George, Westie handlers and breeders. He then purchased a male puppy of the same breeding; while waiting for Aberglen Lucky Lindy to mature, Fred was one of several co-owners of Ch. Holyrood's Hotspur O'Shelly Bay during the first year of his campaign. At the age of 18 months, Lindy was entered in his first show, the 1993 Trinity Valley Specialty, where he was WD and BW for five points; he repeated the win at the California and the Southeast Texas Specialties—three shows, three five-point majors! In October 1993, Lindy won the breed at the first of what would be twelve regional specialties over the next three years. His BBs included Westminster, 1994 and 1995; the WHWTCA Roving Specialty, 1994, and its Annual Specialties in 1994 and 1995; and a career eleven all-breed Bests in Show.

Gail and Gene Miller of Baton Rouge, Louisiana, bought their first Westie in 1990 when only 9 weeks of age; named for his birthplace, A Wee Bit of Dallas Sunshine became their first champion. In 1992 they purchased a young bitch from the Tom Wards; Donnybrook's Jessica was bred to Ch. Holyrood's Hootman of Shelly Bay in 1995, and a bitch from that breeding, the first carrying their Highfield prefix—Lady Airlie—was WB at the 1997 WHWTC of Southeast Texas Specialty. A second bitch from the Wards, Donnybrook Marlie O'HiField, was Best in Sweepstakes at the 1994 Roving; bred to Manley in 1996, she produced Highfield Divine intervention, who was Best Puppy at the 1997 San Francisco Bay Specialty and Best of Opposite in Sweeps and Reserve at the Greater Atlanta Club's first Specialty. In 1995, the Millers joined with Betty and Jim Boso in campaigning Ch. Glengloamin's Rise 'N Shine, who currently holds the Specialty BB record for a bitch.

Marcia Montgomery, Wynecroft, of Nashville, Tennessee, got her first Westie pet in 1971 while in her second year of medical school. Later, after watching the televised Westminster show, Marcia decided she would like a show dog. After several disappointments and the delays caused by her profession, in 1981 she bought both a dog and a bitch from Twila Faye Little; both Storyland's Little Annika and Storyland's Lil' Sandman finished, and

Ch. Crinan Counterpoint, imported from England and owned by Mr. and Mrs. Wendell Marumoto, became a champion the hard way. With his career limited to Hawaii, "Chester" never encountered another Westie in competition and had two BIS en route to his title.

Ch. Hookwood Marquis, owned by Mrs. Richard K. Mellon. *Tauskey*

Am., Can. Ch. Robinridge Macbeth, owned by Rosamond Billett and bred by Mrs. A.S. Monroney. *Tauskey*

the male enjoyed a Specials career that included a Canadian BIS win. Several homebred puppies were finished, but within two generations the bitches ceased to produce and that line ended. In 1988, Marcia went to Montgomery County hoping to buy a finished bitch, but found Holyrood's Hootnanny O'Shelly Bay in the 6-to-9-months Sweepstakes bitch class and purchased her instead. Following advice she read during the 1960s lauding the virtues of line breeding, she has followed such a program to produce several Specialty winners and the culmination of her goals, the BIS bitch Ch. Wynecroft's Wild At Heart, called "GiGi." In her years with the breed, Marcia has owned or co-owned three BIS winners, one of which she bred, multiple Specialty winners and a number of champions, including several homebreds.

Mrs. A.S. (Mary-Ellen) Monroney, of Oklahoma City, Oklahoma, and Washington, D.C., established her Robinridge Kennels in 1935. She owned the first of the breed to obtain an Obedience degree, Robinridge Bimelick, who got both his championship and his CD in 1942 and his CDX in 1943, being trained by Dorothy Hardcastle. Bimelick, a homebred, was whelped June 10, 1940, by Ch. Robinridge MacBeth out of Robinridge Binny. Never without a Westie, Mrs. Monroney died on May 6, 1994, at age 90.

Amelia Musser, Round Town Kennels of Laingsburg, Michigan, purchased her first Westie from Mrs. B.G. Frame in 1963 as a pet. Amelia and her husband, Dan, really became active exhibitors after the purchase of a young bitch from Rose Marie Harris; this bitch went on to become Ch. Rose Marie's Mean Mary Jean and the foundation of Round Town Westies. One of her daughters, Ch. Round Town Critic's Choice, from the English import Ch. Warbonnet's Wolsey, when bred to Dorothea Daniell-Jenkins' Can., Am. Rouge Manabee Zebedee, produced Ch. Wind Town All That Jazz, co-owned by Peggy Haas and Amelia; "Dolly" was bred to the Canadian-owned English import, Eng., Can., Am. Ch. Whitebriar Jeronimo. Two from this litter have been record setters: Ch. Round Town Duke J. Ellington, as a sire of champions, and Ch. Round Town Ella J. Fitzgerald, winner of eight all-breed BIS and the BIS record holder for Westie bitches. In the last ten years, Amelia has campaigned three other males to multiple Bests in Show: Snowbank Starr Shine, Hero's Top Brass and the homebred Round Town Ivan the Terror, who holds the breed record for all-breed Bests.

Susan Napady, Halo Kennels, Portage, Indiana, and her parents, Stella and Tom Napady, purchased their first Westie in 1968 from Dr. Ralph Logan. Although the male puppy, by Ch. Waideshouse Wiloughby ex Ch. Zerbian's White Wash, was intended as a family pet, he went on to be the Group-winning Ch. Kenbrook Wee Thistle. The next year they purchased Reanda Magic Moment from Bergit Zakchewski; "Cricket" finished her championship in 1971 and produced several champions. The first Halo litter arrived in 1970 when Cricket was bred to Bergit's Ch. Rosyles Pirate. Over the last twenty-seven years, more than fifty homebreds have completed their championships, the first of which was Halo's Firecracker. A 1987 breeding

Ch. Snowbank Starr Shine, bred by Martha and Clifford Replogle and owned by Amelia Musser, who turned him over to George Ward for a successful career that included multiple BIS wins. *Booth*

Ch. Doon MacDuff Saint George, owned by Betty Williams and Barbara Nisbet, was a multiple Specialty winner. *Sabrina*

These three Roselle champions were owned by Gloria Roselle and Barbara Nisbet, and all competed successfully during the 1960s. They are (from left) Ch. Roselle Chin Chin, Ch. Roselle Auntie Mame and Ch. Roselle Music Man.

of the Napadys' Ch. Wicken Anjuli of Halo to Ch. Tweed Take By Storm resulted in four puppies, all of whom finished their titles.

Barbara Nisbet was connected with Gloria Roselle in the Roselle program. After moving to Houston, Texas, from New York City about 1968, she was never without a Westie, although she was not actively involved in breeding or showing again until she purchased Doon MacDuff Saint George. Co-bred by Daphne Gentry and Betty Williams, "George" finished in four shows and went on to become a multiple Specialty winner.

Debra Owen, Westies Galore, of Louisville, Kentucky, got her first Westie in 1982 because she thought a picture of one she had seen was "cute." She had a long search to find a puppy, and when Crane's Rachel O'the Hill proved not of show quality, Debbie worked her in Obedience, where she got her CD degree in three shows. Debbie's "Doc"—Ch. Kilkerran Kildare O'Wicket— sired eleven champions, including Specialty and Sweepstakes winners. She has bred three champions.

Claudia Lea Phelps, of Roslyn, Long Island, was one of the earliest proponents of the Westie in the United States and was often referred to as the breed's American sponsor. She obtained her first Westie in 1912 with the purchase of Tam O'Shanter, actually registered in the name of her mother, Mrs. Sheffield Phelps, as were most of her early dogs; their first champion was made up in 1913. Ms. Phelps owned the first West Highland White Terrier to win an all-breed BIS in the United States, Ch. Clarke's Hill Snooker. Between 1913 and 1928, Ms. Phelps imported the best of the English bloodlines, from which she developed her own stock under the Rosstor prefix. She had many of the best dogs in the ring during the late teens and 1920s. She owned the BB winner at the 1926 AKC Sesquicentennial show. She moved to Aiken, South Carolina, and ceased her involvement with the breed in 1929; the dispersal of her stock saw many going to the Edgerstoune Kennels of Mrs. John G. Winant.

Allison Platt, Kirkton Westies, of Baltimore, Maryland, purchased her first Westie—Brynmill Bonnie Kirkton—in 1986 from Tom and June Fraser of Brynmill Westies in Canada. In 1987 Allison bought the bitch that proved to be her foundation, Wee Mack's Kelsey of Kirkton from Eileen McNulty in New York. Kelsey, by the English import Ch. Belash Batchelor Boy at Tervin is now Ch. Wee Mack's Kelsey of Kirkton, TD, CDX, SE, CG and has twice been High in Trial at the WHWTCA annual specialty Obedience Trial. Kirkton Quicksilver Girl, a Kelsey granddaughter, became the fifth of her breed to earn a TDX and the second of her breed to attain an Open Agility title. Another Kelsey grandson, Ch. Kirkton Connecticut Yankee, owned by Kimberly Lohr, earned his Flyball Dog Excellent title and, at his very first Obedience Trial, was High in Trial. The Kirktons are obviously equally at home in the conformation ring, and for all performance activities open to Westies.

Allison Platt's Kirkton Westies took the top spot in the brood bitch class at the 1995 annual Specialty under judge Anne Rogers Clark. Shown here (from left) are Emmaline of Wee Mack, with Allison; Ch. Kirkton Connecticut Yankee, with owner Kimberly Lohr; and Ch. Kirkton Carolina On My Mind, with Tom Juswik. Club president Dawn Diemer presents the trophy. *Ashbey*

Ch. Wee Mack's Kelsey of Kirkton, CDX, TD, SE, was Best Veteran at the 1997 Greater Washington Specialty at age 10. On the same day her granddaughter, Kirkton Nothing Could Be Finer, owned by Daphne Gentry, was Best in Sweepstakes. *Kernan*

Ch. CeannMor Bonny Brae Lass (Ch. Jubilhill Jonathan
ex Ch. Killundine Pinegrove Lass) was the first champion
for Anne Pyle. *Richard Mason*

Anne Pyle, of Richmond, Virginia, decided to add a Westie to her household in the early 1980s. The male she purchased in 1982 subsequently developed severe atopic dermatatis; in 1988 she got a bitch as a companion for
the dog. When "Angus" died at age 8, she decided to become more involved
with the breed and so obtained a bitch from Daphne Gentry in October 1992.
Ch. CeannMor Bonny Brae Lass finished in December 1993 at age 17 months;
from Bonny's first litter to Ch. Doon MacDuff Mark of Stirling, two puppies
became champions, including Ch. CeannMor's Black-Eyed Susan. In 1996,
Anne purchased a Paddyhill bitch in order to run two breeding lines.

Sandy and Ardian Radziwon, of New Castle, Pennsylvania, purchased a
Westie as a companion from Betty Ostrowski in 1981; to their kennel name
of Clydesdale they added Mae Westie. To fulfill a promise to Betty, they started
showing the single bitch puppy in Mae's first litter; not achieving success with
Heather, they decided to show the mother instead. Mae not only got her
championship in 1987 but her CD title and Certificate of Gameness, thereby
earning a Versatile Dog award in 1989. While their dogs have been owner-
handled to Group and Specialty wins, they are most thrilled with finishing
dogs entirely from the Bred By Exhibitor class. In the ensuing sixteen years
since obtaining the original Mae, eighteen champions have borne the Clydesdale prefix.

Mrs. Bertha A. (Roy) Rainey, from Huntington, Long Island, registered
her first Westie in 1911; this dog, Dunvegan Hero, whelped in December 1909
in England, became an American champion in 1915, two years after her
imported Conejo Barone did so.

Martha Strickland Replogle met the Westie as a young child, long before becoming involved with the breed. Each summer she would visit her
grandparents' farm in the Piedmont of North Carolina; on a 1952 visit, she
discovered a new dog living under a sharecropper's cottage. She named the
beautiful small white dog Snowball, and he submitted to her attentions on
many visits in coming years. Twenty-five years later, in a chance conversation with the treasurer of the WHWTCA, she was told about a couple from
New England whose Westie had gotten away from them during a car trip to
Florida early in the 1950s. The same dog? It was 1966 before Martha got
her own Westie; the bitch came from an Air Force couple stationed in Georgia who had purchased both parents while stationed in the Northwest, and
so the dog combined Canadian and American bloodlines: Wallmoore,
Rachelwood, Ben Braggie and Remasais. Moving to Louisville, Kentucky,
shortly thereafter, Martha enrolled Snowbelle in Obedience classes and then
put her into a Conformation match, where she got a Group placement—and
hooked Martha into the show world. Martha met Louisville resident Betty
Williams, who served as a mentor in grooming, showing and breeding; soon
after getting a show-prospect bitch from Betty, Cliff Replogle was transferred
to Florida and their three bitches, now including one obtained from the legendary Dorothea Daniell-Jenkins, moved southward. Among the more than
forty champions carrying the Snowbank prefix was the multiple BIS winner
Snowbank Starr Shine, campaigned to the top of the ranks during the 1980s.

Mr. and Mrs. William B. Rogers imported the finest English stock for
their Nishkenon Kennels in Sherborn, Massachusetts. Their foundation was
Ch. White Adonis, whelped February 19, 1923, by White Demon out of
Greenside Tossy. Their Ch. White Cloud of Nishkenon won her championship in four weeks, culminating with a Group win and an award for Best Bitch
in Show (before the days of BIS awards). Ch. Crivoch Clashmore of
Nishkenon, an import, proved to be an important stud dog. After exhibiting
and breeding Westies for more than twenty years, the Rogers retired to Tennessee late in the 1940s and, while maintaining an interest in the Westie,
moved their activities to field trials.

Gloria Roselle, of Jackson Heights, New York, established Roselle Westies
in the mid-1950s on Triskett, Rannoch Dune and Lawrenton bloodlines. She
bred and owned several dogs who won at the national Specialty level. Resid-
ing in New York and loving the theater, her dogs' names were all associated
with Broadway musicals. With her business partner Barbara Nisbet, she
moved to Houston, Texas, about 1968 and ceased to show and breed. Gloria
died September 17, 1990, and her regional club offers a challenge trophy in
its annual Sweepstakes in her memory.

Anne and Sil Sanders, Rime Westies, of Stanwood, Washington, got their
first Westie in 1971 from Doris Eisenberg of Kar-Ric; although intended as a
pet, he was shown briefly, but without success. They then got a bitch carrying McTwiddles and Maxwelton lines from Doris, although she was not the

Ch. Lite N' Lively's Hello Tollie, owned by Charles and Emilie Schoonover, with her litter by Ch. Arnholme Again and Again. *Montieth*

An appealing study of Tollie and her litter by Ch. Holyrood's Hotspur O'Shellybay. *Montieth*

breeder. Again, they showed Glenmere's Pure Delight; she earned five points toward her championship. By then, the Sanderses were involved in the San Francisco Bay WHWTC and had also met Margaret Barr, who became a real mentor to the couple. "PD" earned her CD and Certificate of Gameness titles and was the dam of Ch. Rime's Alicia Aquena, CDX, TDX, CG—the first TDX Westie and the first Westie to earn titles in four areas of endeavor, shown throughout by Sil. The foundation of their breeding program was Ch. Kar Ric's Luv U Dorie O'Glen, CD, shown in both Conformation and Obedience by Anne. Ch. Rime's Quonquering Hero, UDX, TDX, CG, was the second Westie to earn both the TDX and UDX titles. He was also a Sweepstakes winner and picked up points at two Specialties. Over the years, the Sanderses have owned and/or bred twenty-three champions; in addition, their dogs have earned titles in Obedience, Tracking and Earthdog events.

Nancy Ann Schoch, Windsong Westies, of Pocasset, Massachusetts, by her own description terrified of dogs, showed and bred Silver Persian cats in the 1960s. In 1963, she ventured into the depths of the benching area of the Westminster KC show only because the event followed a large cat show she was attending, and she was fascinated by two little white dogs on a tartan-clad stall. Nine years later she decided to think more about dogs, and it was another year before she found a bitch with the breeding of Ch. Elfinbrook Simon in her background. In April 1973, she purchased Lonsdale Marget from Patricia Storey. Marget provided the impetus for Nancy's involvement with the breed and introduced her to mentors Bettina King, Barbara Langdon, Katharine Hayward and, of course, Patty Storey. Nancy worked with Michael Collings, who brought his Purston Westies from England to Massachusetts in the mid-1970s, using his stud dogs with her bitches and getting dogs carrying the Purston prefix. Ch. Purston Provocateur took Nancy into the Group ring on numerous occasions. The first of four homebred champions was Windsong Challiss MacPherst, who finished entirely from the Bred By Exhibitor class. The most recent champion owned by Windsong is Kenwood Blizzard at Windsong, who was from the last litter bred by Edward McParlan.

Emilie Schoonover, Lite N' Lively, Augusta, New Jersey, was introduced to the breed through Triskett Vogelius, although she had already purchased a companion Westie prior to meeting Triskett. In one of those childhood memories, Emilie reports that when her grandmother first saw "Souch," she told her that when she was only 5 years old, she pointed to a Black & White Scotch calendar and announced that when she grew up, she was going to have a white dog . . . just like that one! It was 1968 when her prediction became a reality. The next year a friend told her he had met a lady who had lots of those dogs who was willing to have her visit and learn how to groom and care for her Westie correctly. Em recalls that the sight greeting her as she pulled into Triskett's drive was "awesome"—ten or so Westies in a bay window barking their greetings! Her memories of Triskett are of a gracious woman with a passion for the breed that she wanted to share. Triskett recommended that Em contact Dorinda Dew when she was ready for her next Westie, and so Tacksman Miracle came to be part of the Schoonover home. She finished her championship and at age 16½, reigns supreme at Lite N' Lively. Emilie gained valuable first-hand experience by working part time at the kennels of leading handler Cliff Hallmark and his wife, Lois, not just in learning to groom but in learning to "read" the feelings of a dog. Sometime later, Emilie bred to Ida Keushgenian's Ch. Orions Man In the Moon and got Ch. Lite N' Lively's Hello Tollie, a winner both in Sweepstakes and class competition at various Specialties during 1991–1992 and multiple Group placements. In the past sixteen years, Emilie and husband, Charlie, have finished thirteen champions, seven of which are homebreds, with a number waiting their turns in the ring.

Linda Servin, Elsinore Westies, of Quincy, Massachusetts, bought her first Westie pet in 1972. Linda's first champion, Ajax of Elsinore, went back to Dreamland breeding through his dam. He was shown to his championship by Edna Cummings, who also taught Linda to trim. The same year, Linda bought Elsinore Tara, her foundation bitch by Ch. Loch Ness MacTavish; Tara finished in Canada but not the United States. Breeding to Watt's the Big Deal, a dog with Dreamland on his sire's side, resulted in two champions: Elsinore Havoc and Elsinore Robin Goodfellow, the first of Elsinore's several Specialty winners. Breeding Havoc to Ajax established the Elsinore line, and over the years there have been twenty-five Elsinore champions. Thirteen dogs have had sweepstakes and/or Specialty wins and six have ranked in the Top Ten. Am., Can. Ch. Elsinore Opus One, the Elsinore standard bearer for the mid-1990s, had multiple Specialty and Group wins, and has shown himself to be a successful producer.

Alice Shepard, Paddyhill Westies, Rancho Mirage, California, in looking for a companion bought her first Westie in October 1982 from Ann Theberge (Ann Marie Rose); showing the bitch as a youngster thoroughly hooked Alice into conformation showing. She then purchased in co-ownership with Pat Darby a young male who finished from the 6-to-9-months puppy class and became her first champion, Cubit Murdoch of Paddyhill. Looking for a foundation bitch, she met Derek Tattersall while he was visiting in San Francisco; a visit to his home in England took place the following year and, in due course, Olac Moonshine came to Paddyhill. "Pip" won a Group third her first time shown; she won the points at a regional Specialty and has produced five champions. Alice is now showing the fifth generation from Pip. Later Alice obtained Crinan Celtic Lullaby from Barbara Hands, who finished and produced well. There have been fifteen Paddyhill champions, most of them homebreds.

Donald McKay Smith, Rothmore, of Cleveland, Ohio, and his wife were probably the first to introduce the breed to the American Midwest with their 1937 purchase of Mheall Dirk, whelped in Scotland in September 1936; the dog finished his American championship during the summer of 1939.

Nancy Spelke, Kintyre, of Pasadena, California, purchased her first Westie from Kathy and Wayne Kompare in 1986; she showed Kilkerran Matinee Idol to his championship. She then obtained "Kutter," officially Kilkerran 'N Wicket A Kut Above, who started his show career in the fall of 1987. He was campaigned during 1988, 1989 and through Westminster 1990, retiring with thirty-seven Group firsts and multiple BIS and Specialty Bests. After finishing Gingerbread Kilkerran Katie, she next campaigned Kilkerran Quintessence, who in 1991 was the number-one Owner-Handled Terrier; "Quin," like Kutter, also had multiple Specialty and all-breed Bests. In 1993, Nancy finished the bitch Whitehaus' Double Trouble, a Quin granddaughter, with all majors, including WB at the Roving Specialty. During 1996, when she was undefeated in breed competition, "Sassy" broke the existing record of forty-two Group wins by a bitch and went on to win her fiftieth Group first before assuming maternal duties. With multiple BIS wins and BB at the 1995 WHWTCA Roving Specialty, Sassy is the top owner-handled bitch in breed history.

Nancy Staab, Gaelforce Westies, from St. Albans, West Virginia, was interested in Conformation showing and in 1984 got Biljonblue Solo of Clansman from the Biljonblue Kennels of Bill Ferrara and John Price, from a litter co-bred by Sylvia Landsman. While Solo never finished, he did get his Companion Dog title. Nancy bred her first litter in 1987, and three of her five champions have been homebred. Of the other two, one, who also has her Canadian championship, is Ch. Gaelforce The Vicar's Wife, who, with multiple Group and Specialty wins in both 1996 and 1997, was nationally ranked both years.

Nancy Stalnaker, Sudoeste Westies, of Scottsdale, Arizona, had two pets succumb at advanced ages within weeks of each other; while her husband thought it might be nice not to have the responsibility of pet ownership for awhile, she set out to find just the right breed. Eventually she narrowed the choice to three breeds, including the Westie. Encouraged by friends to attend her first dog show, Nancy watched the breed and knew then and there that was the dog for her! She followed one of the exhibitors back to her set-up and introduced herself with the statement that she really wanted a Westie. The lady happened to have a puppy available, and so Nancy purchased Nor'Westie's Wee Bear from Margaret "Jean" McAndrews in 1979. Jean served willingly as Nancy's mentor, offering advice, support and encouragement. "Bear" completed her championship and CD degree. Nancy has finished seventeen champions, fifteen homebred, and most owner-handled. Several also hold Canadian, Mexican and International championships.

Patricia Storey, Londsale Westies, of Dedham, Massashusetts, started in Westies in 1966 with the purchase of Westcote Ghillie of Gairloch, who was shown to his championship in 1967 by her 11-year-old son. Completely hooked, Patty purchased a bitch from Thomas and Thelma Adams in 1969. This bitch, Roseneath New Moon, called Laurie, had Wolvey, Branston and

Am., Can. Ch. Gaelforce The Vicar's Wife, a Group and Specialty winner, owned by Nancy A. Staab. *Dog Ads*

Ch. Briarwood Bonnet, owned by Christine L. Swingle. *Shafer*

Ch. Billikin (Edgerstoune Radium ex Edgerstoune Realize), owned by Mrs. Anthony M. Walters and bred by Louise R. Lang. *Tauskey*

Famecheck bloodlines; taller than the Standard allowed, she never finished. Bred first to the Ronald Davises' Jenessey's Myney, a Simon son, a premature litter resulted with but one survivor; the one was Lonsdale Moonbeam, the first of many homebred champions. "Laurie" was next bred to Briarwood Blockbuster, and all three members of that litter finished. In the ensuing years, there have been thirty-two Lonsdale champions, the most recent of which— Londsale Gordon, finished in 1997—represents the ninth generation of homebred champions.

Beverly Sundin, Sun Crest, of Sarasota, Florida, started out with German Shepherd Dogs, but when her dog was diagnosed with hip dysplasia, her husband encouraged her to get a smaller breed; her choice was the Westie. In 1962 she called an old friend from the Chicago area, Georgia DeWitt with the Dee West prefix, and acquired a show-quality bitch. Bee's Honey Bee of Dew West, heavily bred on Cruben Dextor, finished in 1965. Georgia served as Beverly's mentor, advising on breeding the bitch, who became a top producer. After a number of years with the breed, family obligations intervened and Beverly was not active for a dozen years, during which time she lost her original line. Her first effort to obtain a show-quality bitch was not successful, but then she purchased L'Esprits Ms Muffet of Mirage from Gary Gabriel. After finishing, she was bred to dogs bearing the Snowbank prefix and to Ch. Holyrood's Hotspur O'Shelly Bay; she has already produced five champions.

Christine Swingle, Bonnie Brier, of Bristol, Connecticut, bought her first Westie, Briarwood Bonnet, in 1964 from Bettina King and Barbara Langdon; with Roselle and Huntinghouse in her immediate background, "Bonnie" was strongly bred on Simon and Dextor bloodlines. Bought as a companion, Bonnie was what was then referred to as "a good starter dog." Christine accompanied her mentor to shows, and when the day finally came that Bettina handed the lead to Christine, she was hooked! Bred twice, Bonnie completed her championship handled by her owner or Roberta Campbell. From one of Bonnie's litters, Christine kept Bonnie Brier She's Groovin', a champion who was herself the dam of six champions and the Westie her breeder considers to have been the best bitch she ever owned. "Dulcey's" daughter "Luci," Ch. Bonnie Brier Heathertoes, was the dam of five champions, four from one litter. Breeding no more than one litter a year, Christine has finished nineteen champions, of which all are homebreds except for the first, and many are Sweepstakes and Specialty winners. Christine had on occasion painted breed portraits, but while living in California during the late 1980s she began working in clay, and today her sculptures are sought after by breeders as exhibiting the typical breed poses. Her sister Judith, while never having bred a litter, has owned and shown Westies under the Dennie Glen prefix; she is also an accomplished artist, working primarily in pen and ink and oil.

Gordon and Elaine Talbott, Talbott's Westies, of Louisville, Kentucky, got their first Westie from Ginny Frederick in 1974, shortly after their marriage. Talbott's Glen Shar Samson was finished to his championship, groomed by Elaine and shown by Gordon, the combination still used today. Breeding only when they wanted to add another member to their family, they would keep one puppy; in this way, they have finished six homebreds, after Samson. Their bitch, Ch. Talbott's Tattletail, was nationally ranked in 1981, 1982 and 1983, rising as high as number two. Two of her sons, Chs. Talbott's Top Hat and Tails and Talbott's Third Times A Charm, had multiple Group wins, including firsts, to their credit.

Charles and Lee Trudeau, Glencarron Westies, of Stamford, Connecticut, lived in England for ten years; just before their return to the States in 1981 they contacted Mary Torbet of Newtonglen, and within a few months of their return, 6-month-old Newtonglen Fiona arrived. She finished easily, and for the next decade the Trudeaus' breeding program and showing was built on "Jemma's" offspring. She passed away in 1995, at 14. When they lost the last of that line, the Trudeaus obtained Kilkerran Beauty Bewitched from the Kompares, and they are now into the third generation of her progeny. The Trudeaus have finished seven champions, including four homebreds. Their Glencarrons Andromeda garnered her last championship points at the final Westminster Kennel Club event to offer regular classes.

D.A. Tyler, Belmertle Kennels, of Texas, purchased Ch. Charan Minstrel, who sired such dogs as Ch. Shirley Bliss of Belmertle, the oldest bitch to complete a championship, and Ch. Gillette's Lord Tuffington, the first American-bred Highlander to win an all-breed BIS.

Marguerite Van Schaick, of Huntington, Long Island, whose father was long prominent in Collies, registered her first Highlander, Nancy of Springmeade, in 1914. This bitch's line traced within three generations to Athol, Conas and Morven, names of some significance in the history of the breed. From this foundation bitch bred to Conejo Barone, she had her first litter in 1914; in 1916 she obtained Bunty of Springmeade, a daughter of Ch. Rumpus of Glenmere; and the next year she registered her kennel name. Her Ch. Reaside Rex, an import, sired Ch. Springmeade Blackeyed Susan and Ch. Springmeade Rexminimus, the latter a homebred dog that placed in the Group at an all-breed show in 1943 at 10 years of age. Miss Van Schaick was an active exhibitor through the 1940s and continued to breed an occasional litter into the 1950s. Her dogs established the kennels of many prominent fanciers, including Marguerite Vance and film star Charles Ruggles. She died in 1989, still owned by a Westie.

Marguerite Vance, of Indianapolis, Indiana, had the single word Mi as her kennel prefix. Her first Westie was purchased in 1939 from the Donald McKay Smiths in co-ownership with John Hillman, a noted Scottie authority. This bitch, Rothmore's Mheall Dhu, became the first Westie champion in Indiana and the foundation for most of the Westies bred in the area, including the Cranbournes and Wigtowns. She purchased another bitch from the Smiths and, breeding closely on Springmeade and Battison lines, especially after purchasing Ch. Battison Beacon, produced at least ten champions of her own prefix and was the foundation for most of the Midwestern kennels.

Jodine and John Vertuno, Sno-Bilt, of Naperville, Illinois, first had Samoyeds, and Obedience was their first interest in dogs. Wanting a smaller breed, in 1967 they purchased their first Westie, but their actual foundation stock came from the Albert Kayes' Dreamland kennels and resulted in their Sno-Bilt's Aquarius, who won well both as a youngster and a veteran, taking a regional Specialty win as a youthful 7-year-old. Another dog of Sno-Bilt breeding and of which Jodine is justifiably proud, though not herself the breeder, is Ch. Sno-Bilt's Puzzle, sire of over fifty champions and a multiple BIS winner. In more than forty years in the breed, Sno-Bilt has bred over thirty champions.

Triskett Vogelius, of Mendham, New Jersey, based her Triskett kennels on a combination of Cruben and Lawrenton. Her Ch. Triskett's Most Happy Fella won the National Specialty held in Montgomery County in 1959, sired more than fifteen champions and was behind some of the 1960s' leading show dogs, including Roselle, Lawrenton, Donnybrook, Suncrest and Battison.

Mrs. Anthony Walters established Tyndrum Kennels in the 1940s; her brace entry of Tyndrum Crumpet and Tyndrum Dirk won Best Terrier Brace at the 1962 Westminster show—the only time Westies won that honor. A photograph of her Ch. Billikin graced the breed column in the *Pure-Bred Dogs—American Kennel Gazette*. Her breeding helped establish several fanciers, and she was a mentor to people such as Martha Black, Robert Black, Donna Hegstrom and Greg Shively. She died on November 2, 1984.

John T. "Tom" and Billye Ward, Donnybrook Westies, Baltimore, Maryland, got their first Westie from Beverly Sundin while Tom was stationed in Florida with the Coast Guard in 1964. Sun Crest Little Audrey was also their first champion, finishing in 1966. Their first homebred champion came along the next year as Donnybrook's Miss Triskett, named for mentor Triskett Vogelius, finished. Despite a hiatus of almost a decade while their children were pursuing careers on the stage and screen, more than fifty Donnybrook Westies have become champions, usually from the bred-by-exhibitor classes. The Wards initially linebred on Dextor, and then began to blend Whitebriar into that program. The Wards' breeding is behind other successful modern families. They also imported a number of dogs, of which the most successful was the bitch Ch. Whitebriar Jolyminx. After the BIS winner Ch. Whitebriar Jalisker was retired, he came to live at Donnybrook. As this book goes to press the Wards are actively campaigning their latest, Ch. Donnybrook's George, co-owned with Meade Carlson. George was owner-handled to a Best in Show in November 1997.

Mrs. C.K. (Ida) Weaver, of Seattle, Washington, added Westies to her Weaver kennel by obtaining a Ch. Elfinbrook Simon daughter in the early 1960s. She occasionally brought in "new blood" with an import, such as Ch.

Ch. Glengidge Precocious, an owner-handled homebred, was Helene and Seymour Weiss's first Westie champion.

Ch. Glengidge Easy Virtue (Ch. Pillerton Peterman ex Ch. Donnybrook's Eve), owned and bred by Helene and Seymour Weiss. *Ashbey*

Ch. Whitebriar Jaymandie (Whitebriar Jimmick ex Whitebriar Jillsown), imported and owned by Helene and Seymour Weiss and bred in England by Jean Johnson. *Ritter*

Ch. Glengidge Golden Charm (Ch. Dalriada Sam I Am ex Ch. Glengidge Golden Girl, Am., Can. CD), owned by Helene and Seymour Weiss, a multiple Group winner and WHWTCA Sweepstakes winner. *Booth*

Ugadale's Artist's Model. The fancy lost a friend with her tragic death in an automobile accident in October 1972.

Helene and Seymour Weiss, of Brooklyn, New York, have Glengidge Westies. Like many fanciers, Helene—before her marriage—purchased a Westie who, while never shown, did produce the first champion of many to come: Glengidge Precocious, a female whelped in 1971. In 1975 the Weisses purchased Donnybrook's Eve as a puppy, who, when bred to Eng. Ch. Pillerton Peterman, produced the littermates Chs. Glengidge Pickpocket and Glengidge Easy Virtue, from which they continued a strong linebreeding program. The 1969 importation of Whitebriar Jaymandie, who finished in 1972, brought additional strength to Glengidge. Over twenty-five champions—including Sweepstakes, Specialty and Group winners—have come from this hobby kennel. Ch. Glengidge Golden Charm had an excellent career in the early 1990s. A standout as a puppy, "Sari" was Best in the WHWTCA Sweepstakes at Montgomery in 1990. Her record includes ten Group firsts, and she was Best of Opposite Sex at the 1992 Roving Specialty show of the WHWTCA under Dora Lee Wilson.

Judith White bought her first Westie in 1972 from John and Toyoko "Susi" Shafer, who showed and bred at that time under the Toyoko prefix. Judy admits to having shown for five years before getting a single point. Her

Ch. Jubilhill Jellico, owned and bred by Judy White. *Ashbey*

Ch. Honey Hill's Kate of Jubilhill, owned by Judy White. *Ashbey*

Ch. Jubilhill's Jewel (Ch. Whitebriar Jollimont ex Ch. Jubilhill Jade), a Group winner owned and bred by Judy White.

Ch. Doon MacDuff Duncan Dundee, owned by Stanley and Connie Snowden and Betty Williams and bred by Betty Williams and Daphne Gentry, a multiple Group winner and sire of champions. *Brian*

first champion was Pillerton Postman, brought to this county as a young puppy by his breeder, Sylvia Kearsey; "Easy" was ranked in the Top Ten for several consecutive years during the 1970s. Among Judy's accomplishments was retiring the Challenge trophy for Best of Opposite Sex wins at the WHWTCA Roving Specialty, with three bitches: Chs. Jubilhill Jellico, Honey Hills Kate of Jubilhill, and Jubilhill Jewel. Over twenty champions have carried her Jubilhill prefix.

Betty Williams, Doon MacDuff, of Louisville, Kentucky, purchased her first Westie, Doon Highlander MacDuff, early in 1961; her second, a bitch from the legendary Marge Blue, came along the the same year. While Klintilloch Bonnie Lass, a.k.a. Susie, won two large match show Groups, she disliked showing and so was bred to Ch. Klintilloch Magellan; this breeding produced Betty's first champion, Lady Drambuie MacDuff, who finished in April 1968. "Pandy," bred to Ch. Klintilloch Dapper Duffer, led to the first champion to bear the Doon MacDuff prefix. When Ch. Lady Heather Doon MacDuff was bred to the multi-titled Ch. Monsieur Aus Der Flerlage, Ch. Laid Brig-a-Doon MacDuff, a Group winner and sire of thirteen champions, resulted. A Brig great-grandson, Ch. Doon MacDuff Saint George, co-owned with Barbara Nisbet, was a multiple Specialty winner although shown sparingly and always owner-handled by Betty. Ch. Killundine Made In A Dandy Way, co-bred and co-owned with Daphne Gentry, had several Specialty Bests of Opposite Sex, and her son, Am., Can. Ch. Doon MacDuff Duncan Dundee, is a multiple Group winner. Betty has finished forty-two homebred Westies and another four based on her breeding.

Barbara Winans, then of Columbia, Missouri, and the owner of Mr. Mac, the Westie loved by every child in the neighborhood, was introduced to the show world by Elsie and Bob Starkey, in St. Louis. Barbara entered into a co-ownership with Dr. Alvaro T. Hunt of Ch. Bayou Glen's Manchac Mark, who sired her first homebred champion, Westwin's Speaker of the House. Barbara then purchased Ch. Round Town Bo Jangles from the Mussers and, guided by Georgia Harris, Bo achieved a number of nice wins for Barbara. Of late, Barbara has become involved with rescue efforts in the Missouri-Kansas area.

Mrs. John G. Winant (later Mrs. Marion Eppley and still later Mrs. Walter K. Earle) started her Edgerstoune kennels in New Hampshire with stock obtained from Claudia Phelps' dispersal of her Rosstor kennels and augmented it with imports. She was referred to as the bulwark of the breed. Interestingly, Mrs. Winant judged a show in England and placed a Westie bitch BIS; she then arranged to buy the bitch. Brought to the United States, Wolvey Pattern of Edgerstoune made breed history by being the first West Highland bitch to win an all-breed BIS and the first of the breed to go BIS at the Westminster Kennel Club, doing so in 1942 under H.E. Mellenthin, handled by Robert Gorman. "Pattern" was whelped April 20, 1937, by Wolvey Prefect out of Wolvey Privet of Edgerstoune and was bred by Mrs. C.C. Pacey. In addition to Pattern, Mrs. Winant bought many fine dogs from May Pacey's Wolvey Kennels, including Wolvey Pace of Edgerstoune, Wolvey Prophet of Edgerstoune and Wolvey Privet of Edgerstoune—champions all. Another dog she bought was Ray of Rushmoor, who, at the time of her retirement, was the top sire in the breed. Not content to buy, she also bred dogs too innumer-able to identify. She made up more than fifty champions, both imports and homebreds. During the summer of 1954, she astounded many by closing her kennels and dispersing the stock; at that time, she lived at Valley Cottage, New York. Mrs. Winant died on February 15, 1983.

Mrs. William (Florence) Worcester, of Little Falls, New Jersey, started Wishing Well Kennels about 1950 with her daughter Barbara. Among the dogs imported were Ch. Cruben Melphis Chloe, who was BB at Westminster in 1951 and 1952; her son Ch. Cruben Dextor; and of course Ch. Elfinbrook Simon. This kennel, carried into the 1990s—though on a reduced scale—by Barbara, has had seven BIS winners under its banner, more than any other kennel. Mrs. Worcester died in 1974.

Donna Young, Greenbriar, of Dousman, Wisconsin, after looking for a show-quality bitch for more than a year, bought her first Westie in 1970 from the first litter bred by the Napadys; Greenbriar Grenadier finished his cham-pionship in five weeks. She next bought an already-finished bitch, Ch. Reanda Miss Muffet, from Darlene Gralewicz and Bergit Coady. From her second

Ch. Wishing Well's Brigadoon, owned and bred by
Wishing Wells Kennels. *Tauskey*

Ch. Lawrenton Wee Maggie, owned by Wishing
Well Kennels. *Brown*

litter by Grenadier, Tory produced the Montgomery County 1974 Sweep-
stakes winner, Wicken Greenbriar Eagan. Breeding only an occasional litter,
Donna has bred eleven champions over the years. In 1985, she bought from
Marjadele Schiele a Ch. Heritage Farms Jenny Jump-Up granddaughter,
Greenbriar Halli O'the Ridge, who went on to win the Roving Specialty
Sweepstakes in 1986. Her Greenbriar Going My Way was shown only on
Specialty weekends and finished his title with four majors; among his several
champions is the 1996 Montgomery County Winners Bitch, Czarcrest's Solo
O'BryBern.

Janet Zlatoff-Mirsky, Whitesprite, of Elburn, Illinois, got her first two
Westies within six months of each other in 1976: one male from Marjadele
Schiele and another from Joyce Lempke, famed as the breeder of London's
Duffy MacDuf. The younger dog was shown to his Obedience title and
lived past age 17. In 1982, she got a bitch puppy from Jodine Vertuno; this
puppy became Janet's first champion, Sno-Bilt's Daddy's Girl. After she fin-
ished her championship, she produced three of the seven champions bred at
Whitesprite.

Ch. Highlands's Ursa Major, owned by Perry Chadwick.

chapter 4

The Best in Show Winners

When twelve men, each deeply committed to the sport of dogs, met in Philadelphia on September 17, 1884, intent on establishing a Group devoted to that sport, organized dog shows had already been a part of the American scene for a decade. The first show had been held in Mineola, New York, on October 7, 1874; two previous events—one held in Illinois and another in New York, both in June 1874—had not been considered true shows due both to low number of entries and lack of awards made.

These nineteenth-century shows were a far cry from what we know today, and it was not until the 1920s that the standardized procedures now so familiar began to emerge. Under rules initiated in 1923, the various breeds were divided into five Variety Groups; after the Best of Breed dog in each breed had been decided, the best dog within that Group would be determined, and then the best dog in that show would be selected from among those five dogs. Within a year, most clubs were using the Group alignment system. The first club to use the new format to decide its Best in Show winner was the Westminster Kennel Club. Before this procedure was standardized, Best in Show judging took place only when an award was offered; even then, it was considered an unofficial award, technically an "unclassified special prize," and required the decision of between one and five judges from the panel. Because it was an unofficial award, the American Kennel Club did not maintain a record of the dogs who won these awards.

One West Highland White Terrier is known to have garnered a Best in Show during this period of unofficial awards. That Westie was Ch. Clarke's Hill Snooker, a dog considered to be if not the best, one of the best Highlanders of the breed's first years in the United States. Bred by Beatrice E. Greenhalgh, he was whelped in England on December 27, 1913, and imported by Claudia Lea Phelps of Rosstor Kennel fame about 1916; within a year he was an American champion. Like many of the Westies of his era, "Snooker's" pedigree traces back to within three generations of the great English Westie Morven.

West Point Ladas
Ironmouth
Sunshine
Chippings
Chawston Jerry
Hill Crest Meg
Swinger

Ch. Clarke's Hill Snooker

Morven
Cairn Nevis
Corymona
Hill Crest Madcap
Colonsay Calma
Mary of Argyle
Sunshine

Snooker achieved his own place in breed history by taking top honors at the Ladies' Dog Club's seventh annual dog show, which was held at the Beaver Country Day School in Brookline, Massachusetts, on June 17, 1922. This show offered an unclassified special prize for the best dog or bitch; the cash prize of twenty-five dollars was offered by Miss Jean G. Hinkle. Edward B. Chase, from Radnor, Pennsylvania, Dr. Howard W. Church, from Bristol, Rhode Island, and William Prescott Wolcott, from Readville, Massachusetts, were the arbiters of this special award.

To get to the point where he was considered for the award, Snooker had been earlier judged by C.C. Little, of Cold Springs Harbor, New York. There was a breed entry of seven dogs and two bitches, with one dog absent. All the entries were owned either by Miss Phelps or Mr. and Mrs. C.F. Huston Miller, and six had been bred by their owners. The Millers' homebred dog White Frost of Glengarry took the points from the American-bred class, while Ms. Phelps' Rosstor Rhalet took the bitch points. Snooker then got the nod for the breed win over another champion and the winners. Another award offered that day was for the best coat, with the judge given the admonition "to withhold for lack of merit or overtrimming"; that award also went to Snooker.

On the day Snooker won the breed's first Best in Show award, he was 8½ years old and was handled by his owner who has been referred to as the American sponsor of the breed. In a long show career, he was defeated only twice, once by his son Ch. Rosstor the Deil at the Westminster Kennel Club. It was Snooker who was used to illustrate the breed standard in the first years of the breed in this country.

After Snooker's Best, it was almost two decades before another Highlander took top honors at an all-breed show in the United States, this time the 1940 event of the Manchester Kennel Club, a New Hampshire club that dissolved in 1960. This win, too, broke new ground for the Westie as it went to an English-bred bitch, Eng., Am. Ch. Wolvey Pattern of Edgerstoune. "Pattern," bred by Mrs. C.C. (May) Pacey, was whelped April 20, 1937, by Eng. Ch. Wolvey Prefect out of Wolvey Privet of Edgerstoune and was linebred on Eng. Ch. Wolvey Patrician. Shown by her breeder in England, she consistently scored breed wins over champions and easily attained her own championship; one of her wins came under an American judge, Mrs. John G. Winant. With fresh memories of being unable to feed dogs during World War I and with it being all too obvious that another major military conflict was approaching, Mrs. Pacey sold Pattern and a finished male to Mrs. Winant at the end of 1938. The two joined other imports and homebreds at the Edgerstoune kennels near Concord, New Hampshire. After her aforementioned Best in Show win, she continued to be a consistent breed winner and Group placer over the next two years. In 1942 she achieved another distinguished place in breed history by becoming the first of only two Westies, and the only bitch, ever to win top honors at the Westminster Kennel Club show. Handled by Robert Gorman, she achieved this great distinction under judge H.E. Mellenthin.

After the win at Westminster, it was another two years before a Highlander saw the top spot again. After Ch. Gillette's Lord Tuffington's win at an Indiana event in 1944, it was another three years before a Westie went all the way at an all-breed show again; this time, the dog was Ch. Highland Ursa Major, and by winning two all-breed events in 1947, he achieved his own place in breed history by being the first to win multiple Bests in one year. In 1948, he won four all-breed Bests in Show, giving him a record that would not be bested until 1961.

Eight Highlanders have won twenty or more all-breed Best in Show awards. The first was Ch. Elfinbrook Simon, who during 1961 and 1962 won twenty-four Bests. Following "Simon" came Ch. Rannoch-Dune Down Beat, who had twenty-five victories over the years 1965 to 1968. Between 1969 and 1971, Ch. De-Go Hubert had thirty bests. Appearing on the scene to claim his first Best in 1970 was Ch. Purston Pinmoney Pedlar, whose record of fifty held for a quarter century. Ch. Ardenrun Andsome of Purston had thirty-nine Bests between 1974 and 1976. Ch. Holyrood's Hotspur O'Shellybay has fifty-one, won between 1992 and 1995. The record is now held by Ch. Round

Town Ivan the Terror, guided to a record-breaking seventy-six Bests between 1991 and 1995 by handler George Ward for his breeder-owner Amelia Musser. Ch. Hero's Top Brass, campaigned into 1997 under the Round Town banner of Amelia Musser by George Ward, had twenty Bests through 1996.

In 1961, Ch. Elfinbrook Simon took the first of his twenty-four all-breed Bests, won in just a two-year period. He won the Westminster Kennel Club show in 1962, becoming the second and to this point last Highlander to take that classic show. Simon was also the first to achieve double digits in the Bests column.

Simon was bred in England by Mr. and Mrs. H. Mitchell; he was whelped July 20, 1958, by Eng. Ch. Calluna the Laird out of Ichmell Gay Miss. After a less-than-auspicious beginning at his first two shows in the spring of 1959, he was sold to handler Len Pearson, acting for the Wishing Well Kennels of Mrs. Florence Worcester and her daughter Barbara, then of Little Falls, New Jersey. Simon came to New Jersey at 11 months of age and was shown only once that year, at a small show in Pennsylvania, in order to gain Westminster eligibility for 1960.

On February 7, 1960, the day before Westminster, Simon was entered at the Specialty show of the WHWTCA; there, shown by Clifford Hallmark, he was Winners Dog, Best of Winners and Best of Breed under John T. Marvin in an entry of eight dogs, seventeen bitches and twelve champions. At Westminster the next day, he was second in an Open class entry of two and did not go Reserve. Seven weeks later, he was Best of Winners at the WHWTC of Indiana Specialty and the Hoosier Kennel Club all-breed show to finish his championship. Still needing to mature, Simon returned home, although he was shown occasionally by his owner; one of these outings resulted in his first Group victory. His owner also took him to Canada in the summer of 1960, where, on three successive days, he took Best in Show from the classes, finishing his Canadian championship undefeated by any dog of any breed.

To give Simon a chance to prove himself in the show ring, Wishing Well Kennels, late in 1960, turned him over to the celebrated handler George Ward, then preeminent in the Wire Fox Terrier ring. Simon came to Westminster in 1961 and took a Group third, incidentally under the same man who had judged the breed in 1960 (and had not recognized the dog, even with a Reserve). He was shown sparingly during 1961 but, nonetheless, won twelve Bests, the first coming in Muncie, Indiana. In fact, during 1961, Ch. Elfinbrook Simon was not defeated by another West Highland White Terrier.

Simon started 1962 on the highly competitive Florida circuit, where he took four Bests in Show. After some heated discussions (of a friendly nature) between his owners and handler as to whether he would be entered at the Westminster Kennel Club show, it was decided he would be shown. There were twenty entered in the breed under John T. Marvin; after Simon took the purple and gold in the breed ring, he went on to claim the blue in the

Group ring under Fox Terrier authority James A. Farrell, Jr. He entered the Best in Show ring, along with the winning representatives of the other five Groups, to come under the experienced eye of all-breed authority Heywood R. Hartley. There, on February 13, 1962, Simon did what only one other Highlander had ever done before and none have accomplished to date: capture Best in Show at the Westminster Kennel Club, in competition against 2,568 other dogs. He continued to win during 1962, capturing another twelve Bests, the last being his final show at what was then California's largest show, Harbor Cities Kennel Club. Simon, shown sixty-five times, claimed sixty-one breed victories, forty-one Group firsts, twenty-four Bests in Show and four Specialty Bests (three of which were parent club events), after which he was retired to become a house pet and companion for the Worcesters. In June 1968, when he was almost 10 years old, Simon came out of retirement for the WHWTC of California's Specialty and, from the Veteran Dog class, won Best of Breed. Simon died on June 9, 1970.

Ch. Rannoch-Dune Down Beat, the second Highlander to achieve double-digit Bests, was bred by Mrs. Frank B. (Clare W.) Brumby. Whelped on November 23, 1962, he was by Ch. Rannoch Dune Demon out of Rannoch Dune Music. Mrs. B.G. Frame of Wigtown fame purchased Down Beat after he had turned a year old. Guided throughout his career by handler George Ward, "Tommy" took his first best on October 2, 1965, at the Hoosier Kennel Club event in Indianapolis, Indiana, following his breed victory at the Fall Specialty show of the West Highland White Terrier Club of America in a record-setting entry of ninety-one. In a four-year career, Tommy was shown 147 times and took the breed 139 times. In the fall of 1969, he won his twenty-fifth Best, at the same time taking his ninety-ninth Group first, which established another record for the breed. After this win, he was retired to become his owner's house dog. Tommy also earned his Canadian championship, won on one trip to Canada during 1969 where he took six Groups and a single best. Unfortunately, Tommy met a tragic end in September 1972 when he walked through a door inadvertently left open by workmen and was hit by a truck and killed.

Interestingly enough, both Simon and Tommy began their careers with the same shows: the WHWTCA Specialty held the day before the Westminster Kennel Club, Westminster itself, the WHWTC of Indiana and the Hoosier Kennel Club, where both dogs finished their titles (Simon in 1960 and Tommy in 1964). Continuing in the vein of interesting trivia, John Tasker Marvin started Simon out with Winners Dog, Best of Winners and Best of Breed at the WHWTCA specialty in 1960, and he finished Down Beat with the same awards at the 1964 Hoosier Kennel Club event.

In 1971, Tommy's record setting twenty-five Bests were eclipsed by the record of Ch. De-Go Hubert. Whelped August 14, 1966, "Hollis" was the offspring of English-imported parents: Ch. Whitebriar Jalisker and Ch. Whitebriar Jetstar. He was shown to his championship by his breeder, Dean

Ch. Rannoch-Dune Down Beat, owned by Mrs. B.G. Frame and handled to an impressive record by George Ward. He is shown winning BB at the WHWTCA 1967 Specialty under the renowned terrier authority John T. Marvin. *Shafer*

Ch. De-Go Hubert, owned by Jane Esther Henderson, took the occasion of the 1971 Montgomery County terrier classic to prove that, come what may, you can never keep a good Westie down. In the worst of weather, "Hollis" was BIS under Mrs. A.V. Riggs IV and piloted to a muddy finish by handler Clifford Hallmark. *Ashbey*

Hughes, who took him on to a number of Group placements before selling him as a 3-year-old to Jane E. Henderson, who promptly turned him over to Clifford Hallmark. In a three-year period, beginning in 1969, Hollis won thirty Bests, including the 1971 Montgomery County Kennel Club's all-terrier classic (in a downpour) on October 10th.

The dog whose record held for a quarter century was awarded his first Best at the Lexington (Kentucky) Kennel Club in 1970. Ch. Purston Pinmoney Pedlar, bred by Mrs. J.M. Fulford, was by Eng. Ch. Pillerton Peterman out of Pinmoney Pride and whelped in England on January 23, 1968. He was imported in September 1969 for Mrs. Paul (B.G.) Frame. He finished on the 1970 Florida circuit and, though shown sparingly during 1970, picked up six all-breed Bests from seventeen Group firsts.

Dr. Alvaro T. Hunt's memorable English import Ch. Ardenrun Andsome of Purston was by Whitebriar Jonfair out of Ardenrun Agitator. He was bred by Mr. C. Oakley in England, where he was born on June 13, 1972. He was purchased by Dr. Hunt for a purported 9,000 dollars and turned over to the professional handler Dora Lee Wilson for a career that would include numerous successes. "Andy" got his first Best at the Des Moines Kennel Club show on September 8, 1974. Mrs. Wilson guided him to a total of thirty-nine Bests over a three-year period, including the 1976 Montgomery County all-terrier show over an entry of 1867 dogs. Andy bested 164 in the breed under Mrs. Barbara Keenan and then got the nod in the Best ring from Heywood R. Hartley, the same judge who awarded Simon the 1962 Westminster Best. Andy was retired the day after getting his last Best under Robert J. Moore in December 1977; in retirement he resided with Roberta Mocabee at her Happymac Kennels in California, where he was used extensively at stud.

For a decade and a half after Andy's retirement, the breed was consistently represented in the Best in Show column, but there was no big winner until the 1990s, when two dogs sharing a similar pedigree appeared on the scene.

Ch. Holyrood's Hotspur O'Shellybay, whelped January 28, 1990, was bred by Marilyn Foster and Judy Francisco; he was by Ch. Holyrood's Here Comes the Son out of Ch. Holyrood's Ms. Mayhem. During 1992, "Ted" was campaigned under the ownership of Marcia Montgomery, Florence MacMillan, Gary Gabriel, Marilyn Foster and Randell Dickerson; during 1993 he was campaigned by Dr. Montgomery, Frederick Melville, Mrs. Foster and Mr. Dickerson. He ended his career under the ownership of Mrs. Foster and Mr. Dickerson. Ted became the holder of the number-two spot in the record book with back-to-back Bests on February 11 and 12, 1995, at the Central Indiana and Hoosier Kennel Clubs shows. His last show—Hoosier—also gave him his 156th Group win.

Ch. Round Town Ivan the Terror, whelped August 14, 1989, was by Ch. Holyrood's Hootman O'Shelybay out of Ch. Round Town Sugar Plum (whose

Ch. Purston Pinmoney Pedlar, owned by Mrs. B.G. Frame, was one of the breed's foremost winners during the early 1970s. His wins include BIS at Montgomery County in 1972.

Ch. Ardenrun Andsome of Purston, owned by Alvaro T. Hunt, MD, was a popular winner during the mid-1970s. He won the Terrier Group at the 1975 Westminster show and was BIS at a very wet Montgomery County in 1976 under Heywood R. Hartley.

dam holds the breed record for most Bests in Show won by a bitch). "Ivan" finished his championship at the Hatboro Dog Club in October 1990 under Edward Keenan, and his first Best came at the Kennel Club of Columbus, Indiana, on March 19, 1991, with Mrs. Jane Forsyth giving him the nod in the Group ring and Mrs. Michelle Billings the coveted red, white and blue. He tied the Pedlar dog's record of fifty Bests at the Kennel Club of Columbus, Indiana, show in August 1993 and broke the record at the Tennessee Valley Kennel Club in November of the same year. His seventy-sixth and last career Best came on February 26, 1995, with Mrs. Jane Forsyth awarding him Best at the Panama City (Florida) event.

Ch. Hero's Top Brass, sired by Ch. Round Town Ivan the Terror out of Ch. Hero's Lady Sarah and bred by Mrs. R.S. Pajak, was born January 17, 1994. He is owned by Amelia Musser of Round Town Kennels and handled by George Ward. Through the end of 1996, he has won twenty-one all-breed Bests.

The all-terrier classic, the Montgomery County Kennel Club's show held in October near Philadelphia, Pennsylvania, has been claimed by a Highlander on five occasions. The first Montgomery won by a Westie was the 1960 edition, when Barbara J. Worcester's Ch. Symmetra Snip, a 3-year-old import sired by Eng. Ch. Symmetra Skirmish out of Symmetra Serener, took the honors under George Hartman. Snip, bred by B. Taylor and V. Davidson, was handled by Clifford Hallmark to three all-breed Bests as well. In 1971, Montgomery was claimed by Jane E. Henderson's Ch. De-Go Hubert, again with Clifford Hallmark on the other end of the lead; the breed nod was given by judge Terence P. Bresnahan, while the Best came from Mrs. Augustus Riggs IV. The next year, 1972, George Ward guided Mrs. B.G. Frame's Ch. Purston Pinmoney Pedlar to the red, white and blue rosette awarded by Dr. E.S. Montgomery after getting the breed purple and gold from Mrs. Heywood R. Hartley. In 1974, Clifford Hallmark was again on the lead of the winner, this time Mr. and Mrs. George Seemann's Ch. Braidholme White Tornado of Binate, a ten-time all-breed Best winner. Pointing to the Irish-bred import called "Nikki" was W.W. Brainard, Jr. As mentioned earlier, the last time the nod went to a Westie was at the 1976 show, when Dora Lee Wilson brought Dr. Alvaro Hunt's Ch. Ardenrun Andsome of Purston to the Group ring for Heywood R. Hartley to take to the top.

After Ch. Wolvey Pattern of Edgerstoune's all-breed wins in 1940 and 1942, it wasn't until 1951 that a bitch took top honors again. During the 1950s two bitches won three shows, but no bitch took an all-breed Best in Show during the 1960s. The first show during the 1970s in which the nod was given to a bitch was in 1973. The first bitch to win multiple Bests within a single year was Ch. Heritage Farms Jenny Jump Up. Born April 18, 1973, "Jenny" was by Ch. Monsieur Aus Der Flerlage out of Ch. Merryhart Sweet Pea. Bred by N. Johnson, Jenny was owned by Mrs. Marjadele Schiele and co-owned by Shirley Jean O'Neill. Jenny was sent to the whelping box

Ch. Heritage Farms Jenny Jump Up, owned by Marjadele Schiele, began her successful career after most dogs are retired. A multiple Specialty winner, her record includes two consecutive Best of Breed at the Westminster KC in 1978 and 1979. *Booth*

Ch. Celtic's Cory, owned and bred by Nils and Monica Carlson, at one time held the group record for Westie bitches. *Alverson*

before the Conformation ring; in fact, she whelped eighteen puppies before being entered in her first show in the fall of 1977. She finished her championship in just four weekends. In 1978 Jenny became the first Westie bitch to go Best in Show in twenty-two years and the first American-bred bitch to take a Best in twenty-seven years. In a single year, she won four all-breed Bests, capably handled by Landis Hirstein. At age 10 she got her Companion Dog title, and at age 13 her Certificate of Gameness. Jenny died on April 28, 1989, just ten days following her sixteenth birthday.

In 1984 and 1985 Am., Can. Ch. Celtic's Cory (Ch. Loch O Fee's Pirate Ransom x Ch. Loch O Fee's Celie), owned by her breeders Nils and Monica Carlson, won five all-breed BIS, including back-to-back events. The next year Ch. Round Town Ella J. Fitzgerald, who had taken a single show in 1982, came out of the whelping box to win seven shows over a two-year period for her breeder Amelia Musser. "Ella" was by Eng., Can., Am. Ch. Whitebriar Jeronimo out of Ch. Wind Town All That Jazz and whelped June 18, 1981. After Ella's retirement in 1987, it was not until 1995 that a bitch took another all-breed Best. Ch. Whitehaus' Double Trouble, bred by Shirley Goldman and Shirley Jean Niehaus, also made a place in breed history by being the first bitch to win a Best, handled by her owner, Nancy Spelke. "Sassy," whelped August 7, 1992 and sired by Ch. Shirl's Jolly Jack out of Shirl's-Whitehaus Quiddity, established another record in 1996 when she won her fiftieth Group 1, besting the eleven-year-old record of forty-two held by Ch. Celtic's Cory.

Two bitches each won a single Best during 1996: Ch. Glengloamin's Rise 'N Shine and Ch. Wynecroft Wild at Heart. The latter, "Gigi," was bred by Marcia Montgomery and co-owned by her breeder and Crecia C. Closson, Crannog Westies. Whelped October 17, 1993, she was handled by Kathleen Ferris. "Stacee," bred by Randell Dickerson and Bill Green, was by Ch. Holyrood's Hotspur O'Shelly Bay out of Ch. Glengloamin's Fancee Free. Whelped on September 14, 1992, she is owned by Gail and Gene Miller, Highfield Westies, and Dr. James and Elizabeth Boso, Glengloamin Westies, and is handled by Bergit Coady. Stacee picked up another all-breed Best early in 1997.

BEST-IN-SHOW WINNERS

Year	Dog's Name		Owner(s)
1922	Ch. Clarke's Hill Snooker	1	Rosstor Kennels
1940	Ch. Wolvey Pattern of Edgerstoune*	1	Mrs. John G. Winant

Ch. Round Town Ella J. Fitzgerald, owned and bred by Amelia Musser, holds the all-breed BIS record for Westie bitches with eight awards. Her wins also include the WHWTCA Specialty Best of Breed at Montgomery County 1986 under Joan Graber. *Booth*

Ch. Wynecroft Wild at Heart, owned by Dr. Marcia A. Montgomery (her breeder) and Crecia C. Closson, has won well during the mid-1990s in the hands of Kathleen J. Ferris.

Ch. Klintilloch Molly Dee, the second BIS Westie bitch.

Ch. Pinmoney Puck, owned by Wishing Well Kennels and Marjadele Schiele, was one of six BIS offspring of the legendary Ch. Pillerton Peterman.

Ch. Whitebriar Jalisker, an import owned by Mr. and Mrs. Herman Fellton, was a strong winner and sired the memorable Ch. De-Go Hubert. He was shown by Michelle Billings. *Gilbert*

1942	Ch. Wolvey Pattern of Edgerstoune*	1	Mrs. John G. Winant
1944	Ch. Gillette's Lord Tuffington	1	Ben Gillette
1947	Ch. Highland Ursa Major	2	Perry Chadwick
1948	Ch. Cranbourne Arial	1	Mrs. John T. Marvin
	Ch. Highland Ursa Major	4	Perry Chadwick
1949	Ch. Cranbourne Arial	2	Mrs. John T. Marvin
	Ch. Highland Ursa Major	1	Perry Chadwick
1950	Ch. Cranbourne Arial	1	Mrs. John T. Marvin
1951	Ch. Klintilloch Molly Dee*	1	Mrs. S. Marge Blue
1952	Ch. Humby's Dipper	2	Mrs. Almary Henderson
1953	Ch. Cranbourne Atomic	1	Mrs. John T. Marvin
	Ch. Cruben Dextor	1	Barbara Worcester
1954	Ch. Cranbourne Atomic	1	Mrs. John T. Marvin
	Ch. Cruben Dextor	2	Barbara Worcester
	Ch. Shiningcliff Donark Dancer*	1	Robert Lowry
1955	Ch. Cravat Coronation	1	William Worley
1956	Ch. Cranbourne Alexandrite	2	Mrs. John T. Marvin
	Ch. Cruben Flashback	1	Barbara Worcester
	Ch. Shiningcliff Donark Dancer*	1	Robert Lowry
	Ch. Tulyar of Trenean	1	Barbara Worcester
1957	Ch. Cruben Flashback	1	Barbara Worcester
	Ch. Culbahn Garry	1	B.F. & N. Crawford
	Ch. Wigtown Talent Scout	1	Mrs. B.G. Frame
1958	No BIS was won by a WHWT in this year.		

1959	Ch. Wigtown Talent Scout	1	Mrs. B.G. Frame
1960	Ch. Symmetra Snip	3	Barbara Worcester
	Ch. Wigtown Talent Scout	1	Mrs. B.G. Frame
1961	Ch. Elfinbrook Simon	12	Wishing Well Kennels
1962	Ch. Elfinbrook Simon	12	Wishing Well Kennels
	Ch. Klintilloch Mercator	1	Robert & Robert Momberger
1963	Ch. Whitebriar Journeyman	2	Mrs. Barbara Sayres & Mrs. Sally Hudson
	Ch. Wolvey Pickwick	1	Mrs. E.K. Fischer
1964	Ch. Tumbleweed's High Hopes	1	Mrs. Carl Furhmann
	Ch. Wolvey Pickwick	1	Mrs. E.K. Fischer
1965	Ch. Maxwelton Freshman	1	Robert Lowry
	Ch. Rannoch-Dune Down Beat	1	Mrs. B.G. Frame
	Ch. Tamlor's Danny O'Dunoon	1	R.H. Gustin
1966	Ch. Forest Glen Simon Sez Be Brisk	1	Mrs. C.C. Fawcett
	Ch. Rannoch-Dune Down Beat	4	Mrs. B.G. Frame
1967	Ch. Rannoch-Dune Down Beat	5	Mrs. B.G. Frame
	Ch. Whitebriar Jalisker	3	Mr. & Mrs. H.L. Fellton
1968	Ch. Alderbrook Jolly Roger	1	Dr. Lois G. Dickie
	Ch. Alpinegay Impresario	2	Mrs. G.F. Church
	Ch. Huntinghouse Little Fella	1	Katharine Hayward
	Ch. Rannoch-Dune Down Beat	11	Mrs. B.G. Frame
	Ch. Ugadale's Artist's Model	1	Mrs. C.K. Weaver

1968	Ch. Whitebriar Jalisker	9	Mr. & Mrs. H.L. Fellton
1969	Ch. Alpinegay Impresario	4	Mrs. G.F. Church
	Ch. D and D's Dead Ringer	1	Mr. & Mrs. R.L. Hanna
	Ch. De-Go Hubert	8	Mrs. Jane Esther Henderson
	Ch. Lymehill's Birkfell Solstice	4	Wishing Well Kennels
	Ch. Monsieur Aus Der Flerlage	2	Bergit Zakschewski
	Ch. Rannoch-Dune Down Beat	4	Mrs. B.G. Frame
	Ch. Whitebriar Jalisker	1	Mr. & Mrs. H.L. Fellton
1970	Ch. Alpinegay Impresario	1	Mrs. G.F. Church
	Ch. De-Go Hubert	16	Mrs. Jane Esther Henderson
	Ch. Lymehill's Birkfell Solstice	1	Wishing Well Kennels
	Ch. Purston Pinmoney Pedlar	6	Mrs. B.G. Frame
1971	Ch. De-Go Hubert	6	Mrs. Jane Esther Henderson
	Ch. Purston Pinmoney Pedlar	6	Mrs. B.G. Frame
	Ch. White Oaks Lover Boy	1	Dr. & Mrs. G.G. Meisels
1972	Ch. Pillerton Peterkin	1	Mrs. Constance Jones
	Ch. Pinmoney Puck	1	Mrs. Marjadele Schiele & Wishing Well Kennels

	Ch. Purston Pinmoney Pedlar	13	Mrs. B.G. Frame
	Ch. Wiloglen's Willoughboy	2	Allan & Marlene Kotlisky
1973	Ch. Braidholme White Tornado of Binate	1	Mr. & Mrs. G.H. Seemann
	Ch. Highlands Angus	4	Dr. A.T. Hunt
	Ch. Pinmoney Puck	7	Mrs. Marjadele Schiele & Wishing Well Kennels
	Ch. Purston Pinmoney Pedlar	20	Mrs. B.G. Frame
	Ch. Purston Polly Perkins*	1	Mrs. Constance Jones
1974	Ch. Ardenrun Andsome of Purston	9	Dr. A.T. Hunt
	Ch. Braidholme White Tornado of Binate	9	Mr. & Mrs. G.H. Seemann
	Ch. Highlands Angus	2	Dr. A.T. Hunt
	Ch. Keithall Pilot	1	Mrs. Joanne Glodek
	Ch. Pinmoney Puck	1	Mrs. Marjadele Schiele & Wishing Well Kennels
	Ch. Purston Pinmoney Pedlar	5	Mrs. B.G. Frame
1975	Ch. Ardenrun Andsome of Purston	19	Dr. A. T. Hunt
	Ch. Commander of Tintibar	1	Mrs. Constance Jones
1976	Ch. Ardenrun Andsome of Purston	11	Dr. A.T. Hunt
	Ch. B-J's Sir Becket	1	Anita J. Becky
	Ch. London Duffy MacDuf	2	Bobbe London & Bergit Coady

1977	Ch. B-J's Sir Becket	3	Anita J. Becky
1978	Ch. Heritage Farms Jenny Jump Up*	4	Mrs. Marjadele Schiele
	Ch. Purston Primate	8	Dr. A.T. Hunt
1979	Ch. Donnarry's Robby of Lochsend	1	Dr. Hazel Norris
	Ch. Purston Primate	1	Dr. A.T. Hunt
1980	Ch. Keri of Thistle Ridge*	1	Lupe Flores
	Ch. Purston Merrymick	5	Dr. A.T. Hunt
	Ch. Seamate	1	Mrs. Peggy Lewis
1981	Ch. Donnarry's Robby of Lochsend	1	Dr. Hazel Norris
	Ch. Kenwood's Measure for Measure	2	Ed McParlan
	Ch. Olac Mooncloud	1	R. L. Hanna, R. Widden & W. Webb
	Ch. Skaket's Candy Man	1	Nancy & Mitzi Gauthier
1982	Ch. Cripsey Brigand	1	Gerald Ireton
	Ch. Kenwood's Measure for Measure	1	Ed McParlan
	Ch. Kilbrannon Curtain Up	1	Mr. & Mrs. G.H. Seemann
	Ch. Olac Mooncloud	1	R.L. Hanna, R. Widden & W. Webb
	Ch. Pagan Ghost	1	Mr. & Mrs. G. H. Seemann
	Ch. Round Town Ella J. Fitzgerald*	1	Amelia E. Musser
	Ch. Sno-Bilt's Puzzle	1	Jodine Vertuno

	Ch. Whitecrest Sir Andre	1	Helmut & Jutta Buchele
1983	Ch. Kenwood's Measure for Measure	1	Ed McParlan
	Ch. Pagan Ghost	3	Mr. & Mrs. G.H. Seemann
	Ch. Sno-Bilt's Puzzle	2	Jodine Vertuno
1984	Ch. Celtic's Cory*	2	Mr. & Mrs. Nils Carlson
	Ch. Mac-Ken-Char's Irish Navigator	4	Joanne & Jaimi Glodek
	Ch. Pagan Ghost	4	Mr. & Mrs. G. H. Seemann
1985	Ch. Celtic's Cory*	3	Mr. & Mrs. Nils Carlson
	Ch. Glenfinnan's Special Brew	1	Mary L. Charles
	Ch. Glenncheck May Be*	1	Pat Darby & Barbara Keenan
	Ch. Jopeta Jamie Macpherst	1	Ed McParlan & Michael Collings
	Ch. Kilkerran D'Artagnan	2	Kathleen & Wayne Kompare
	Ch. Mac-Ken-Char's Irish Navigator	2	Joanne & Jaimi Glodek
1986	Ch. Mac-Ken-Char's Irish Navigator	3	Joanne & Jaimi Glodek
	Ch. Round Town Ella J. Fitzgerald*	5	Amelia E. Musser
1987	Ch. Mac-Ken-Char's Irish Navigator	1	Joanne & Jaimi Glodek

1987	Ch. Round Town Ella J. Fitzgerald*	2	Amelia E. Musser
	Ch. Snowbank Starr Shine	1	Amelia E. Musser
	Ch. Tweed Take By Storm	1	Gary R. Gabriel & Florence W. MacMillan
	Ch. Waterford of Wyndam	1	Gary R. Gabriel & Florence W. MacMillan
1988	Ch. Kilkerran 'N Wicket A Kut Above	1	Nancy Spelke, Laura T. Moreno & Kathleen Kompare
	Ch. Sallydean's Duglad of Damara	1	Sheila Ehmann
	Ch. Snowbank Starr Shine	2	Amelia E. Musser
	Ch. Tweed Take By Storm	11	Gary R. Gabriel & Florence W. MacMillan
	Ch. Waterford of Wyndam	2	Gary R. Gabriel & Florence W. MacMillan
1989	Ch. Holyrood's Hootman O'Shelybay	5	Dr. James & Elizabeth Boso
	Ch. Kilkerran 'N Wicket A Kut Above	2	Nancy Spelke, Laura T. Moreno & Kathleen Kompare
	Ch. Luann's I'm For Keeps	1	Susan L. Simpson
	Ch. Pilot of Keithall	1	Martha W. Black
	Ch. Snowbank Starr Shine	1	Amelia E. Musser

	Ch. Tweed Take By Storm	7	Gary R. Gabriel & Florence W. MacMillan
1990	Ch. Ashgate Alistair of Trewen	2	Angeline F. Austin & Martha W. Black
	Ch. Crinan Counterpoint	2	Wendell Marumoto
	Ch. Holyrood's Hootman O'Shelybay	3	Dr. James & Elizabeth Boso
	Ch. Principal's Macgyver	2	Robert & Susan Ernst
1991	Ch. Biljonblue's Burlington Burt	1	Jerry & Paul Magee
	Ch. Holyrood's Hootman O'Shelybay	2	Dr. James & Elizabeth Boso
	Ch. Kilkerran Quintessence	4	Nancy Spelke & Kathy Kompare
	Ch. Round Town Ivan the Terror	11	Amelia E. Musser
	Ch. Windswept's Frederic	1	Patricia A. Caswell
1992	Ch. Crinan Counterpoint	1	Wendell Marumoto
	Ch. Holyrood's Hotspur O'Shellybay	13	Marcia Montgomery, Florence MacMillan, Gary Gabriel, Marilyn Foster & Randell Dickerson
	Ch. Kilkerran Quintessence	1	Nancy Spelke & Kathy Kompare
1992	Ch. Round Town Ivan the Terror	20	Amelia E. Musser

1993	Ch. Holyrood's Hotspur O'Shellybay	27	Marcia Montgomery, Frederick Melville, Marilyn Foster & Randell Dickerson
	Ch. Round Town Ivan the Terror	26	Amelia E. Musser
1994	Ch. Aberglen Lucky Lindy	4	Fred Melville
	Ch. Holyrood's Hotspur O'Shellybay	9	Marilyn Foster & Randell Dickerson
	Ch. Playboy O'Peter Pan	1	Thomas H. & Barbara Barrie
	Ch. Round Town Ivan the Terror	18	Amelia E. Musser
1995	Ch. Aberglen Lucky Lindy	7	Fred Melville
	Ch. Hero's Top Brass	1	Amelia E. Musser
	Ch. Holyrood's Hotspur O'Shellybay	2	Marilyn Foster & Randell Dickerson
	Ch. Round Town Ivan the Terror	1	Amelia E. Musser
	Ch. Whitehaus' Double Trouble*	3	Nancy Spelke
1996	Ch. Acreages Bold Bonus	1	Joanne Tucker
	Ch. Glengloamin's Rise 'N Shine*	1	Gail & Gene Miller & Dr. James & Elizabeth Boso
	Ch. Hero's Top Brass	20	Amelia E. Musser
	Ch. Wynecroft Wild at Heart*	1	Crecia C. Closson & Dr. Marcia Montgomery
1997	Ch. Glengloamin's Rise 'N Shine*	1	Gail & Gene Miller & Dr. James & Elizabeth Boso

Ch. Sweet Sound's King of Rock N' Roll	1	Robert & Susan M. Ernst
Ch. Mac-Ken-Char's Ashscot Liberty	1	Joanne & Jaimi Glodek
Ch. Donnybrook's George	1	Meade W. Carlson & John T. Ward

* *Indicates a bitch.*

Ch. Kilkerran 'N Wicket a Kut Above, owned by Nancy Spelke (pictured), Laura Moreno and Kathy Kompare, was owner-handled by Nancy to an impressive show record that included multiple all-bred BIS and Specialties. *Missy Yuhl*

Ch. Kilkerran Quintessence, owned by Nancy Spelke and Kathy Kompare, was yet another from these fanciers that made a host of top wins handled by his amateur co-owner—no mean feat in the highly competitive Terrier Group. *Missy Yuhl*

chapter 5

The Specialty Winners

The West Highland White Terrier was recognized as a breed by the American Kennel Club on September 21, 1909. Just eight months later, on May 28, 1910, fanciers held the breed's first Specialty show—an event in which only one breed competes—in Greenwich, Connecticut; an entry of twenty-five came out for James Mortimer, then an AKC director, to judge. On October 24, 1911, fanciers brought fifty-two Westies to the national Specialty show in Convent, New Jersey, to pass under the eye of Henry T. Fleitmann, a Sealyham Terrier breeder. Even though these first two events drew large entries, it was not until 1923 that another Specialty show was held. At none of these early Specialty shows was one Westie selected as the Best Dog; since 1926, however, Specialty shows have produced a Best in Specialty show winner, a placement that is coveted by breeders and owners alike.

For twenty years there was only one Specialty show each year, and that one was put on under the auspices of the parent club for the breed, the West Highland White Terrier Club of America. At the end of World War II, travel restrictions eased and an element of prosperity returned to the American scene. Dog fanciers—not just of Westies, but of all breeds—established local organizations devoted to the betterment of their respective breeds and the holding of Specialty shows. For Westies, the first club to hold its own regional show was the Central West Highland White Terrier Club, established in the summer of 1946 in Indianapolis, Indiana. In the half century since, fanciers from New England to Hawaii, from Houston to Chicago, and all points in between have come together, and as of 1997 there were twenty-one clubs, seventeen of which hold their own Specialty shows. In 1959, the parent club added a second Specialty show to the agenda so that there are now nineteen annual occasions on which West Highland White Terriers show themselves to their admirers in the important spotlight of a Specialty.

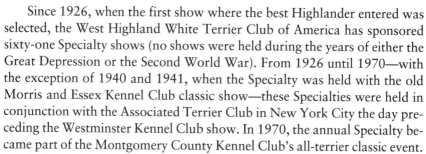

Since 1926, when the first show where the best Highlander entered was selected, the West Highland White Terrier Club of America has sponsored sixty-one Specialty shows (no shows were held during the years of either the Great Depression or the Second World War). From 1926 until 1970—with the exception of 1940 and 1941, when the Specialty was held with the old Morris and Essex Kennel Club classic show—these Specialties were held in conjunction with the Associated Terrier Club in New York City the day preceding the Westminster Kennel Club show. In 1970, the annual Specialty became part of the Montgomery County Kennel Club's all-terrier classic event.

In those sixty-two shows, forty-nine different Westies—thirty-eight dogs and eleven bitches—have been victorious. Of those forty-nine, seventeen were bred by their owners and eleven were handled by their owners, and nine of those twelve were breeder-owner-handled.

The first Best in Specialty Highlander was W.B. Rogers' imported bitch White Cloud of Nishkenon (White Smasher ex White Sylvia); she repeated her 1926 win in 1927 as a champion. A short, cobby bitch, she was set upon by three or four other bitches and killed in June 1931, just a month shy of her seventh birthday. After those first two shows, four years passed without another Specialty show being held. The 1932 and 1933 events were won by imports bearing the Cooden prefix and owned by Mrs. William Dexter, founder of the Heather Hill kennels. The 1934 show was won by a homebred from the Edgerstoune kennels of Mrs. John G. (Marion) Winant. Between 1934 and 1954, Highlanders owned or bred by Mrs. Winant won ten of the fifteen Specialty shows held. Included among these was the 1940 winner, Ch. Wolvey Pattern of Edgerstoune, the bitch who made breed history by being the first Westie to go Best in Show at Westminster Kennel Club.

The first of the five shows won by other than Edgerstoune-bred or -owned Westies in this period went to Ch. Robinridge Commodore, owned and bred by Mrs. A.S. (Mary-Ellen) Monroney; though not carrying the Edgerstoune prefix, the dog traced to that kennel as both his sire and dam were Edgerstoune, his sire being the 1936 Specialty winner. Unfortunately, this first Specialty win was also the last win for a promising dog as, when his crate was opened the morning after the show, he was found dead. This tragedy, fortunately, did not deter Mrs. Monroney, the wife of a senator from the state of Oklahoma. She had started in the breed by purchasing a number of bitches from Mrs. Winant in 1935 as the foundation of her Robinridge kennels; she also purchased Ch. Cooden Sheriff of Edgerstoune, an outstanding stud dog whose presence in the Midwest would be strongly felt in future years.

With war looming on the European horizon as the 1930s drew to a close, English and Scottish kennels found they would have to reduce their stock. With memories of destroying dogs because of inadequate food supplies during World War I fresh in too many minds, the alternative was to sell them to North America; thus, importation on a scale not seen in twenty years started.

Although the war was not felt in the United States to the same extent that it was in Great Britain, the attention of the world was on matters other than sporting events in the first half-decade of the 1940s, with dog shows all but ceasing during the period. A number of breeders were able to maintain their stock and breeding programs, though on a greatly reduced scale, so that when shows were resumed at the end of the Second World War, the breed had its stalwarts as well as a number of new enthusiasts. Foremost among those old retainers was Mrs. William Dexter, who at this point was the person who had the longest involvement with the West Highlander, having been breeding and showing since the 1920s with bloodlines based on Wolvey Poacher. While she was not exhibiting at the level of her pre-war degree, her Heather Hill–bred dogs were still to be contended with during the latter half of the 1940s.

Many of the new enthusiasts of the breed who entered the show ring in the second half of the 1940s include the "Who's Who of Westiedom," both in people and dogs. The 1948 WHWTCA Specialty was won by the Canadian-bred Ch. Highland Ursa Major, owned by Perry Chadwick. Again, though not carrying the Edgerstoune name, he was bred on Edgerstoune lines, as his dam was Edgerstoune Stardust and his sire had both a Robinridge sire and dam, both of whom were Edgerstoune-bred. Ursa Major went on to fame as a sire and a multiple Best in Show winner. In 1950, Ch. Cranbourne Arial set another record as being the first Westie to be handled to a Specialty win by his breeder-owner-handler, Mrs. John T. (Bea) Marvin. The Marvins started with Wire Fox Terriers early in the 1930s but purchased a Westie in 1943 and, from there, their involvement with the breed is history. Arial was the first of the three homebred dogs Mrs. Marvin owner-handled to all-breed Bests in Show.

The 1951 Specialty was won by Ch. Cruben Melphis Chloe, a bitch owned by another name synonymous with the history of the breed in America: Barbara J. Worcester (later Sayres, then Keenan), who along with her mother, Mrs. Florence Worcester, established Wishing Well Kennels in Little Falls, New Jersey, in the late 1940s. Under the Wishing Well Kennels banner, Barbara Keenan has owned, bred and shown Westies for almost fifty years. The last of the dogs not of Edgerstoune breeding to win one of the first twenty Specialty shows for Westies was also owned by Barbara Worcester, and that dog was Ch. Cruben Dextor, an import whelped in England on January 17, 1950. This dog, by Eng. Ch. Hookwood Mentor out of Ch. Cruben Melphis Chloe, was one of the most prominent stud dogs of the period, having sired more than twenty-five champions in at least three countries: England, Canada and the United States.

The second half of the 1950s were marked by the stellar achievements of two dogs: Cruben Moray (later known as Cruben Moray of Clairedale), owned by Claire K. Dixon and handled by Robert Gorman, and Roseneath

Ch. Cranbourne Arial, owned and bred by Mr. and Mrs. John T. Marvin, was handled to a host of top wins at Specialties and all-breed shows.

Ch. Cruben Dextor, owned by Barbara Worcester, was BB at the 1953 WHWTCA Specialty following by two years his mother, Ch. Cruben Melphis Chloe, who made the same win. An influential stud during the early 1950s, he was sire by Ch. Hookwood Mentor. *Tauskey*

Ch. Roseneath White Knight, owned and handled by T.S. Adams, was BB from the classes at the WHWTCA Specialty in 1957 under Mrs. William Dexter (right). Mrs. Dexter was one of the Westies' great supporters during and after World War II. Mrs. Florence Worcester completes this historic grouping. *William Brown*

White Knight, owned by Thomas S. Adams. Both won the Specialty from the classes, the former in 1955 and the latter in 1957, handled by his breeder-owner of Ontario, Canada. Both returned to claim the win again, Moray in 1956 and 1958 and Knight in 1959, again handled by Mr. Adams.

The WHWTCA Specialty shows of the 1960s started with a win from the classes by Elfinbrook Simon, an import for the Wishing Well banner. Simon repeated the win in 1962. And what can be said about this dog other than that which has been said in referring to him as "the imcomparable one"? As a sire and as a show dog, he had no equals in his time; while the records he established have been surpassed in the almost thirty years since his death, he remains a legend within the breed and is likely always to be so.

Twice more in the decade of the 1960s the breed winner came from the classes: the bitch, Dina-Ken's Little Pip, in 1961 and the male, Glenhaven Ceasar, in 1965. Twice also dogs from Canada were declared victorious: Dina-Ken's Little Pip, breeder-owned by the Albert Kayes, and Ch. Whitebriar Journeyman, an import co-owned by Sally Hudson of Sallydean Kennel fame and Barbara Sayres. Twice again, the winning dog had been bred by its owner: the Barbers' Glenhaven Ceasar and Katharine Hayward's Ch. Huntinghouse Little Fella. Twice the winner was handled by the owner, as Albert Kaye was on the lead of Dina-Ken's Little Pip and Barbara Sayres on Journeyman. And

Ch. Dina-Ken's Little Pip, owned by Mr. and Mrs. Albert Kaye, was BB at the WHWTCA Specialty in 1961 from the classes.

Ch. Whitebriar Journeyman (Eng. Ch. Famecheck Gay Crusader ex Whitebriar Juana), owned by Sally Hudson and Barbara Sayres and bred by Mrs. J.H. Daniell-Jenkins. *Brown*

Ch. Camcrest Andsurely Trouble, owned by Carol C. Greenwald and bred by Sandy Campbell and Carol McKay, has had a remarkable career. Twice BB at WHWTCA Specialties, her first such win came in 1993 from the classes. She repeated in 1996 under John T. Ward. *Lindemaier*

twice the same dog won: Simon in 1960 and 1962, and Ch. Rannoch-Dune Down Beat, bred by Mrs. Frank B. (Claire) Brumby and owned by Mrs. Paul (B.G.) Frame, who won in 1966 and 1967.

Of the eight dogs who won the ten shows during the 1970s, four were imports and four were bred in the United States; of the latter four, two were owned by their breeders and one of those—the veteran bitch Ch. Briarpatch Raggamuffin—was shown by her owner to the win. Of the four imports, two wore the Purston prefix while another wore this prominent English kennel name as an affix, but none of the three shared either breeders or breeding in the immediate generations. The other winners, Ch. Braidholme White Tornado of Binate, owned by the George H. Seemanns, and Ch. Ardenrun Andsome of Purston, owned by Dr. Alvaro T. Hunt, each had impressive show records.

Eight dogs again shared wins at the ten shows held during the decade of the 1980s, with the only double winners being Ch. Skaket's Candy Man, who won in 1981 at the age of 2 years and again in 1988 from the Veterans class, and Ch. Pagan Ghost. Four of the winners from this decade were bred by their owners, and three of the four were handled to their wins by their breeder-owners. Two of the other three winners were imports, and the last winner of the 1980s was also the first winner of the 1990s.

Ch. Holyrood's Hootman O'Shelybay, owned by Dr. James and Elizabeth Boso, had a long successful career in top all-breed and Specialty competition. His last WHWTCA Specialty BB came in March 1997 from the Veteran's class. *Callea*

Ch. Glenfinnan's Something Dandy, owned by Dr. James and Elizabeth Boso, was BB at the 1991 WHWTCA Specialty from the Veteran's class under judge William Ferrara. *Callea*

Ch. Aberglen Lucky Lindy, owned by Frederick Melville, has a long list of Specialty triumphs all over the United States. *Callea*

The 1990s also saw a winner come from the Veterans class and a young class bitch, Camcrest Andsurely Trouble, go to the top from the Bred-by-Exhibitor class; the same bitch returned as a champion three years later—after whelping three litters—to take the Specialty win again. In so doing, she became the first bitch to win two national Specialties since the first two Specialties in 1926 and 1927 were won by White Cloud of Nishkenon, whose first win also came before she was a champion. The 1990s also saw a sequence in which three generations went to the top at the national Specialty, starting with the son, Ch. Holyrood's Hootman O'Shelybay in 1990 (who had also won in 1989), followed by the father, Ch. Glenfinnan's Something Dandy from the Veterans class in 1991, and continuing with the Hootman son, Ch. Aberglen Lucky Lindy, in 1994 and 1995.

Forty-nine different Highlanders have taken top honors at the sixty-two specialties held under the auspices of the WHWTCA; of these forty-nine, seventeen were bred by their owners, twelve were handled by their owners, and eight of the eleven were handled by their breeder-owners. One person, Mrs. John G. Winant, owned nine of the twelve different winners; another, Barbara Keenan, had four dogs account for five wins. Two ownerships had four wins: Both Mr. and Mrs. George H. Seemann and Dr. Alvaro T. Hunt had two dogs that won twice each. Three persons won on three occasions: Mrs. Claire Dixon, whose dogs were shown under the Clairedale Kennel name, won three events—all with the same dog—while Mrs. Paul (B.G.) Frame and James and Elizabeth Boso each had three wins, both with two different dogs. Seven individuals owned dogs that each had two wins, with four of those seven being bred and handled by their owners.

Upon membership request, a second parent club-sponsored competition was added in 1959. Of the thirty-seven shows held since the initiation of a Roving Specialty, twenty-eight different dogs have taken top honors, and of those twenty-eight, twelve repeated national Specialty wins. Eleven of the twenty-eight were bred by their owners, twelve were handled by their owners and five were handled to the wins by their breeder-owners.

Mrs. Paul (B.G.) Frame's dogs won six of the thirty-seven shows, with one dog—Ch. Rannoch-Dune Down Beat—winning on four occasions. Her other wins came with her homebred Ch. Wigtown Talent Scout and Ch. Purston Pinmoney Pedlar, "the Pedlar dog," as he was known during his career. The Wishing Well Kennels of Barbara Keenan had three wins, all with different dogs and all of whom were imports. Breeder Edward McParlan took his Ch. Kenwood's Measure for Measure to three consecutive wins between 1979 and 1981 to retire the long-offered Ch. Waideshouse Willoughby Memorial Trophy. James and Elizabeth Boso's Ch. Holyrood's Hootman O'Shelybay won the Rovings held in 1990, 1991 and 1997, thereby retiring the English Champion Pillerton Peterman Memorial Trophy and bettering by one "Manley's" double wins at the national level. Two persons each had two wins: Dr. Alvaro T. Hunt's Ch. Purston Primate's win in 1978 matched

Ch. Kenwood's Measure for Measure, owned and bred by Ed McParlan, shown here in his last WHWTCA Specialty BB, Montgomery, 1983, under judge Seymour Weiss, handler Vicki Barker. *Gilbert*

Ch. Pagan Ghost, owned by Mr. and Mrs. George Seemann, was one of the breed's foremost standard bearers during the early 1980s. He is shown here winning BB at the WHWTCA Specialty at Montgomery County under John T. Marvin, handler Cliff Hallmark. *Gilbert*

his national win the same year, while his Ch. Purston Peacemaker won in 1976; Melinda Lyon and Daphne Gentry's Ch. Lair O'Lyon's Killundine Chip, handled by Ms. Lyon and bred by Ms. Gentry, took back-to-back wins in 1982 and 1983. Of the twenty-three Highlanders who had one victory each, nine have also won a national Specialty.

Regional organizations were formed around the country as interest in the breed increased following the end of the Second World War. The first club was formed in the Indianapolis, Indiana, area in 1946; named the Central West Highland White Terrier Club, it held its first show that fall. Within a year, it had changed its name to the West Highland White Terrier Club of Indiana, and it is today the oldest of the twenty-one regional breed clubs. A club was formed near Chicago, Illinois, at about the same time as the Indianapolis club came into being, but this group disbanded within two years. In 1951 a club was formed in the Los Angeles area; the West Highland White Terrier Club of California is the second oldest regional club and has been sponsoring shows since 1953. The West Highland White Terrier Club of Northern Ohio, concentrated in the Cleveland area, was holding Specialty shows by 1967. Thus, twenty years after the reorganization of the WHWTCA, there were three regional Specialty clubs—two in the Midwest and one in California—holding shows in addition to the national and roving Specialties.

In 1973, the number of regional Specialties doubled, with clubs in Dallas, Chicago and Houston all holding their first shows. By 1978, clubs in San Francisco, New York and Washington, D.C., had been added to the list and by 1984, groups of fanciers had formed Specialty-giving clubs in Baltimore, Denver and Pittsburgh. Within another five years, clubs centered around Seattle, Detroit and Philadelphia were added to the ever-growing list. That number stayed constant until the mid-1990s, when in the successive years of 1995, 1996 and 1997, clubs in northern New Jersey, Phoenix and Atlanta were added to the line-up of Specialty-sponsoring organizations. Clubs in Hawaii, Austin, the New England region and Connecticut support fanciers and their interests but do not, as of this writing, sponsor shows.

In the fifty years that these clubs have held Specialty shows, there have been 340 such events. Sixty-one dogs have accounted for 226 of the possible victories, with 114 dogs having one win each. Ch. Mac-Ken-Char's Irish Navigator (Ch. Keithall Pilot ex Mac-Ken-Char's Wild Irish) has won top honors at thirteen regional club Specialties. "Gregory," handled throughout his career by co-owner/breeder Jaimi Glodek, with her mother Joanne providing moral support, won his first regional Specialty at the WHWTC of Northern Illinois in June 1984 and his last in April 1991, when he won at the WHWTC of Southeastern Michigan as a 10-year-old veteran. In between he won at the WHWTC of Northern Ohio in 1984 and 1986, WHWTC of Southeast Texas in 1985 and 1987, WHWTC of Greater Washington in 1985

Ch. Country Boy Rootin Tootin, owned, bred and handled by Linda McCutcheon, is the winner of multiple Specialty Bests. *Booth*

Ch. Orion's Mercury, owned and bred by Ida and Joe Keushgenian, is an owner-handled Group and Specialty winner. *Joe C*

Ch. Elsinore Opus One, owned, bred and handled by Linda J. Servin, has won a number of Groups and Specialty Bests including the WHWTCA 1996 Roving under judge Wayne Kompare.

and 1986, WHWTC of Greater Baltimore in 1986 and 1987 and Western Pennsylvania WHWTC in 1985 and 1986. His last win from the regular classes was at the WHWTC of Northern Illinois in 1987, where he had won his first regional Specialty.

Just barely behind Gregory in the win column is Ch. Aberglen Lucky Lindy (Ch. Holyrood's Hootman O'Shelbay ex Lanarkstone Winter Solitude), who won twelve regional events between October 1993 and June 1996. "Lindy's" first win came at the WHWTC of Greater New York; during 1994 he won at the San Francisco Bay WHWTC, Trinity Valley WHWTC, WHWTC of Southeast Texas, Greater Denver WHWTC and again at the WHWTC of Greater New York. In 1995 he repeated his victories at the San Francisco Bay and Denver clubs and added a win at the WHWTC of Indiana. Shown only during the first half of 1996, he started the year with his third consecutive win at the San Francisco Bay WHWTC and followed the next week with his second win at the WHWTC of Indiana; he also claimed the breed win at the WHWTC of California in June 1996. Lindy has been shown for Frederick C. Melville by his breeder, Sally George.

Lindy's sire, Ch. Holyrood's Hootman O'Shelbay (Ch. Glenfinnan's Something Dandy ex Ch. Holyrood's Ms. Mayhem), bred by Judith Francisco and Marilyn Foster, won nine regional Specialties for his owners, James and Elizabeth Boso, between March 1990 and August 1992. He had five victories in 1990, at the San Francisco Bay WHWT, WHWTC of Indiana, WHWTC of California, WHWTC of Southeast Texas and WHWTC of Greater New York. In 1991, "Manley" won three regional Specialties: San Francisco Bay WHWTC, Trinity Valley WHWTC and the WHWTC of Northern Illinois; and in 1992 he won a single Specialty event, the WHWTC of Southeast Texas.

Two Highlanders each have won eight regional Specialty shows: Ch. Pagan Ghost ("Jamie"), between September 1982 and September 1985, and Ch. Mac-Ken-Char's Battle Star ("Popeye"), between May 1993 and August 1995. Jamie (Ch. Olac Mooncloud ex Purston Pagan Princess), owned by Mr. and Mrs. George H. Seemann, was bred by James R. Sanders and handled throughout his career by Clifford Hallmark. He was victorious at the WHWTC of Greater New York for the four consecutive years that he was campaigned, and had wins at the WHWTC of Greater Washington and WHWTC of Western Pennsylvania in 1983 and the WHWTC of Greater Baltimore in 1984 and 1985. Popeye (Ch. Mac-Ken-Char's White Shadow ex Mac-Ken-Char's Star Gazer) was bred by his owners, Joanne and Jaimi Glodek, and handled by Jaimi to wins at the final show of the WHWTC of Greater Baltimore in 1993 as well as the WHWTC of Greater Washington and the William Penn WHWTC that same year; during 1994, he was victorious at the WHWTC of Greater Washington, William Penn WHWTC and the WHWTC of Southeast Texas. During 1995 he had wins at the Trinity Valley WHWTC and the WHWTC of Northern Ohio.

Ch. Ashgate Lochmaddy, owned by Gary Gabriel. *Petrulis*

Ch. Pilot of Keithhall, owned by Martha Black, won the WHWTCA Specialty at Montgomery County in 1988 under British authority Sheila Cleland. *Klein*

Ch. Lor-E-L's Snickers Bar-None, owned by Judy Arenz and bred by Barbara and Larry Robertson, is a multiple Group and Specialty winner. *Fallen Images*

One dog had victories at seven regional Specialty events: Ch. Glenfinnan's Something Dandy (Ch. Whitebriar Jeronimo ex Ch. Craigty's Something Special), bred by Mary Lowry Charles and owned by James and Elizabeth Boso. During 1986, "Nicky" won at the San Francisco Bay WHWTC, the WHWTC of Northern Illinois and WHWTC of Southeast Texas; in 1987 he had victories at the Western Pennsylvania WHWTC, the WHWTC of California and WHWTC of Greater Denver; his single 1988 victory was at the San Francisco Bay WHWTC. Nicky is the sire of Ch. Holyrood's Hootman O'Shelybay, who has nine regional Specialty victories; Manley, in turn, is the sire of Ch. Aberglen Lucky Lindy, who currently holds the number-two position for the most Specialty Bests.

Five Highlanders have won six regional Specialty events: Ch. Rannoch Dune Down Beat, who had one win each in 1964 and 1966, and two wins each in 1967 and 1968—achieved at a time when there were only two regional clubs offering Specialty shows; Ch. London's Duffy MacDuf, who had two wins in 1974, one in 1975 and three in 1976; Ch. Mac-Ken-Char's White Shadow, who had five wins during 1990 and one in 1992; Ch. Holyrood's Hotspur O'Shellybay, who had two wins in 1992, three in 1993 and one in 1994; and, finally, the bitch Ch. Glengloamin's Rise 'N Shine, who, in 1994, achieved her first win from the classes, then added five wins in 1995 and one in 1996.

Three West Highland White Terriers have won five regional Specialties. At a time when there were only two Specialty-giving regional clubs, Ch. Highland Ursa Major, in winning five shows between 1947 and 1949, won five of the first six regional Specialty shows held. Ch. Purston Pinmoney Pedlar won at the WHWTC of Indiana shows held in 1970, 1971, 1972 and 1973; he rounded off his five with a 1974 victory at the WHWTC of Northern Illinois show. Ch. Jack the Lad of Jopeta from Purston had five wins in 1987 and one in 1989.

Ten Westies have each had four regional Specialty wins; another ten have each had three victories, while twenty-seven have had two regional Bests each. Included among those with three wins are the bitches Ch. Heritage Farms Jenny Jump Up, with two wins in 1978 and one in 1979, and Ch. Glenncheck May Be, whose three wins came in 1985. The bitches with two wins are Ch. Whiskybae Duces Tecum, who won at the Trinity Valley shows in 1981 and 1982; Ch. Glengloamin's It Had To Be You, winning twice in 1992; and Ch. Wynecroft Wild at Heart, with two wins in 1996. At least seventeen bitches have won one regional Specialty show.

BEST OF BREED

WHWTCA ANNUAL SPECIALTY SHOWS

Date	Dog's Name	Owner(s)
Feb 10, 1926	White Cloud of Nishkenon*	Mr. & Mrs. W.B. Rogers
Feb 9, 1927	Ch. White Cloud of Nishkenon*	Mr. & Mrs. W.B. Rogers
Feb 10, 1932	Cooden Slave of Heather Hill	Mrs. William Dexter
Feb 11, 1933	Cooden Skua of Heather Hill*	Mrs. William Dexter
Feb 10, 1934	Edgerstoune Rastus	Mrs. John G. Winant
Feb 10, 1935	Leaside Larkspur*	Mrs. John G. Winant
Feb 9, 1936	Ch. Edgerstoune Roughy	Mrs. John G. Winant
Feb 9, 1937	Edgerstoune Rebel	P. Mullinnit
Feb 9, 1938	Wolvey Privet of Edgerstoune*	Mrs. John G. Winant
Feb 12, 1939	Ch. Robinridge Commodore	Mrs. A.S. Monroney
May 25, 1940	Ch. Wolvey Pattern of Edgerstoune*	Mrs. John G. Winant
May 31, 1941	Ch. Edgerstoune Royalty	Mrs. John G. Winant
Feb 10, 1948	Ch. Highland Ursa Major	Perry M. Chadwick
Feb 12, 1949	Ch. Pamela of Hillandale*	Mrs. John G. Winant

Feb 12, 1950	Ch. Cranbourne Arial	Mrs. John T. Marvin
Feb 11, 1951	Ch. Cruben Melphis Chloe*	Barbara J. Worcester
Feb 9, 1952	Brisk of Branston of Edgerstoune	Mrs. John G. Winant
Feb 8, 1953	Ch. Cruben Dextor	Barbara J. Worcester
Feb 7, 1954	Ch. Edgerstoune White Raider	Mrs. Marion Eppley
Feb 13, 1955	Cruben Moray	Clairedale Kennels
Feb 12, 1956	Ch. Cruben Moray of Clairedale	Clairedale Kennels
Feb 10, 1957	Roseneath White Knight	Mr. & Mrs. T.S. Adams
Feb 9, 1958	Ch. Cruben Moray of Clairedale	Clairedale Kennels
Feb 8, 1959	Ch. Roseneath White Knight	Mr. & Mrs. T.S. Adams
Feb 7, 1960	Elfinbrook Simon	Wishing Well Kennels
Feb 12, 1961	Dina-Ken's Little Pip**	Mr. & Mrs. Albert A. Kaye
Feb 11, 1962	Ch. Elfinbrook Simon	Wishing Well Kennels
Feb 10, 1963	Ch. Famecheck Viking	Margaret Jensen
Feb 9, 1964	Ch. Whitebriar Journeyman	Sally Hudson & Barbara Sayres
Feb 14, 1965	Glenhaven Ceasar	Joseph R. & Donna K. Barber
Feb 13, 1966	Ch. Rannoch-Dune Down Beat	Mrs. B.G. Frame

Feb 12, 1967	Ch. Rannoch-Dune Down Beat	Mrs. B.G. Frame
Feb 11, 1968	Ch. Huntinghouse Little Fella	Katharine Hayward
Feb 9, 1969	Ch. Incheril Ischa of Pennyworth	Pennyworth Kennels
Feb 8, 1970	Ch. Vimy Ridge Money Man	Liz Hallmark
Oct 10, 1971	Ch. De-Go Hubert	Jane Esther Henderson
Oct 8, 1972	Ch. Purston Pinmoney Pedlar	Mrs. B.G. Frame
Oct 7, 1973	Braidholme White Tornado of Binate	Mr. & Mrs. George H. Seemann
Oct 6, 1974	Ch. Braidholme White Tornado of Binate	Mr. & Mrs. George H. Seemann
Oct 5, 1975	Ch. Ardenrun Andsome of Purston	Alvaro T. Hunt
Oct 3, 1976	Ch. Ardenrun Andsome of Purston	Alvaro T. Hunt
Oct 9, 1977	Ch. B-J's Sir Becket	Anita Becky
Oct 8, 1978	Ch. Purston Primate	Alvaro T. Hunt
Oct 7, 1979	Ch. Briarpatch Raggamuffin*	Barbara Goss
Oct 5, 1980	Ch. Purston Merrymick	Alvaro T. Hunt
Oct 4, 1981	Ch. Skaket's Candy Man	Nancy & Mitzi Gauthier
Oct 3, 1982	Ch. Pagan Ghost	Mr. & Mrs. George H. Seemann
Oct 9, 1983	Ch. Kenwood's Measure for Measure	Edward McParlan
Oct 7, 1984	Ch. Mac-Ken-Char's Irish Navigator	Joanne & Jaimi Glodek
Oct 6, 1985	Ch. Pagan Ghost	Mr. & Mrs. George H. Seemann

Oct 5, 1986	Ch. Round Town Ella J. Fitzgerald*	Amelia Musser
Oct 4, 1987	Ch. Pilot of Keithhall	Martha W. Black
Oct 9, 1988	Ch. Skaket's Candy Man	Nancy & Mitzi Gauthier
Oct 8, 1989	Ch. Holyrood's Hootman O'Shelybay	James & Elizabeth Boso
Oct 7, 1990	Ch. Holyrood's Hootman O'Shelybay	James & Elizabeth Boso
Oct 6, 1991	Ch. Glenfinnan's Something Dandy	James & Elizabeth Boso
Oct 4, 1992	Ch. Highlands Honey Hill's Excaliber	James Riggs & Naomi Engers
Oct 9, 1993	Camcrest Andsurely Trouble*	Sandy Campbell
Oct 8, 1994	Ch. Aberglen Lucky Lindy	Frederick Melville
Oct 7, 1995	Ch. Aberglen Lucky Lindy	Frederick Melville
Oct 6, 1996	Ch. Camcrest Andsurely Trouble*	Sandy Campbell
Oct 5, 1997	Ch. Mac-Ken-Char Ashscot Liberty	Joanne & Jaimi Glodek

*indicates a bitch

BEST OF BREED

WHWTCA ROVING SPECIALTY SHOWS

Date	Dog's Name	Owner
Oct 4, 1959	Triskett's Most Happy Fella	Triskett T. Vogelius
Aug 28, 1960	Ch. Wigtown Talent Scout	Mrs. B.G. Frame
Oct 8, 1961	Ch. Elfinbrook Simon	Wishing Well Kennels

Sept 22, 1962	Ch. Rhianafa the Rock	Mrs. Jean Goddard
Sept 29, 1963	Ch. Whitebriar Journeyman	Barbara Sayers & Sally Hudson
Oct 4, 1964	Ch. Rannoch-Dune Down Beat	Mrs. B.G. Frame
Oct 2, 1965	Ch. Rannoch-Dune Down Beat	Mrs. B.G. Frame
July 30, 1966	Ch. Glenhaven Ceasar	Joseph R. & Donna J. Barber
Oct 8, 1967	Ch. Rannoch-Dune Down Beat	Mrs. B.G. Frame
Aug 24,1968	Ch. Rannoch-Dune Down Beat	Mrs. B.G. Frame
1969	No Roving Specialty Show Held	
Oct 4, 1970	Ch. Lymehills Birkfell Solstice	Wishing Well Kennels
1971	No Roving Specialty Show Held	
June 3, 1972	Ch. Monsieur Aus Der Flerlage	Bergit Zakschewski
Feb 24, 1973	Ch. Purston Pinmoney Pedlar	Mrs. B.G. Frame
June 2, 1974	Ch. Braidholme White Tornado of Binate	Mr. & Mrs. George H. Seemann
Mar 29, 1975	Ch. Merryhart Sound Off	Neoma & James Eberhardt
June 3, 1976	Ch. Purston Peacemaker	Alvaro T. Hunt
Mar 27, 1977	Ch. B-J's Sir Becket	Anita Becky
Feb 25, 1978	Ch. Purston Primate	Alvaro T. Hunt
June 17, 1979	Ch. Kenwood's Measure for Measure	Edward McParlan
June 21, 1980	Ch. Kenwood's Measure for Measure	Edward McParlan

May 24, 1981	Ch. Kenwood's Measure for Measure	Edward McParlan
May 28, 1982	Ch. Lair O'Lyon's Killundine Chip	Melinda Lyon & Daphne Gentry
Mar 26, 1983	Ch. Lair O'Lyon's Killundine Chip	Melinda Lyon & Daphne Gentry
April 14, 1984	Ch. Olac Moondrift	Pat Darby
May 18, 1985	Ch. Mac-Ken-Char's Onederboy	Joanne & Jaimi Glodek
Mar 16, 1986	Ch. Round Town Ella J. Fitzgerald*	Amelia Musser
Aug 7, 1987	Ch. Tweed Take By Storm	Gary Gabriel & Florence MacMillan
Aug 6, 1988	Ch. LuAnn's I'm For Keeps	Susan L. Simpson
June 3, 1989	Ch. Honey Hill's Magnum	Joseph P. & Naomi K. Engers
April 29, 1990	Ch. Holyrood's Hootman O'Shelybay	James & Elizabeth Boso
June 22, 1991	Ch. Holyrood's Hootman O'Shelybay	James & Elizabeth Boso
June 14, 1992	Ch. Holyrood's Hotspur O'Shelybay	Marcia Montgomery, Gary Gabriel, Florence MacMillan, Marilyn Foster & Randell Dickerson
Aug 13, 1993	Ch. Holyrood's Hotspur O'Shelybay	Frederick Melville, Marcia Montgomery, Marilyn Foster & Randell Dickerson

Aug 20, 1994	Ch. Aberglen Lucky Lindy	Frederick Melville
July 15, 1995	Ch. Whitehaus' Double Trouble*	Nancy Spelke
April 14, 1996	Ch. Elsinore Opus One	Linda J. Servin
March 8, 1997	Ch. Holyrood's Hootman O'Shelybay	James & Elizabeth Boso

* *Indicates a bitch.*

chapter 6

The Top Producers

Any study of top-producing West Highland White Terrier dogs and bitches since the introduction of the breed into the United States requires looking at the number of champions produced within the same period. The first champion Westie was Cream of the Skies, who won his championship during 1909. This dog, born on October 4, 1907, in England, was imported by R.D. Humphreys and Philip Boyer, early fanciers of the breed who lived in Mt. Kisco, New York. His sire was Ossian and his dam, Sky Lady; although Sky Lady was also imported by Messrs. Humphreys and Boyer, she did not produce another champion.

Between 1910 and 1919, thirty Westies won their championships, each out of a different dam. These thirty were sired by twenty-five dogs, as four dogs produced multiple champions in this decade: Dunollie Admiral with two, Ch. Rhuellen of Glenmere in 1913 and Ch. Greenwich Chief in 1914; Athol with two, Ch. Wayside Glenmhor Model in 1912 and Ch. Walpole Witch in 1917; Dunvegan Chief with two, Ch. Ornsay Rhoda in 1912 and Ch. Dunvegan Hero in 1915; and Lagavulin with three, Ch. Walpole Witty in 1913, Ch. Scotia Chief in 1914 and Ch. Butterscotch in 1915. Most of the dogs that became champions were whelped in England; the first American-bred champion was Rumpus of Glenmore, who finished in 1913 as a 2-year-old. His breeder, Robert Goelet who had Glenmere Kennels in Chester, New York, imported both his sire, Kiltie of Glenmere, and his dam, Rhuellen of Glenmere, from England.

Between 1920 and 1929, thirty-three Westies completed their championships. Ch. Clarke's Hill Snooker, who won the breed's first Best in Show in 1922, added two champions to the one he had sired earlier; two other dogs, Ch. Rosstor the De'il (one of Snooker's three champion get) and Ch. White Adonis, each sired three champions, while Inverailort Whitewash and Ch. Rosstor Rajus each sired two. During this decade there was at last multiple produce from bitches, with Rosstor Rhoda becoming the first bitch with multiple champions when Ch. Rosstor Rattray finished in 1923, the year following Ch. Rosstor Duguid. The second bitch to produce two champions was Rosstor Rayne, when Ch. Nishkenon Tess, finishing in 1927, joined her full-litter sister in this distinction, Ch. Nishkenon Wee Lass, who had finished during the previous year.

During the 1930s, forty-nine Westies were made up as champions, with twenty-six of those being sired by only seven dogs. Four dogs—Cooden Sirdar, Wolvey Patrician, Ch. Reaside Rex and Sandy of Roweford—each produced two champions, while Ch. Edgerstoune Roughy sired four champions during the decade and would add two more to his record in 1941. Wolvey Poacher, an English champion, sired five American champions, to which three more would be added by 1942. In addition, Ch. Ray of Rushmoor, who had been imported by Mrs. John G. Winant to add to the impressive stud force available at her Edgerstoune Kennels, sired ten Westies—all but one bearing her estimable prefix—who finished their championships between 1934 and 1939.

On the distaff side, eight bitches accounted for nineteen of the forty-nine Westies who finished their championships during the 1930s. Six bitches—Cooden Security, Rosstor Priscilla, Ch. Ornsay Vera of Edgerstoune, Springmeade White Heather, Edgerstoune Epoch and Ch. Wolvey Pace of Edgerstoune—each produced two champions, while Ch. Clint Casserole was responsible for three and Rosalie of Rushmoor four, a number to which she would add one in 1942 to become the first bitch to produce five conformation champions in the United States. Twice in this decade, litter mates won their championships and when, in 1941, Robinridge Cherie finished, she made breed history as being the third of a litter to finish, the other two being Chs. Robinridge Commodore and Countess. This litter was bred by Mrs. Almer Stillwell (Mary-Ellen) Monroney of Oklahoma City, Oklahoma; the sire was Ch. Edgerstoune Roughy and the dam, Ch. Wolvey Pace of Edgerstoune. Whelped April 10, 1936, the litter consisted of three males and three bitches.

Between 1940 and 1949, eighty Westies obtained their championships, with the number hitting the double digits for the first time in 1947 when eleven finished. Leading the top-producing sires were Ch. Battison Beacon, who produced seven champions, two of whom also had Obedience degrees; Ch. Charan Minstrel, with six, including the Best in Show–winning Ch. Gillette's Lord Tuffington, the first American bred BIS winner; and Ch. Edgerstoune Radium and Ch. Heather Hill Partridge, each with four champion get.

Can. Ch. Belmertle Aldrich sired three American champions during the 1940s, and five dogs each sired two champions: Ch. Gillette's Lord Tuffington, Ch. Wolvey Parole (an import), Ch. Robinridge MacBeth, Ch. Cruben Silver Birk (an import) and Ch. Springmeade Rory.

Three bitches each produced three champions during this decade. Ch. Prairiecrest Lolly Polly and Edgerstoune Star Dust each had litter mates that finished in addition to one from another litter, while Ch. Bermertle Alba had three champions out of three litters. Robinridge Binny, Ch. Edgerstoune Starlet and Ch. Yowell's Little Bit of Sugar each produced two champions.

One hundred ninety-three Westies attained championship status with the American Kennel Club between 1909 and 1949; in the next ten years, that number was exceeded by one-third as 253 Westies won their championships. The numbers increased from that point: During the 1960s, 613 Westies finished; in the 1970s, 1,156; during the 1980s, 1,573; and in the first seven years of the 1990s, 1,044 Westies had become champions. As the numbers of champions increased, so did the numbers of top producers.

During the decade of the 1950s, one dog alone stands out: Eng., Am. Ch. Cruben Dextor, who sired nineteen champions—a number to which more would be added during the 1960s. "Dextor" was bred in England by Dr. and Mrs. A. Russell, who started their Cruben Kennels at the end of World War II and operated them with some success for more than a dozen years. Whelped January 17, 1950, Dextor completed his English title early in 1951 and was shortly thereafter purchased on behalf of Barbara Worcester and Wishing Well Kennels. A multiple Specialty winner and a multiple all-breed Best in Show winner, Dextor can be found in the background of many of today's most prominent Westies.

While the number of champions produced by other dogs pales when studying Dextor's record, in previous decades these dogs would have been leaders. Six dogs each sired six champions during the 1950s: Ch. Crinan Hector of Clairedale, Ch. Wishing Well's High Tide, Eng. Ch. Hookwood Mentor, Ch. Shiningcliff Simon, Ch. Cranbourne Arial and Ch. Cruben Cranny of Edgerstoune; two of these—Ch. Crinan Hector of Clairedale and Ch. Wishing Well's High Tide—would add to their totals, with other champions finishing in the 1960s. Three other dogs each sired five champions: Ch. Shiningcliff Sim, who would add to his list during the 1960s, Ch. Highland Mercury and Ch. Highland Castor.

The multiple Best in Show bitch Ch. Shiningcliff Donark Dancer proved herself in the whelping box as well as the show ring by producing six champions, all carrying the Maxwelton prefix of her owner, Robert Lowry, during the 1950s, with another finishing early in 1960. Three bitches—Ch. Klintilloch Margee, Ch. Oh Mi Cindy of Elmview and Ch. Moonbeam's Heather McTwiddles—each produced four champions in this decade, with Ch. Klintilloch Margee having another to finish in 1960. Seven bitches each produced three champions: Ch. Wolvey Piquet of Clairedale (with another finishing in 1960), Ch. Hookwood Banneret, Cruben Fancy, Wishing Well's Candida, Ch. Heatherbelle Miss Muffet, Ch. Glencaven's Imp and Ch. Belmertle Imogene.

Just as the 1950s were dominated by Dextor, the 1960s were dominated by another of the dogs imported by the Worcesters' Wishing Well Kennels: Ch. Elfinbrook Simon. By the end of the decade, his number of champions

Ch. Mac-Ken-Char's Irish Navigator (left), owned and bred by Joanne and Jaimi Glodek, left his indelible mark on the breed as a great winner and, more significantly, as its top producer. He is shown here winning BB at the Baltimore Specialty under judge Robert Shreve. His son Ch. Glengidge Mayor Mac-Ken-Char (center) was BW on this day from the puppy class en route to his title, while BOS went to Ch. Glengidge Plum Candy, dam of the BW. *Kernan*

Ch. Pillerton Peterman at age 12 with his owner-breeder, Sylvia J. Kearsey. This remarkable dog sired six BIS winners, five of which came from England before he did. *Gilbert*

was reaching towards fifty, a number he surpassed early in the 1970s. His record stood for almost a quarter of a century. Wishing Well Kennels housed an impressive stud force during this period, and several of their dogs sired multiple champions, though none entered double figures: Ch. Tulyar of Trenean, who had sired seven champions by 1963, and Ch. Loch Crest Highfalutin, owned with the Harry Grindles, whose record of fifteen champions finished by 1970 would undoubtedly have been higher had he lived beyond 1969. Dogs bearing S. Marge Blue's Klintilloch prefix collectively accounted for more than thirty champions during the decade, while those with Claire W. Brumby's Rannoch-Dune prefix, again collectively, accounted for another two dozen. It was only fitting that, in their latter years, these two stalwarts of the breed combined their kennels—one formerly resided in Indiana and the other in New York—in Arizona.

Two bitches, Ch. Rannoch-Dune Merrilee and Ch. Wigtown Margene, each accounted for five new champions during the 1960s, with Margene establishing the foundation for the Kar-Ric Westies. Ch. Ellis Bonnie Lady Argyle, Ch. Kar-Ric's Gamble, Ch. Klintilloch Cinderella and Ch. Wishing Well's Water Baby each produced four champions and a number of bitches each produced three, among whom were Ch. Bee's Honey Bee of Dew West, Ch. Brisk of Forest Glen, Ch. Donnybrook's Miss Triskett, Ch. Famecheck Lucky Charm and Ch. Klintilloch Medallion.

In the last twenty-five years, more than 3,700 Westies have won their championships. Sixty dogs have sired ten or more champions; an even dozen have thus far accounted for twenty-five or more champions, while another three dogs have sired fifty or more AKC champions. Finally, one dog—Ch. Mac-Ken-Char's Irish Navigator—has been credited with siring well over one hundred champions, a record that surely will stand for some time. Listed, in ascending order, are those Westies with twenty-five or more champions: FCI Int., Ber., Mex., Can., Am. Ch. Skaket's Candy Man UDT, TT, CG; Ch. Ugadale Artist's Model; Ch. Lymehill's Birkfell Solstice; Eng. Ch. Pillerton Peterman; Ch. Royal Tartan Glen O'Red Lodge; Ch. Olac Mooncloud; Ch. Whitebriar Jollimont; Ch. Glenfinnan's Something Dandy; Ch. Sno-Bilt's Eliminator; Ch. Tweed Take By Storm; Ch. Whitebriar Jeronimo, and Ch. Holyrood's Hootman O'Shelybay. Ch. Elfinbrook Simon, whose record in the mid-1950s stood until recently; Am., Ber. Ch. Sno-Bilt's Puzzle and Ch. Ardenrun Andsome of Purston have each sired more than fifty champions, with "Andy" accounting for more than seventy.

The record-holding producer Ch. Mac-Ken-Char's Irish Navigator was whelped October 14, 1980, at the Mac-Ken-Char Kennels of Joanne and Jaimi Glodek in Severn, Maryland. His sire was the imported Ch. Keithall Pilot, a Best in Show winner in Puerto Rico, and his dam Mac-Ken-Char's Wild Irish, who, though never finished herself, produced six other champions in addition to "Gregory." He finished his championship at the 1982 Indiana Specialty and went on to become a multiple Best in Show winner, a multiple

Am., Nordic Ch. Tweed Take By Storm, owned by Gary Gabriel and Florence MacMillan and bred in Sweden by Birgitta Hasslegren. A top winner after arriving in the United States, he provided a useful outcross for American bloodlines. *Missy Yuhl*

Eng., Am., Can. Ch. Whitebriar Jeronimo, owned by Mr. and Mrs. Thomas Fraser and bred by Mrs. J.E. Beer, was another who won well and proved his ability as a producer. *Missy Yuhl*

Ch. Sno-Bilt's Puzzle, owned and bred by Jodine Vertuno, had a number of all-breed and Specialty wins and produced quality offspring for his owner and other fanciers as well. *Olson*

Ch. Liberty's Chairman of the Board, owned and bred by Linda Leavelle, has sired a number of the 1990s' top winners, including the BB winners at Montgomery County in 1996 and 1997.

Specialty Best in Show winner, and, of course, a sire of note. Gregory died in June 1995 but, due to technological advances in the field of reproduction, may still have progeny unborn that will complete their championships, adding to their sire's total.

Within the same time period—1970 to the present—eighty bitches have produced five or more champions, with at least six of these having produced eight each. Four bitches, three owned by Mr.and Mrs. Wendell (Twila Faye) Little, have each borne ten or more champions. Merryhart Chastity, bred by James and Neoma Eberhardt but owned by the Littles, produced ten champions from breedings to Chs. Merryhart Honest John, Jerome of Whitebriar and Merryhart Aspen Abel, while their Heritage Heidi of Storyland, who was bred by Shirley Jean O'Neill, produced ten champions from her breedings to dogs including Chs. Jerome of Whitebriar and Storyland Sweetheart.

Ch. Imperial's Mata-Hari, owned by Jutta and Helmut Buchele, produced eleven champions from breedings to four different dogs. "Kristie" was bred by Janet Marley Parcel of Illinois; her sire was the Paul McAndrews' Am., Can. Ch. Nor'Westie's Wee Charger and her dam was Ch. Imperial's Blast of Melrose. She was born in May 1978 and, as a 4-month-old, went to the Bucheles, then living in Tempe, Arizona. Among her eleven champions were two Best in Show winners, one American and one Japanese. From her breeding to Ch. Ardenrun Andsome of Purston there were three champions: Whitecrest Little Diadem, Whitecrest Sir Andre and Whitecrest Eris of Shanavail; bred next to Ch. Purston Merrymick, she produced two champions: Whitecrest Mickey Spillane, who also finished in Japan, and Whitecrest

Merryhart Chastity, owned by Mr. and Mrs. Wendell Little, is the dam of ten champions.

Bel-West's Buttercup, owned by Mr. and Mrs. Wendell Little, is the breed's top-producing bitch, with thirteen champion offspring.

Ch. Jerome of Whitebriar, an English import owned by Mr. and Mrs. Wendell Little, nicked well with his owners' (and others') bitches, making him a successful producer.

Ch. Bar-Dan's Naughty But Nice, owned by Barbara Krotts, is the dam of seven champions.

Ch. Bonnie Brier She's Groovin', owned by Christine Swingle, at 9 months. She went on to be the dam of six champions.

Ch. Roselynde Radiant Star, owned and bred by Gwendolyn Law, had a fruitful show career, and as a producer she had five champions from one litter of seven. *Booth*

Shanty Chantilla. Four champions resulted from her breeding to Am., Ber. Ch. Sno-Bilt's Puzzle: Whitecrest Pride N Joy, Whitecrest Imperial's Legacy, Whitecrest Stirling Sonsy and Whitecrest Stirling Pride, the latter two of whom also finished in Canada. Finally bred to Ch. Cripsey Brigand, she produced two champions: Whitecrest Stirling Rocky and Whitecrest Regal-West of Moy. Following her success as a brood bitch, she was retired to house pet status; Kristie died in the fall of 1992, shortly after being diagnosed with cancer of the spine.

The all-time record in the breed is held by Bel-West's Buttercup, who produced thirteen champions. Born March 26, 1980 and bred by Harold Heubel, she was sired by Eng., Am. Ch. Ardenrun Andsome of Purston out of Ch. Purston Primemover. Her first two litters were co-bred by Mr. Heubel and Mr. and Mrs. Wendell (Twila Faye) Little; subsequent litters were in the ownership of the Littles and bore their Storyland prefix. Her progeny include Chs. Bel-West's Bonnibelle, Bel-West's Ballyhoo, Bel-West's Bit O'Heaven, Storyland Sweetheart Roland, Storyland Lady Rowena, Storyland Little Cinderella, Storyland Little Bear, Storyland Sir Ivanhoe, Storyland Richard Lion-heart, Storyland Princess Aurora, Storyland Mary Poppins, Storyland Baron of Brynmill and Storyland Sleepy Time Gal. From her three breedings to Ch. Jerome of Whitebriar there were seven champions; a single breeding to Ch. Jonpick of Whitebriar resulted in four champions, and she had one champion with Ch. Storyland Robin Hood. After her retirement from the whelping box, Buttercup was placed in a single-dog companion home, where she died in 1993 at the age of 13.

As the twentieth century draws to a close, veterinary advancement in the field of reproduction technology will undoubtedly bring a new element to top producers' records. With the use of fresh-cooled semen, difficulties around weather and transportation can be met, while frozen semen is making it possible for a dog no longer living to produce new champions.

chapter 7

Grooming the Westie Pet

By George Harris
Diagrams by Ann Priddy

In today's world of busy lifestyles, just finding enough time to fit everyday commitments into your schedule is sometimes all you can manage. Finding the hours needed to groom your Westie properly is more than most pet owners can manage. Thus, more and more pet owners have turned to the professional pet groomer to take care of their Westies' cosmetic needs.

As Westie popularity increased, some people saw breeding these dogs as a fad and a money-making opportunity to be mass produced to fill a demand. Such individuals never see the Westie in the same vein as do concerned breeders. Rather, these so-called breeders produce puppies just for the income generated and take no steps to protect the breed. Their practice of mass production without attention to health or pedigrees has created some problems within the breed.

The principal area of concern when discussing grooming involves the skin. This chapter will offer some assistance in this area. It will address first what you—the owner—can do in maintenance grooming at home, and then what you should be able to expect from your local pet groomer.

As an owner, start working on the basic grooming of your Westie as soon as he joins your household. In all likelihood, your new Westie will be a young puppy, and his breeder has already given him a good introduction to grooming. Be certain that you make your dog's grooming time an enjoyable period, a time in which he garners considerable attention. Your basic home grooming includes bathing, cleaning and trimming ears, trimming nails, brushing and combing the coat and, last but not least, basic dental care.

The most expensive piece of equipment you will require is a grooming table and arm. If, however, you do not wish to invest in a table and arm, you can make a tabletop by attaching a piece of rubber matting to a ¼-inch plywood board and placing that on a level surface, such as a washer or dryer. You will need to attach the dog's leash to a hook in the wall or ceiling, or you might prefer to have an assistant hold the leash taut while you groom. (This last can be tedious for all concerned unless grooming sessions are very brief.) If you make grooming sessions enjoyable for your Westie, he may eventually not need to be restrained in any way.

The hand tools you will need for grooming can be purchased from most grooming or pet supply stores or through pet catalogs. You will require a soft slicker brush, a pin brush, a "Greyhound" comb, a pair of blunt-end scissors, a pair of thinning shears, a pair of nail trimmers, Kwik Stop™ or another coagulant and a hand-held hair dryer. You will also want a toothbrush and toothpaste made especially for use on dogs.

Step 1

At least once a week, thoroughly brush your Westie, using a soft slicker brush that will stimulate both the hair and skin. Brush the body coat straight back from the head to the tail, and then brush the tail from its base to the tip. Next, brush the sides downward into the skirt; then brush the legs, the chest and the rear, always in a downward motion. Hold your dog up by its front legs and brush the center of the skirt. Then, brush the hair on the head forward toward the eyes and nose. After you have thoroughly brushed your Westie, repeat the process, this time using your comb. First use the wide end of the comb and then the small end, repeating the same process as you used with the brush. This will assure there are no snarls in the body coat. *See Diagram 1.*

Step 2

Now that your Westie is well brushed out, use your blunt-end scissors to trim the hair from the top fourth of the ears. *See Diagram 2.* Next, check the ear canals for any excessive hair growth or wax accumulation. You may use forceps to remove such hair. If there should be wax in the ear canals, use a good ear wash that can be purchased either from your vet or pet supply store. Using cotton swabs or cotton puffs saturated with the ear wash, wipe all the little crevices you can see until they are clean. Be careful not to go any deeper in the ear canal than you can see. If either the ear or the ear wax is smelly or dark in color, consult your vet, as either symptom may indicate the presence of infection or an infestation of ear mites.

Step 3

Trimming the nails frightens most owners and as a result, many allow their dogs' nails to get too long. If your dog's nails are long enough to hit the ground before the pads do, then every time he takes a step, the base of the nail is painfully pushed back into the paw. If the nails are that long, the dog is forced to walk on the back of his pads, instead of squarely on his pads.

Diagram 1. Proper direction in which to brush a Westie coat.

Diagram 2. Trimming ears. For those who have difficulty in getting both ears to match, trimming one ear with the dog facing the groomer and the other ear with the dog facing away often does the trick.

Diagram 3. Cutting nails.

Diagram 4. Correctly trimmed foot.

Ideally, a Westie should have black nails, but if your dog has white nails, as do so many, you can see the blood line, or quick; with black nails the quick will not be visible and you will have to guess where the quick is. *See Diagram 3.* Taking one toe at a time, press the toe firmly between your index finger and thumb, in effect forming a tourniquet; your knuckle should turn white from the pressure. First approximate how much of the nail needs to be taken off; then, using the nail clipper, make a straight up-and-down cut. Before releasing the toe, check the end of the nail to see if there is any bleeding. If there is, apply an ample amount of coagulant to stem the flow. Continue the tourniquet while applying the coagulant, and for a minute or so after, to allow the bleeding to subside. Repeat this until all nails, including the dewclaws (if present), are trimmed. If your dog's nails have grown extremely long, you may have to tip them once a week; this will drive the blood line back until you have the nails at a proper length. Once this is accomplished, trimming the nails once every couple of weeks should be sufficient.

Many owners prefer to grind their dogs' nails, either using a tool designed for the purpose or a Dremel™ grinding tool. The trick here is to accustom your Westie to accepting the use of the grinder. After shortening the nails, use your scissors to trim any excess hair from around the feet and between the pads. The foot should have the appearance of a circle. Refer to diagram 4 for the proper manner to achieve this appearance.

Step 4

In years past, owners were told to use cornstarch or white grooming powders as cleansing agents for a dirty Westie. Today, however, with skin problems a concern and with the constant problem associated with fleas, it is best to use shampoos and conditioners developed especially for the harsh terrier coat. Your vet or groomer can recommend the proper product, basically a tearless whitener shampoo for harsh coats.

While the dog is in the tub, you might want to express its anal glands. The anal sacs are on either side of the rectum and must be checked on a regular basis. Holding the tail out of the way and with a large piece of cotton or

Diagram 5. Location of anal glands.

paper towel over the anus, place the thumb of your right hand behind one sac and the middle finger behind the other, and slowly press fluid out through the anus. *See Diagram 5*. The less active your dog is, the more often the sacs need to be checked. If you feel you need a demonstration before trying this procedure, ask your vet or an experienced groomer to help you.

After you have expressed the anal sac, wet your dog and apply the shampoo; use your fingers to scrub and then rinse thoroughly. Use a conditioner on the head, skirt and legs, and rinse thoroughly again. The conditioner will help undo any snarls and reduce the static electricity in the hair.

Step 5

Towel dry the dog until it is just barely damp. Then use the same brushing method as shown in *Diagram 1*. Use a hand-held hair dryer, remembering always to point the dryer in the direction you want the hair to lie. *Diagram 6* shows the direction in which the dryer should be pointed. Dry the body first, then the skirt, legs and head. When the coat is thoroughly dry, comb through as earlier instructed.

If your Westie has dry, flaky skin, oily skin or a dermatitis problem due to allergies or flea bites, consult your vet or groomer for the proper shampoos. An oatmeal shampoo is best for a dog with either sensitive or very dry skin, while an all-natural shampoo provides the best attack against fleas. The fewer strong chemicals present in the shampoo, the better it is for your dog. Shampoos containing tea tree oil have given excellent results.

Step 6

Another maintenance project you can undertake at home involves your Westie's teeth. Start getting your Westie used to having its teeth brushed as a young puppy. You can purchase a canine toothbrush and toothpaste from

Diagram 6. The hair should be dried in the same direction as it is brushed.

your vet or pet supply shop. Some toys have been especially designed to remove canine plaque. Do not attempt to scale your own dogs' teeth, but do have them checked at least once a year by your vet.

Step 7

When you take your Westie to a professional groomer, do not hesitate to ask questions. Many groomers do not have a great deal of experience with Westies, and you need to feel as comfortable with your pet groomer as you do with your own hairdresser or barber.

The groomer is that one person who can do what very few pet owners can—the clipping and scissoring of your Westie to give it that finished look. Remember that a clippered Westie will never look like a hand-stripped Westie, but it can still look well-groomed.

If you feel energetic and ambitious and wish to clip your Westie yourself, you will need, in addition to the equipment already described, an Oster™ A-5 electric clipper fitted with a #5F blade, a #4F blade and a #10 blade, a pair of 46-tooth single serrated thinning shears and a pair of finishing shears or scissors.

They say one picture is worth 10,000 words, so we will use seven pictures and *Diagrams 7-A* through *7-F* to guide you through clipping and scissoring your Westie. If you wish to hand strip your Westie, refer to Chapter 8, "Grooming the Westie for the Show Ring." Whichever method you use to groom your Westie, remember: Be patient, and take your time.

GROOMING CHART FOR PET TRIMMING A WEST HIGHLAND TERRIER

7A-1

7A-2

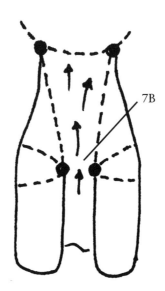

7B

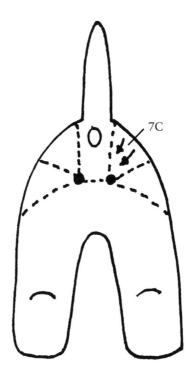

7C

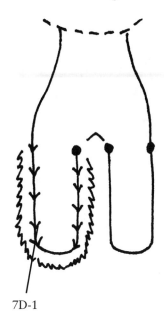

7D-1

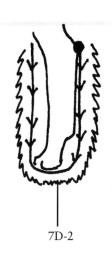

7D-2

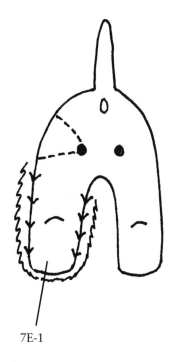

7E-1

7E-2

7F-1

7F-2

7F-3

chapter 8

Grooming the Westie for the Show Ring

By Georgia Harris
Diagrams by Ann Priddy

There are as many different methods to prepare a Westie's coat for show as there are people who hand strip. This chapter we will show you, with diagrams, one method. Neither the information nor the method in this chapter is original. Over the years, I have worked with and observed some of the finest Westie groomers in this country, and I have taken everything I learned and applied it to a way that best suits me. You must do the same with what you are shown in this chapter. Good depth perception and good hand-eye coordination are very helpful when stripping a Westie.

Let's start with the equipment you will need. It is very important that your grooming table and arm be at the proper height. If the table and dog are too tall or too short for you to work comfortably, you will feel this in your back and arms. Using PVC pipe on its legs is an inexpensive way to raise your table to a comfortable height. The basic hand tools you need are listed in the chapter on pet grooming. The stripping aids I prefer are Dr. Scholl's Corn and Callus Remover™ (with white handle); a fine, medium and coarse stripping knife; and last, but certainly not least, your thumb and index finger. Many different styles and shapes of stripping knives are on the market. I do not recommend one brand over another, as you must make your own choice, based partly on the comfort of the knife in your hand. You will find that dipping your fingertips in a small quantity of harsh grooming powder while you are trimming will help to pull the hair more easily.

The basic maintenance grooming that should be done on a regular basis is covered in the chapter on pet grooming. This includes cleaning ears, trimming nails, expressing anal glands, cleaning teeth and bathing.

When you first start stripping either a puppy or a young dog, take frequent breaks to avoid tiring either your dog or yourself, keeping your patience and your Westie's tolerance threshold intact.

145

Ch. Killundine I'm Texas Terra Too (Ch. Glen Finnan's Cadence ex Ch. Killundine Shortbread Made), owned by Leila Livengood and Daphne Gentry, presents a lovely study of a well-conditioned Westie in good trim and ready for the show ring. *Richard Mason*

The dog is right, the trim is wrong. This is a dog of obvious quality, but trimmed more like a Scottish Terrier than West Highland White. From this photo it is easy to see why such a trim is completely wrong for a Westie. *Tauskey*

Start by placing your grooming table in front of a large mirror. The mirror will allow you to see what you are accomplishing as you strip. Be certain you have plenty of light and that no shadow falls on the table.

Before starting, here are the terms that will be used in the discussion of show grooming:

Hand stripping: Pulling the hair out by the roots with your fingers.

Carding: Holding the skin taut with one hand and, using a medium stripping knife in the other hand, slowly but firmly pulling the knife over the body towards the tail to pull the undercoat out.

Undercoat: The soft, downy coat under the harsh coat.

Blending, or tapering: Stripping from an area of shorter to longer hair without leaving a line.

Finger: Refers to thumb and index finger.

Dorsal strip: The area from one inch on either side of the spine, including the spine, extending from the base of the skull, between the ears, to the front side of the base of the tail.

Dips: Low areas in the structure, most often seen behind the withers and above the elbows.

Now that you are set up to strip your Westie, you must consider the method to be used. The instructions in this chapter are for a right-handed person; if you are left-handed, simply reverse the instructions.

To pull the dorsal strip, use your left hand to hold the hair straight out from the body, and with your right hand pull the visibly longest hair first. When you have finished with that length, go to the next length, never pulling too much at a time. Proceed slowly and stay in one area until you are done. Remember that the hair on the dorsal strip grows toward the tail and that even though you are holding the hair straight out, you will pull it slightly towards the tail. Always pull the dorsal strip with your fingers. On the other areas of the body where you pull hair, whether with your fingers or with a knife, there is a special way to do it in order not to hurt the dog. Just above or in front of the area you will strip, gently roll some of the skin firmly into your left hand to keep the skin in the area tight; by doing this, pulling out the hair will not hurt the dog. Check often to be sure you are getting the roots and not breaking or cutting the hair. The root end of each hair you pull out should have a tiny round ball on it. If you twist your wrist while pulling hair, you will increase the chance of having broken or cut hair and leaving the root in the skin.

At this point, the pattern for the fully grown coat should be set; this is achieved by stripping out the body coat completely. In pattern setting, all the outer coat on the body is stripped off in a short period of time to uncover the dog's individual structure. The undercoat is left intact. This allows the faults, as well as the good points of the dog's conformation, to be seen. Pattern setting, therefore, shows where more undercoat must be left to fill in dips and those areas where the hair must be kept short and thinner. All this is done to achieve that smooth, balanced look so sought after in the show ring at this time.

Never work on a freshly washed jacket. If you must bathe your Westie, wait a few days before you start stripping. Remember, you will also get a better grip on the hair you are stripping if you apply grooming chalk to your fingers before starting to pull.

While too-frequent bathing of the jacket of a Westie being shown is not recommended, the head, legs and skirt should be kept clean and free of stains. Bathe these areas whenever necessary.

It is now time to start following the directions accompanying each diagram. In the following diagrams, the arrows indicate the direction in which the hair is to be pulled. The large dots in some of these indicate the presence of a natural cowlick. Try to complete all the steps shown in the diagrams within a two-week time frame. Upon completion, your Westie's coat will be short, but in about twelve weeks it will be ready to show.

Diagram 1. Trimming the dorsal strip

A. Side view

B. Top view

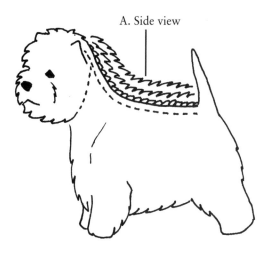

Diagram 2. Trimming the jacket

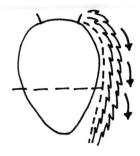

A. The coat is blended and layered along the sides of the rib cage from behind the withers to the set-on of the tail.

B. Schematic front view of rib cage showing graduated coat length.

Diagram 3. Trimming the front

A. The coat is blended from very close to fairly long in this area.

B. The elbow must not be trimmed too closely.

Diagram 4. Trimming the rear

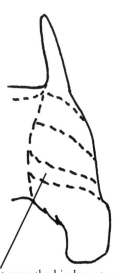

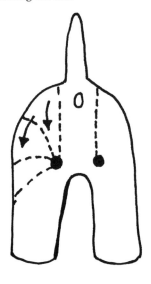

A. The coat over the hindquarters is trained backward.

B. Schematic rear view of properly trimmed rear.

Diagram 5. Trimming under the neck

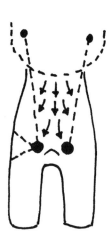

A. This hair is trimmed quite closely and is blended into the natural cowlicks as shown.

B. Front view

Diagram 6. Trimming the head

A. The modern trim imparts a circular look.

B. Schematic to show "section" trimming of the Westie head.

C. The long hair on the outside of the face frame is pulled as shown.

D. Front view of foreface showing the direction hair is pulled.

E. The hair around the eyes is pulled in the direction of the arrows. The eyes should be readily visible, but the brows should be dense and abundant.

Diagram 7. Trimming the front legs

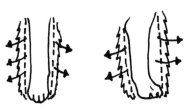

B. The dotted line indicates the correct length.

A. The legs should be pulled to encourage density rather than length.

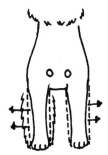

D/E. Front and side view of front legs showing direction to pull.

C. Front view showing excess hair to be pulled.

Diagram 8. Trimming the hind legs

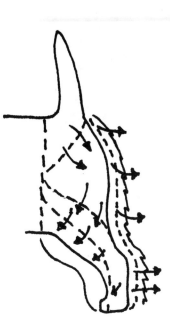

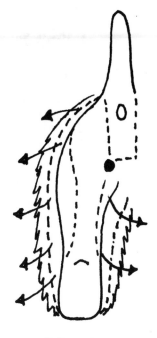

A. Side view showing hair to be pulled
and the desired direction.

B. Rear view

Diagram 9. Trimming the underside

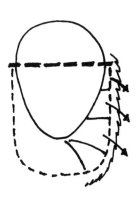

A. Side view showing point of origin, length and
angles of furnishings.

B. Schematic front view of rib cage
showing the proper blending.

Diagram 10. Trimming the tail

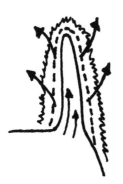

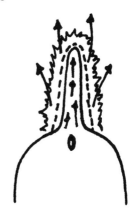

A. Side view of tail showing direction
hair is pulled.

B. Rear view

Diagram 11. Training the coat

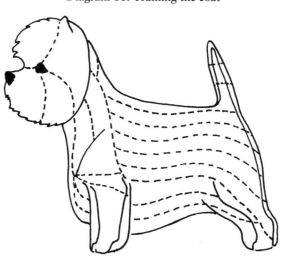

The dotted lines indicate the direction in which the coat
is trained to grow.

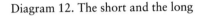
Diagram 12. The short and the long

All the hair above the dotted line is shorter than the hair on the legs and skirt. The two areas are joined by artful blending.

Now that you have completed stripping your Westie, wait two weeks; then start all over again, except this time take off only the hair that looks out of place. Continue this every two weeks. About six weeks after the completion of the original stripping, you will really start to see the hair grow. At this point, start repeating the steps every week. This approach is called *rolling the coat*, and it is possible to keep a Westie in show coat indefinitely by rolling the coat properly and consistently.

The Westie Standard calls for 2 inches of coat for a dog in prime condition, but that does not mean 2 inches overall. The properly trimmed show coat must be artfully tapered and sculpted from $\frac{1}{8}$ inch to 2 inches on various areas of the body. Ideally, the finished result will not show any obvious demarcation from short to long; this is what is meant by the requirement for blending, which you will find in the General Appearance and Coat sections of the breed Standard.

When your Westie goes into the ring, the first feature that will be noticed is the coat and what was done with it. In preparing your Westie for the ring, think of yourself as an artist in the process of sculpting a masterpiece. Take your time, be patient, and if you get off schedule with your stripping, back the coat off by slowly pulling a little more hair than the diagrams call for until you are back on track.

Up to now I have spoken only about chalk, or grooming powder, as a means of helping grip the hair when pulling it. Chalk can also be used to give the head, legs and skirt a fuller appearance—*only* on the day your Westie is being shown. Never leave the chalk in the hair once you have shown your dog. Rinse the chalk out and dry the hair you have washed. Remember, the chalk is used to clean, help dry and fluff. Do not leave excessive amounts in the hair. Chalk is considered to be a foreign substance and may cause the dog carrying it into the ring to be excused. Under no circumstances should chalk be seen or felt in the coat by the judge.

Hair sprays, gels and mousse-type dressings, like chalk, are all considered foreign substances by the AKC dog show rules. If you strip your Westie properly, you should not have to use these enhancers. But, if you do, avoid overkill—use them in the strictest moderation.

Happy stripping!

chapter 9

Training the West Highland White Terrier
By Allison Platt

INTRODUCTION

"You can't train Westies, they're stubborn."

"They're so cute, why would you want to force them to do anything?"

"If you compete, you can't expect very high scores."

"If Westies are good at performance activities, why aren't there more of them competing?"

"Get a Golden!"

These are all commonly held opinions about training a West Highland White Terrier. But they are wrong! Whether you want to have a well-behaved pet, get out with your dog and participate in exciting activities with enjoyable people or score High in Trial at an all-breed Obedience Trial, you can achieve any of these goals with the right dog, using the right training and handling techniques. This chapter will discuss evaluating your dog for performance activities, obtaining a puppy with performance in mind, what to look for in training classes and specific approaches to training Westies. Chapter 10 will introduce the various types of performance activities in which you and your Westie can participate, and how to find out more about the activities that interest you.

Understanding how to train Westies should be guided by an understanding of the job they were bred to perform. Westies were originally bred to help farmers in Scotland hunt and kill rodents and small mammals, such as foxes and badgers, that damaged crops and preyed on farm animals. To do this, Westies had to be both tenacious and courageous; they had to work independently of humans in order to "go to ground" into the animals' dens; and they had to cooperate within their pack in order to hunt and kill their quarry. Selection for these traits has given the breed a disposition that is brave and independent, self-confident and strong-willed, yet not quarrelsome or

It is easier to be noticed in performance activities with a Westie! In 1995, 136 Golden Retrievers obtained their Utility titles, while only two Westies did. This is Angeline Austin and Eastfield Saltcoat Sea Spray, CDX, who shared the thrill of obtaining their third Utility leg and UD title at the National Specialty in October 1996.

It helps when training a Westie to remember that the breed was meant to hunt independently of humans. Here Ch. Harridale Go-To-Ground Biff, CG, and Ch. Benchmark Little Cloud, CG, CD, investigate a groundhog den. *Anne Budge*

aggressive. Because of these characteristics, many people assume that Westies are not interested in pleasing their owners enough to mind them, and certainly not inclined to excel in Obedience competition.

Westies are also small in size and quite adorable, leading many people to incorrectly assume they would be great lap dogs or accessories and that they would require little training. In fact, if Westies are indulged they will often quickly train their owners and take over the house, sometimes exhibiting dominant behavior until it becomes a problem. Many inexperienced owners are very surprised that these cute little dogs are most definitely not lap dogs, and sadly, these same owners are often the ones most likely to give up their Westies because they can't do anything with them.

All Westies require in order to be well-behaved is a strong yet fair human "pack leader"; without this, their independence can cause problems. Because so many people acquire Westies without understanding their basic terrier nature, the breed has in some quarters earned a reputation as hardheaded and difficult to train.

Compare the qualities bred into terriers with those bred into other breeds, and an effective approach to training will begin to emerge. Dogs bred to herd or work in other ways for and with their human partners must look to them for guidance in order to accomplish their assigned mission. Such breeds are often thought to be ideally suited for performance activities because their drive to please their owners is so strong. And in fact, these types of dogs—Golden Retrievers, Border Collies, Shetland Sheepdogs and Poodles—often excel at performance activities.

But you want a Westie! Westies can do as well as these more popular performance breeds if you understand what motivates them and learn to train them using methods that leave their terrier disposition intact. In defense of Westies and other terriers, when compared to the more popular performance breeds, it is likely that one of the reasons so many Goldens and Poodles excel at performance activities is that there are so many more of them in the general canine population.

Terriers are the numerically smallest Group in terms of AKC registrations, so it follows that fewer participate in dog sports. Also, if a person is primarily interested in performance activities rather than in a particular breed, they will probably choose a breed that has demonstrated success in those activities rather than taking a chance on a breed with less of a track record. It is encouraging that many well-known Obedience trainers are now beginning to choose unusual breeds for high-level competition. This demonstrates that appropriate training techniques can succeed with any breed of dog.

One big advantage of training a lesser-known breed is that it is easier to excel. For instance, in 1995 136 Golden Retrievers received their Utility title (the third level of AKC Obedience titles), while only two Westies did. The Sheltie with the most High in Trial scores in a given year (i.e., highest-scoring dog at an all-breed or Specialty Obedience trial) probably showed nearly every weekend to achieve that distinction, while the highest-scoring High in Trial Westie may have won the honor with only one or two HIT scores!

Every Westie should at least attend puppy kindergarten and basic Obedience classes with its owner so that the dog learns manners and the owner learns how to be "top dog" to his or her Westie and train him in a fair and effective manner. Basic Obedience training, taught correctly, will not interfere with the Westie's sunny disposition or ruin the dog for conformation, as some breeders maintain. Done correctly, it will make your dog welcome wherever it goes and give him confidence in all types of new situations.

WHERE CAN I TAKE CLASSES?

The best place to learn more about performance activities is probably an all-breed dog club that includes Obedience training or a club that specializes in dog training. Many such clubs are member or licensed clubs in the AKC, and you can find out about those near you by calling the AKC or by asking your dog's breeder or someone who shows dogs in your area. There are also an increasing number of private training clubs not affiliated with the AKC or other dog registries, and many of these are excellent places to train your dog.

Clubs are the best way for a beginner to be introduced to dog training because they usually have several instructors who may have different views on training, allowing you to evaluate different techniques and see what works best for you and your dog. In addition, training clubs often offer classes in a variety of performance activities, so you can take a puppy or basic Obedience class and also learn more about Tracking, Agility or Flyball. If you are interested in a club or training center, ask whether you can sit in on a class before signing up. Ask questions about the club's training philosophy and what the feeling is about training terriers. Ask if there is a particular instructor who is better at training small dogs and/or terriers. Avoid harsh training methods or instructors who maintain there is only one correct way to train all types of dogs.

EVALUATING YOUR WESTIE FOR
PERFORMANCE ACTIVITIES

Perhaps you already have a Westie and are considering taking him to Obedience classes or learning more about Agility or another dog sport. Your dog may be a beloved companion, a new puppy, a "teenager" or rescue dog with a few bad habits or a recently finished champion who is young, fit and bored! Because Westies are highly active, intelligent, curious and playful dogs, they need some positive way to expend all their excess energy, and if they don't get it, you may find that they are getting into mischief around your home!

But before you sign your dog up for Obedience classes or any of the other activities outlined in the next chapter, you should make sure that your dog is

Before you train your Westie, be sure he is fit and able to handle the physical stress required by the activity. This is Ch. Skaket's Candy Man, UDT, CG, owned by Nancy Gauthier and Mitzi Beals. Twice BB at Montgomery County, he earned his UD title at 11 years of age. *Nancy Gauthier*

healthy and reasonably fit and that he can handle the physical stress required by the activity that interests you. Most training facilities will require that the dog be current on all its vaccinations. The dog should also be checked by your vet to be sure it is healthy—an infected ear or other problem can keep a dog from being able to concentrate enough to learn. The dog should not be overweight or underweight. Overweight dogs in particular are more likely to injure themselves when they suddenly become more active.

You must also evaluate whether your dog has any physical limitations that should be considered in choosing an activity for the two of you. If the dog is older, be sure he is not arthritic and that his vision and hearing are not impaired. If you find that these conditions exist, it may still be possible to train your dog, but you must do so with an understanding of any limitations the dog may have.

An activity such as a beginning Obedience class can be a great first performance activity for you and your dog. The basic control and handling skills you learn will be necessary for any other activities in which you might be interested, and it will allow your dog to get into shape gradually, so that by the time you are ready to graduate and move up to the next level of Obedience or on to other activities, you will both be more prepared. Activities such as vigorous walks with your dog are also a good way to get in shape for more demanding activities. At the more advanced levels of all

In the advanced levels of all performance activities, the dogs will excel only if they are in excellent condition. Princess Maggie Kate, NA, CD, shown here jumping through the tire on an Agility course, swims regularly to stay fit. Maggie is owned by Sheila Mehring. *4U2C*

performance activities, the dogs will do well only if they are in excellent condition. And in activities such as Agility, you must run the course with your dog, so you will quickly discover that you also need to be in good condition!

However, even if you or your dog have some limitations on your mobility, there are still many enjoyable activities in which you can participate successfully—and many wonderful people who will help you learn new skills and form a much closer bond with your Westie while having a great time. If you decide to compete in any of the activities described in the next chapter, you will discover that, unlike in conformation classes, where only one male and one female can win, everyone who achieves a set minimum score qualifies, or wins. There is still competition, especially at the higher levels, but there is also a great deal of camaraderie and the basis for friendships that will last a lifetime.

ACQUIRING A WESTIE WITH PERFORMANCE IN MIND

Perhaps you haven't yet found the perfect Westie for you, but you are very interested in participating in Obedience, Agility or other activities with your dog. The many books and articles that advise you how to go about finding the right Westie also apply if you are interested in acquiring a Westie for performance, with a few additional considerations. As the literature recommends, you should find a reputable breeder, ask lots of questions and be willing to wait for the right puppy or older dog. Most responsible breeders, once they are satisfied that you will be a good owner, will discuss with you honestly the strengths and weaknesses of their line. Let the breeder know that you are particularly interested in performance and that you want a dog with a good temperament and no genetic history of physical problems that might inhibit its ability to compete. Visit the breeder's home and ask to see the dam of the litter or proposed litter, as well as the sire and other closely related Westies from the same line, if possible.

Westies, like all breeds, have some genetic and congenital problems that responsible breeders are working hard to eradicate. You should ask the breeder from whom you plan to acquire a dog about these and listen carefully to his or her replies, with the understanding that no one has ever bred a perfect dog and the best breeders are those who acknowledge the problems they have and work to correct them.

However, there are a few problems in the breed that could potentially keep your Westie from participating in performance events. Some Westies (and many other breeds) have problems with luxated patellas (dislocated kneecaps), and a few have problems related to their hips, as well. Problems with patellas in particular often go undetected for many generations in small dogs, because if the dogs are not physically stressed problems may not appear at all, or not until later in the dog's life. Symptoms include a reluctance to jump above a certain low height easily negotiated by a normally sound Westie, intermittent lameness and soreness in one or both back legs. You cannot tell by examining a young puppy if it will have this problem, but a history of the problem in the line is certainly of concern, and lack of adequate rear angulation in the puppy or either of its parents is sometimes an indicator. You should also ask if any dogs in the line have ever had any hip problems. The best protection against this and other structural problems is to connect with a breeder who makes soundness an important priority.

Some Westie breeders have little interest in performance, which is unfortunate, since sound temperament and correct structure should be fundamental to Westies' succeeding in the show ring as well as in performance activities. If a breeder glosses over any structural problems, or maintains there are no genetic problems in his or her line, it might be best to find another breeder.

If you are seeking a puppy with performance in mind, look for a sound puppy that is confident in all types of situations. This 8-week-old Kirkton puppy, bred by Allison Platt, is confidentally approaching an unknown object (a wheelbarrow!) on one of her first adventures outdoors. *Allison Platt*

On the other hand, there are many Westie puppies who may have a fault that eliminates them from the show ring but would not interfere with their ability to participate in performance activities. A bad bite, retained testicles, an ear that will not stand up or a less-than-ideal tailset or coat will not keep a Westie from being a great Agility or Tracking dog or a treasured companion.

Sound temperament is also important to success in performance activities, and an overly shy or aggressive nature can be a considerable training challenge. Temperament is formed by the interplay of genetics and the environment (especially the early environment) of the puppy. Although Westies have been bred for over a century to have certain characteristics that make up breed "type," if you know several Westies, you have probably observed that there is a great deal of variation in temperaments within the breed (as within all breeds). Careful observation of many litters of Westies over the years has led this breeder to the conviction that, like humans and other animals, each Westie is born with a distinct personality that can be modified, but not fundamentally altered, by its environment. Dominance, aggression, shyness and attraction to people seem to be inborn, and whether these traits become problems or strengths can often be influenced both by early socialization and by proper training and handling.

Ask the breeder how the puppies are raised and socialized. Ideally, the litter from which you acquire your puppy should have been handled frequently and gently from birth, and the puppies should be carefully introduced to an ever-widening array of stimuli as they grow through their first few months. Different noises, men and women of different ages, infants and children (well-behaved and supervised!), a variety of dogs in a variety of sizes (*also* well-behaved and supervised!), different places and ground surfaces—all help the puppy become well-adjusted, stable and ready to learn.

Many breeders temperament-test their puppies before placing them in new homes to determine which puppy would be best in a particular situation. Very experienced breeders may not perform specific tests, but their years of experience allow them to understand the puppies' personalities as they develop. The formal tests are fairly accurate predictors of some important personality traits such as dominance, attraction to people, retrieving ability, touch and noise-sensitivity, chase instinct and response to strange objects. A good candidate for a performance home might be a puppy that scored high on attraction to people, ran to investigate a strange object, ran to a thrown object and brought it back and was *not* very aggressive or sensitive to noise. The tests are not infallible, however (for instance, one of the puppies might not have been feeling well or might have been tired when tested), and are not a substitute for careful observation over a period of weeks or months.

There are many opinions on the ideal time to take your new puppy home in order for it to become "bonded" to you. Westies are highly adaptable individuals, and most breeders agree that they can become bonded to their new owners at any age as long they receive the care and affection they desire in their new surroundings, just as they did in their birth homes. Breeders vary in the age at which they will release puppies to their new owners. If you are not experienced in breeding and raising Westies yourself, put your confidence in the breeder's experience more than on popular wisdom on this subject.

AN APPROACH TO TRAINING YOUR WESTIE

This section presents an approach to training that the author has found to be successful in training her Westies and many other breeds of dogs. The approach can be explained most easily by using examples from Obedience training, but the general philosophy also applies to other performance activities, and even to the breed ring. Tracking, Earthdog tests, Agility and Flyball are all taught almost exclusively through the use of positive reinforcement rather than with corrections, and this is the method advocated for teaching

Tracking, Earthdog tests, Agility and Flyball are all taught almost exclusively with positive reinforcement. Here Kirkton Quicksilver Girl, TDX, NA ("Sprite"), has indicated an article on a TDX training track and receives well-deserved praise and food rewards. *Sue Ammerman*

your Westie Obedience, as well. Training techniques specific to the other performance activities will be covered in Chapter 10.

Many years ago, when Obedience training first became popular, the only method taught was what is now fondly remembered as the "jerk and choke" method. This method produced results, but not happy working dogs, and especially not happy working terriers. Currently those methods that incorporate positive reinforcement and/or food incentives are more popular. There is a vast and bewildering array of books, trainers, tapes and seminars on Obedience training techniques and on training techniques in general. As you learn more about training, you will be able to adapt parts of different techniques into your own training methods, but at the beginning, a simple positive-reinforcement method combined with techniques tailored to small dogs should get you and your Westie off to a good start.

The fundamental approach to training any dog should include the following elements:

- Always maintain a positive attitude
- Understand the importance of correct timing

The importance of a positive training attitude becomes clear at the higher levels of competition, where the dog must work away from the handler. Shown here is Ch. Rime's Quonquering Hero, UDTX, owned by Sil and Anne Sanders. "Mr. Q" is the first UDTX (Utility Dog-Tracking Dog Excellent) Westie in history. *Sil Sanders*

- Be consistent
- Set goals for yourself and your dog, and follow through on them
- Realize that you are half of the team, and that your dog is not the only one on the team who must learn new skills.

In addition to these approaches and skills, there are particular methods that seem to work better for Westies and other small terriers than more conventional training formats:

- Use food or other positive reinforcement techniques to teach the dog
- Correct only *after* your dog understands what you expect of him or her
- Do not overtrain
- Use techniques appropriate for a small dog.

Let's look at each of these elements more closely.

POSITIVE ATTITUDE

Training should be a positive experience for you and your Westie. If you are not getting the results you want, especially when you begin training, it is probably because the dog is confused rather than because he has decided to ignore or defy you. Always assume at first that the dog does not understand, and help him to learn. Even when you are certain that the dog *does* understand and is making the decision not to obey, your attitude should calmly convey to him: "Perhaps you didn't understand me, but that was a command and *not* a request. Let me help you." Then, when it does as you ask, praise the dog lavishly, reward and play with him and go on to something else. Do not train when you are frustrated or angry. This is particularly important when training terriers: If training is no fun for them, they will either physically or mentally leave the situation, and they are less likely than other dogs to forgive and forget. The result of training in anger or with too much force is a Westie that may obey, but looks (and probably *is*) unhappy about it.

TIMING IS EVERYTHING

One of the most common problems with novice trainers is poor timing of both reinforcements and corrections. Correct timing is definitely a learned skill, and one that requires practice and good hand/eye coordination. Often when you teach a dog a new skill, you do it by luring him into doing what you want with food or by using your leash to gently guide him. For instance, if you want the puppy to sit, you can take a food morsel and move it over the pup's nose and back towards his ears. If the food is out of reach, the dog will look up at it, and lean backwards until it is natural for him to sit. At the exact moment he sits, the trainer should say "GOOD SIT!" in a happy voice and give the puppy the food reward. Very quickly, the pup will learn to associate sitting with the word "sit," a happy tone of voice and a food reward.

However, if your timing is off, so that the pup sits but then gets distracted by something and gets up before you reinforce the sit, your praise and the food are not associated with the correct action and the dog has not learned anything. If you must correct the dog because he did not do what you asked (once you are sure he understands the command), it is essential both to give the correction at the *instant* the dog fails to obey and to remember that the *instant* the dog corrects himself and does what you ask, you must *praise the dog!* Then the dog will remember the praise and not the correction. Correcting too late, or praising too late or not at all, only confuses the dog and makes him unresponsive.

BE CONSISTENT

Many novice handlers make the mistake of teaching their dogs commands, but not insisting that they always be obeyed. For instance, if you are teaching your dog the "come," you must use that command only if you are sure you can enforce it. Do not call your dog in from the yard with this command if he can decide not to come and there is nothing you can do about it, because you have then taught your dog that he can decide whether or not to obey you (use another phrase like, "let's go inside"). Do not train your dog while doing something else, so that you are likely to become distracted. If you ask your dog to lie down and stay, and then get distracted and don't react

When training, it is essential to define your goals. If you wish to compete successfully in Obedience, you must be precise in your training techniques to ensure that your handling and your dog's performance are the best they can be. Here, Bella Vista's Indyan Summer and handler Stephanie Capkovic demonstrate a near-perfect heel position.

when the dog gets up and wanders off, the dog has learned you don't really mean what you say! No dog, and certainly no Westie, will respect you as a pack leader if he can decide whether or not to obey you.

SET GOALS AND FOLLOW THROUGH

In order to begin training your Westie, first evaluate your goals for participation in the activity you have chosen. Is your goal simply to get out and do some fun activity with your dog? Are you interested in competing in Obedience Trials, but not too concerned about high scores? Or do you want to compete for high scores and obtain advanced titles? Each of these goals is absolutely valid, but each will require a different approach, amount of time and level of commitment. Your goals may also change over time: You may decide to take an Obedience class for fun and later become interested in competition. You may take basic Obedience and then decide you would rather learn Tracking or Agility. If you are training your first dog, and/or your first Westie, experimenting with different activities is desirable and may lead you to the one sport for which you and your Westie are best suited. You may also end up loving one sport so much that you just have to acquire a second dog so you can continue to train (watch out, now you are really hooked!).

Whatever your goal, if you decide to take a class it will be of value only if you put forth the effort required to learn. You cannot go to class once a week, never practice outside of class and expect your dog to progress.

If you decide that your goal is to earn a CD (Companion Dog title—the first-level Obedience title) with your dog, it might be possible, with frequent practice and a willing dog, to be prepared to compete within, say, six months. If, on the other hand, you want advanced titles and want to compete for national placements in Obedience, it could easily take two years of training to be ready to compete for a CD. Clearly your expectations of yourself and your dog, and your commitment of time and energy, will differ according to your ultimate goals.

TRAIN YOURSELF

It is important to understand that the handler must learn a distinct set of skills for each of the sports outlined in Chapter 10. You need to know the rules of each sport and to learn how best to train your dog to perform the skills needed.

In Tracking, for instance, you must learn what scent is and how it operates on different surfaces and under a variety of environmental conditions. You must also learn how to teach your dog which scents to follow and which to ignore.

In Agility, you must safely introduce your dog to many new skills, such as climbing a six-foot A-frame and balancing on a teeter-totter. You must learn how to handle your dog around an Agility course, off-lead and at high speed.

Because human scenting ability is not equal to that of dogs, positive reinforcement methods are the *only* methods that work to train a dog for Tracking. "Sprite" has finished her TDX training track and earned her rewards: abundant praise, treats and time to play with her favorite glove. *Sue Ammerman*

In the upper levels of Obedience, you must teach your dog to heel at your side, sit, stand, lie down and come without speaking a word to it. You must know how to prepare your dog before going in the ring, and once you are in the ring you must know the sequence of exercises, what behavior is acceptable for both you and your dog and what behavior will mean you will not qualify (i.e., earn a "leg" toward an Obedience title).

And finally, while learning the skills you need and teaching your dog the skills he needs, you should both enjoy the training. Otherwise, what is the point of doing it?

USING FOOD AND OTHER POSITIVE REINFORCEMENT TECHNIQUES

Before training with food and other *inducive* methods became popular, there were few Westies who did well in Obedience. This is probably because, since Westies are intelligent individuals, their reaction to being forced to do anything for no understandable (to them) reason was to go and hide when the training lead was produced. If it is true that people are like their dogs, those who own terriers can probably understand this reaction perfectly. Some dogs have such a strong drive to please humans that they will forgive the force to get the praise, but terriers are not usually among them. The terrier's attitude towards training, and life in general, might be expressed most bluntly as "What's in it for me?"

What should be "in it" for your Westie is a chance to do interesting things and go places with you (his favorite person), along with rewards, praise and playtime for a job well done. These are motivators that a terrier can understand. And in fact, they are motivators that all breeds of dogs can understand.

Using food is an excellent training technique because it is something the dog understands immediately, and it is also simple to understand and master as a beginning technique for the novice handler. There are other methods, of course, and as you become more adept at handling you will probably incorporate some of these into your training methods.

In the old methods of dog training (still used by some trainers), you would have taught the dog to heel by pulling it into position with a choke collar, and then (hopefully) praising it in the "heel position." This method taught the dog skills through *negative reinforcement*; that is, it only learned by doing something wrong and being corrected, not by being right and being praised.

With food, you can teach the dog to heel by employing *positive reinforcement*. With the dog at your left side, show it the food and walk forward so that that the dog is lured into following you in the heel position. As soon as the dog begins to follow, you positively reinforce the behavior by praising the dog, naming the desired behavior ("Good heel!") and giving a food reward. This is an oversimplification of the method, and the techniques are best applied under the guidance of an experienced instructor, but the advantages of teaching with positive reinforcement are obvious, especially to any self-respecting Westie!

It is important to understand that the spoken praise and the named behavior are just as important as, and perhaps even more important than, the food. The food is used to shape the behavior in a positive way, but over time the praise should become the *primary* reinforcement and the food reward should become more randomly offered as the dog progresses in its training. While there is no need to ever completely eliminate food rewards from your training, the food must not become a constant bribe that is required before the dog will perform; you have missed an important step if this occurs.

As the dog progresses, you must also learn to distinguish between confusion, a decision not to obey and various levels of response. If the dog is confused, do not reward him; on the other hand do not correct him, but instead help him to understand. If the dog decides not to obey a command, correct the dog but *do not reward the behavior*. Many novice handlers are so programmed to feed their dogs that they will correct the dog for not obeying and then feed him! There should also be *levels* of praise and rewards. If the dog is trying hard to learn a new skill but having difficulty, try praise and a food reward for each small improvement. If you then continue to help the dog a few more times until he gets it *just right,* you should feed *several pieces* of food, praise the dog *enthusiastically,* break off working on that exercise for the day and perhaps take a short "play break." This will *really* motivate him to try harder the next time.

Another positive reinforcement you can use is toys. For instance, many Westies love "squeaky rats" made out of rabbit fur, so if your dog has just worked hard and performed brilliantly, break off training for a few minutes and throw the toy for your dog. This relieves the stress of training and makes it much more fun for the dog. Many trainers discover which toy is their dog's favorite and reserve it as a reward during training (squeaky rats are a good example of a toy to reserve for training, because if you give one to a Westie for more than a few minutes, fur will fly!).

What type of food should you use? Actually, the choice is yours. Many trainers use cooked hot dogs cut up into small pieces, but any soft food that the dog really likes (such as cheese or soft cat treats) will work. You can vary what you use from time to time to keep the dog from getting bored with the same thing. Try apples or carrots once in a while. Kibbles and biscuits are *not* recommended because the dog has to stop and chew before it can get back to training. It is also important to use *very small* pieces of food. Dogs do not distinguish between small and large pieces of food—a treat is a treat to them— and larger pieces will only cause unnecessary weight gains.

Be careful about where you store your food during training sessions. If you always keep treats in your left pocket, for instance, you will discover that your dog is paying more attention to your pocket than to you. It is for this reason that many trainers hold their treats in their mouth—so that the dog's attention is on *them*. Many novice handlers are not enthusiastic about this method, however, and if that applies to you, you will have to find a convenient place to keep the food you will use without distracting the dog.

USING CORRECTIONS IN TRAINING

It will sometimes be necessary to correct your dog. If you begin training with positive reinforcement, your dog will probably learn the skills you desire fairly quickly while maintaining a positive attitude toward its training. At some point, however, terriers being as they are, you will give your dog a command, he will hear and understand the command, but he will decide that there is something else more important that he has to do at that particular moment. At that moment, you must correct your dog if you want it to understand that when you give a command, it must be obeyed—then! Perhaps this sounds harsh, but if you think it is, consider the "down" command: If your dog is off-leash and about to run into your driveway while someone is backing out and does not see it, do you want the dog to decide whether or not it will obey your "down" command?

As discussed in the earlier sections of this chapter, attitude and timing are essential to effective corrections and to maintaining a positive attitude toward training. The correction should be done quickly, calmly and with the minimum amount of force needed to get the point across. And the correction should *always* be followed by praise when the dog responds as you wish. If

Just as this bitch teaches her puppy good manners, so must
you, as the Westie's pack leader, learn to teach your pup
using rewards, along with fair and well-timed corrections.
Appropriate corrections followed by praise will not cause
the pup to resent you any more than he resents his mother.
Allison Platt

the dog does *not* respond to the correction (yes, Westies can *occasionally* be
stubborn), you must set up the situation again and correct again until the dog
responds in the appropriate manner so that you can end your training session on a positive note.

Corrections are nearly always more painful for the novice handler to give
than they are for the dog to receive (when done correctly). Learning to give
corrections properly is another skill best learned under the guidance of an
experienced trainer. When dogs are corrected swiftly and appropriately and
then praised lavishly for obeying, nearly all will happily wag their tails and
generally demonstrate their pleasure in having made their trainers happy. If
your Westie does not, you should wonder whether your correction was too
harsh or whether it didn't understand the command the first time.

It is useful to understand a little about how dogs learn in order to know
when it is appropriate to correct, as well as when you should instead help the
dog. Students of dog behavior have observed that in the course of learning,
dogs will often appear to master a skill fairly quickly but then seem to forget
it briefly before they truly understand it. The theory is that short-term memory
and long-term memory are stored in different parts of the brain (as in humans). When introducing a new skill, you must repeat the exercise often

enough to allow the dog to "move" this skill from short-term to long-term memory. And as we all know, moving is traumatic and causes all of us to forget things! Because of this, you should not be frustrated or annoyed with your dog if yesterday he seemed to know an exercise perfectly, but today has forgotten it completely. Knowledge of this learning process will be very helpful in training if it allows you to give your dog the benefit of the doubt and show him the exercise one more time rather than rush to give a correction. As stated earlier, if your Westie does not know what you want and you correct him needlessly, it will not easily forgive and forget!

Another important observation about how dogs learn is that they seem to associate the *place* where they learn something with the *skill* they are learning. Since dogs don't use language as we do, they seem to think contextually, so if you teach your dog to down-stay in your living room, then give it the down-stay command in your yard, it may not immediately get the connection between the two. This is the reason for the often-heard lament of novice handlers to their trainers: *"But he does it perfectly at home!"* And perceptive trainers know when they hear this that it may be true. To ensure a consistent response to your commands, you must "proof" them in a variety of places and with all types of distractions before you can expect a consistent response from your Westie star performer.

TRAINING IS NOT BOOT CAMP

Your Westie will definitely *not* learn more quickly if you drill him for hours. All you will achieve is a bored and unhappy dog who *has learned* to hate training. If you are working on the sit command and your dog does it correctly five times in a row, then praise him and go on to something else. If you are having difficulty with an exercise, you may need to work on it a little longer, but as soon as the dog has done it correctly, don't do it ten more times to be *sure* it understands. Instead, praise and end the session or work on something else. At the next training session, begin that exercise with higher expectations of what the dog knows. In this way you can progress a little each time you train. When you begin training a young or "green" dog, there is no reason to train for more than fifteen to thirty minutes per day.

USE TRAINING TECHNIQUES APPROPRIATE
FOR THE SMALL DOG

Training a small dog presents a unique set of challenges that need to be taken into account if your training is to succeed. Because training a small dog is different from training a large one, it is desirable to have an instructor who understands the difference and helps you to devise training methods that work effectively.

One of the major differences is that *you* must be more careful in training. If you are moving quickly with your dog, for instance in Obedience

Windermere of Rosewood, CDX, TD, CG, shown here with her owner-trainer Mary Bell, was the second recipient of the Versatile Dog Award offered by the WHWTCA.

heeling or on an Agility course, it is easier to step into or on the dog inadvertently and either frighten him, make him shy away or even injure him (or yourself).

If you are interested in Obedience competition, you must be precise in your movements and body language. In heeling, for instance, it is much more obvious if a small dog is not in "heel position." The AKC rules state that in the heel position the dog should be about 6 inches from your leg, but 6 inches away with a German Shepherd Dog looks very different from 6 inches from a West Highland White! Similarly, if you are calling the dog to a sit in front of you (the Obedience recall), it is supposed to sit *within reach*, but that position is very different for a small dog and a large one. A small dog sitting 10 or 12 inches back will look very much farther away than a large dog at the same distance.

You can also make your dog sit too far out or too far to the side if you lean over the dog too much. It is better to bend from the knees than to lean over, because the dog generally learns to watch your face for approval and commands, and if you are leaning over your dog can see better from farther out. Since you probably will initially use food to teach the dog to heel, you must position the food far enough down toward it to get its attention. By the time you learn to hold the food in the correct position without leaning over or bending toward your dog, while moving forward and watching it, you will probably have a sore back and neck and begin to feel like a contortionist!

As you progress, there are many aids you can use to help train your small dog. In Obedience, you can use techniques such as chutes to bring the dog in straight, or dowels that allow you to put the food near the dog without bending over. In Agility, you can teach your dog how to navigate the weave poles using shorter poles, so you can more easily lure the dog through with food or guide it with a leash. These and many other techniques can be learned from trainers or devised on your own as you gain more knowledge of training and how your particular dog learns.

One last, but very important, consideration for training the small dog is the need to be aware of the potential problems you may encounter with big dogs and their handlers. Such problems can occur anywhere—on a walk, at a show or in a training class. Because Westies have a large self-image (Westies think they are giant dogs in small bodies!), they seldom take kindly to being rushed at by large dogs. If your dog is dominant, it may snap at the large dog; and even if your Westie is gentle and submissive, such an experience is not likely to add to its level of confidence.

Unfortunately, many large dog owners see nothing wrong with allowing their dogs to run up to your Westie at a gallop (*"He just wants to play!"*), and will even be offended if your Westie tries to defend itself. There may *not* be a problem, but it is better to be careful, since it is likely that at some point you will encounter a large dog that is aggressive towards smaller dogs. In such a situation, your Westie could be seriously hurt, or at a minimum psychologically shaken. When you are in a place where there are strange dogs, be sure to keep a close eye on your dog and other dogs. Insist that the owners of strange dogs not allow them to rush or lunge at your dog, even in play, until the dogs are acquainted and you are sure they will get along. (Note: Some puppy classes encourage off-lead play during or after class. This is *not* recommended for your Westie or other small dog.) This cautious approach to other dogs is especially important when your Westie is young: If you protect him from bad experiences when he is young, you will be training him to be calm and friendly with dogs of all kinds throughout his life.

Ch. Rime's Alicia Aquena, CDX, TDX, CG, owned and bred by Sil and Anne Sanders, was the first TDX Westie and the first Westie to earn titles in Conformation, Obedience, Tracking and Terrier Trials. This versatile "superachiever" was handled throughout by Sil.

chapter 10

Performance Activities for You and Your Westie
By Allison Platt

The he major organized performance activities available to you and your Westie include Obedience Trials, Agility, Tracking Tests, Earthdog Tests and Flyball. These activities are offered by the AKC and/or other dog registries and by other organizations that exist to promote a particular dog sport. This chapter will present the basic concept and purpose of each activity and direct you to sources of further information.

This chapter also gives the names of Westies and their owners that have obtained titles in the various dog sports. In the longer-established sports, only the dogs with higher-level titles are listed, since in Obedience alone, for example, nearly 900 Westies have earned CD degrees! The listings are further limited to AKC titles, because they include the most complete statistics on titles. Many thanks to the Performance Committee of the West Highland White Terrier Club of America for its Herculean record-keeping, and for making the official records available for this book.

OBEDIENCE TRIALS

Obedience trials have been the premier performance activity for dogs and their handlers for more than fifty years. The advantage of choosing to train your dog in Obedience, besides owning a well-behaved dog, is that you can usually find classes and trials almost anywhere you live. Even in a fairly isolated location, hundreds of books, tapes and seminars are readily available that can help you train on your own. To begin with, all you and your dog will need is a collar and a 6-foot lead. As you progress, you will need additional equipment, but this will not be a consideration for at least the first year.

Obedience is meant to demonstrate the dog's ability to work with its handler in useful ways. Many of the exercises incorporate tasks that are equally relevant to all breeds (e.g., scent discrimination), while others reflect origins in tasks useful for Working and Herding dogs, such as the "go-out" and directed jumping (skills that might be used to send a herding dog out to gather a flock of sheep). Westies can learn these skills as well as any dog, and although some Obedience judges are said to have difficulty taking a small dog in Obedience seriously, it is probably also true that just as many judges are completely charmed by seeing a happy working Westie in their ring.

Both the American Kennel Club and the United Kennel Club offer competition for Obedience titles at their shows (UKC titles are preceded by a "U-," as in U-CD or U-CDX). Both are similar, although they differ in some details. Both offer (in ascending order of difficulty) Novice classes where the CD (Companion Dog) title may be earned, Open classes where the CDX (Companion Dog Excellent) title may be earned and Utility classes where the UD (Utility Dog) title may be earned. For each of these titles, your dog must qualify three times at three separate shows under different judges. A *qualifying score* means that the dog has earned at least half the allowed points for each exercise and has earned a minimum of 170 points overall out of a "perfect" score of 200.

The AKC also offers UDX (Utility Dog Excellent) and OTCh (Obedience Trial Champion) titles. A UDX title is gained after the UD title by qualifying in both Open B and Utility B classes at ten shows. An OTCh title is gained after the UD title by earning first or second place in the Utility and Open classes and accumulating points at each show based on the number of dogs defeated in each class until the dog accumulates a total of 100 points (including at least one first place in each class, plus an additional first place in either class, under three different judges). The UKC does not offer a title equivalent to the UDX, but its U-OCH is very similar to the AKC OTCh, except that points are awarded based on scores, not on the number of dogs defeated.

The Novice (CD) level is meant to test the dog's ability to perform basic Obedience tasks, such as heeling on and off lead, standing for examination, coming when called and staying quietly in a sit or down position within sight of the handler. Nearly all Westies are capable of achieving a CD title.

At the Open level (CDX), the dog performs all the exercises off lead, and many of the exercises require the dog to leave the handler's side in order to perform them. The exercises include heeling off lead; retrieving an object (a wooden or plastic "dumbbell" made to fit comfortably in the dog's mouth) thrown by the handler both on the ground and over a high jump; a "drop on recall," in which the dog must drop to the ground on a command from the handler while being called in to the handler; a recall over a broad jump, which is a series of very low boards; and a longer down-stay and sit-stay than is performed in the Novice class with the handler out of sight of the dog. If the handler is willing to put in the time to train, most Westies can obtain a CDX title.

The Directed Retrieve exercise in the Utility class is an example of an exercise meant to demonstrate the dog's ability to work with its owner in useful ways. Again, this is Ch. Rime's Quonquering Hero, UDTX ("Mr. Q"), owned by Sil and Anne Sanders, returning over the high jump. *Sil Sanders*

The Utility (UD) level of competition requires the dog to think and work independently of the handler to the greatest degree. As with the highest-level title in most dog sports, this title is not easy to obtain, and it requires both a strongly motivated handler and a dog who enjoys training. The exercises include a heeling exercise that is executed entirely with hand signals; a scent discrimination exercise in which the dog must choose the article with the handler's scent on it from among eight similar articles; a directed retrieve where the handler uses a voice and hand signal to send the dog to retrieve one of three gloves; a "moving stand" exercise where the dog must stop during a heel exercise at a command from the handler (who then leaves the dog), be examined by the judge and return to the heel position from the stand at a command from the handler; and finally, a directed jumping exercise where the dog is sent across the length of the ring at a command from the handler, sits on command, and then takes a jump to the right or left, depending on the signal from the handler.

Basic Obedience is essential before beginning any training in the other dog sports. Agility, for instance, requires that each dog complete the course on command and off lead. This is Kirkton's Conundrum, NA, SE ("Drummer"), owned by Lynn Stonesifer and Allison Platt. *J. Brimmer*

Only a handful of Westies have ever won an all-breed High in Trial score. This is Dawn's Bright N' Early ("Piper") and Margaret Schrader after the team won HIT with a score of 197$\frac{1}{2}$ in November 1989. *Klein*

The best way to understand the sport and the requirements of each level of competition is to go to Obedience trials and watch, or volunteer to steward (help the judge in the ring). If you go to observe, it is best to watch several dogs in each class in order to understand the skill levels required, the order of the exercises and the range of performances usually seen in each class. If you train through an Obedience club, you can also volunteer to steward, which will give you experience in the ring and allow you to learn first hand how the exercises are judged.

In recent years the number of dogs in AKC Novice "A" classes (classes for dogs *and handlers* who have never attained an Obedience title before) has been declining, probably because Agility and other new events are gaining in popularity. It is this writer's opinion, however, that basic Obedience training is essential before beginning training in the other dog sports. Obedience teaches the owner basic handling and communication skills and teaches the dog basic commands essential for control and teamwork. Examples of Obedience skills needed in the other dog sports are numerous: In Earthdog Tests at the upper level, a dog must be recalled from the tunnel; in Agility a dog must sit, down, jump, turn and negotiate various pieces of equipment on command and off lead; in Tracking a dog must indicate and/or retrieve the scent articles when it finds them. Many clubs require successful completion of a basic Obedience course before admitting a dog to training for other activities.

WESTIE OBEDIENCE TITLE HOLDERS

Westies have participated in Obedience competition from the beginning of its establishment as an AKC performance event in the 1930s. The first West Highland White Terrier recorded as attaining a CD title was Ch. Robinridge Bimelick, who achieved both his CD degree and conformation championship in 1942. Since then, Westies have earned nearly 900 CDs, more than 200 CDXs, more than 50 UDs, 3 UDXs and 1 OTCH.

As a sign of the increasing popularity of Westies in Obedience, the West Highland White Terrier Club of America introduced Obedience as one of the events offered at the 1992 national Specialty. Participation and the percentage of dogs qualifying has increased steadily since then. In 1992, there were seventeen entries and four qualifiers; in 1995, there were thirty-six entries and seventeen qualifiers, and in 1997, there were thirty-nine entries and twenty-three qualifiers.

The "High in Trial" Westies (i.e., the highest-scoring dogs in regular classes) since the inception of Obedience at the national Specialty in 1992 include:

OBEDIENCE TITLE HOLDERS

Year	Dog's Name	Owner(s)
1992:	Glover's Duke of Winchester, UD (from Utility B)	Michael & Renee Glover
1993:	Bonnie Baby Kins, CDX (from Open B)	Margaret Kipp Bushnell
1994:	Ch. Wee Mack's Kelsey of Kirkton, CD, JE (from Open A)	Allison Platt
1995:	Ch. Wee Mack's Kelsey of Kirkton, CDX, TD, SE (from Open B)	Allison Platt
1996:	Leman Clodie, CD, JE (from Open A)	Ginette Lemieux
1997:	Happymac's Rhythm N Blues, TD, JE (from Novice B)	Renee Glover

There has been only one year since the inception of the national Obedience competition that any Westie has qualified for High Combined honors: Glover's Duke of Winchester, UD, owned by Michael and Renee Glover, achieved this distinction in 1993, from the Open B and Utility B classes.

Westies are now seen in Obedience competition more frequently than ever before. It is interesting to note that in the 1950s there was one UD title earned; in the 1960s, there were three; in the 1970s, four; in the 1980s, eighteen; and so far in the 1990s, over twenty. Listed below are the Westies with titles of UD or above:

UD TITLES

Year	Dog's name	Owner
1956:	Barr's Katie McLeod	Margaret Barr
1964:	Ch. Mac-A-Dac Jack Straw	Bonnie Miller
1967:	Ch. Crest-O-Lake Twinkle Toes	(unknown)
	Prince's Magnificent Sultan	(unknown)
1972:	Barr's P. Pringle	Margaret Barr

1974:	Alfie	(unknown)
	Davenport's Jigger of Scotch	Darlene Cox
1977:	Wee Honey Hall	Mildred & Reuben Hall
1980:	Ka-Le's Heather Hildegard	L. Hilliard & K. Nordeen
	Maxwelton's Hopscotch Lass	Laraine & Karen Moffa
	Norsk Skotte Daisy	Roberta Sundrud
1981:	Skaket's Chunkies	Ernest & Nancy Gauthier
	Tartin's Popcorn Treat	Laraine & Karen Moffa
1982:	Rob Roy MacDuff II, TD	Maribeth McMahon
1983:	Cameron's Carole	Barbara Lee Giese
	Castlemilk's Darby Don't	Ted & Linda Terroux
1984:	Scottlands Fiona	Monique Courtois
1985:	Schrader's McSam	Charles & Margaret Schrader
	Twinky's Shadow	Bonnie Fruzen
	Wee Duke The Poacher	David & Kathie Ward
1986:	OTCh Dee Dee's Heather	Delores Ehnes
1987:	Darcie Mae of Chatange	Richard & Marilyn Bennett
	Hall's Scotch Mist	Mildred & Reuben Hall
	Natos' Tuff Stuff By the Banker	Judy & Melissa Roth
	Strathdon Tallyho O'Cameron	Cindy Ashlock
	Ch. Renie's Jiminy Kricket	Lorraine Reilly

1990:	Maggie of Witmer Manor	Virginia Witmer
	Scotdale's Wendy Ann	Marilyn Manning
1991:	Ch. Skaket's Candy Man, TD CG	Nancy Gauthier & Mitzi Beals
	Wynzalot's Kachina Doll	Judy & Melissa Roth
1992:	Bonnie Baby Kins	Margaret Kipp Bushnell
	Glover's Duke of Winchester	Michael & Renee Glover
	Sherrus Duncan of Riverbluff	Yedda & Robert Gorman
	Sherrus Muffin Edmonson	Andrea Edmonson Cox
1993:	Jessie's Cotton Candy	Alice & John Ward, Sr.
	Scotdale's Little Heartthrob	Marilyn Manning
	Tipton's William McKinley	Stephen & Teresa Tipton
1994:	Brianna Scruffy D and E	Sherron Corner
	Clanblair Piper O'Peter Pan	Mary Kuhlman
	Gingerbread Laddie's Buttons	C.S. Casey & M.E. Champagne
	Sioux Snow Angel	Marilyn Manning
	Sir Spencer the Merryheart	James & Teresa Wilson
1995:	Happymac's Duke of Bertshire	Michael & Renee Glover
	Ch. Rime's Quonquering Hero, TDX	Sil & Anne Sanders
1996:	We-Hi-Te Miss Snow Bunny	Marcia Harrison
	Ch. BCK's Meghan Mac Bounce	Alice Reis

	Eastfield Saltcoat Sea Spray	Angeline Austin
	Bonnie Bluebell	Jane Vollers
1997:	Biljonblue's Prince Digger	George C. Harris, Jr.
	Sherrus Watts In a Name	Yedda Marks
	Ch. Leman Clodie, CD, JE	Ginette Lemieux

There were only three UDX and one OTCh Westie as of the end of June 1997. The UDX Westie dog/handler teams are Sir Spencer of Merryheart, owned by James and Teresa Wilson, who earned their title in 1995, and Sioux Snow Angel, owned by Marilyn Manning, who earned their title in 1996; and Ch. Rime's Quonquering Hero, TDX, owned by Sil and Anne Sanders and handled by Sil, who earned their title in 1997. The UDX title has been available only since 1993, and several UD Westies have legs towards this title, so more UDX titles can be expected in the near future. Dee Dee's Heather, owned and handled by Delores Ehnes, earned the singular distinction of becoming an Obedience Trial Champion in 1990. Earning an OTCh is extremely difficult, and as competition improves over time, it is becoming progressively more difficult to do so.

There have been several Westies who have earned other Obedience honors, including all-breed High in Trial scores. Statistics on these records are a little more difficult to find, but one handler who has done very well with her Westies is Margaret Schrader, with Dawn's Bright N' Early ("Piper"). The team won an all-breed HIT score in November 1989, with a score of 197½. They also placed from the Novice class at both the Eastern Regional and the Classic Obedience competitions in 1990. The Regionals are national Obedience competitions that can be entered only if a dog has earned three scores averaging 193 or above in the particular class. Each competition consists of three shows, and the winners are the dogs with the highest number of total points from the three (600 possible points total). Only dogs that place in the three Regionals can compete in the Classic. Margaret and Piper place sixth at the Regional, losing only six points out of 600, and third in the Classic, losing only three points out of 600. Piper is the only West Highland ever to place in either competition.

AGILITY

Agility was invented in England as an entertainment at the Crufts dog show in 1979. Since then it has become enormously popular and is now the fastest-growing dog sport in North America, England and Europe. The sport is modeled on equestrian jumping competitions, but has evolved to become a unique sport designed to showcase canine Agility, speed and teamwork with

Agility is the fastest-growing dog sport in North America, England and Europe and the most exciting to watch. Here Kirkton Quicksilver Girl, TDX, NA ("Sprite"), starts down the A-Frame in competition.

The teeter-totter is one of the most difficult obstacles in Agility. The dog must learn to climb the board and stop just past the balance point to tip the board down and run off at the far end. "Drummer," with handler Lynn Stonesifer, shows the fitness required. *J. Brimmer*

their owners. Agility is one of the most entertaining dog sports to watch and one of the most challenging for both handler and dog. It is a sport at which small dogs can excel, and an increasing number of Westies are being seen participating in Agility.

The judge designs a unique course for each level of competition. The course consists of jumps and "obstacles," and the dogs, who are further divided into classes by height, must complete it in a set amount of time and in the proper sequence. Faults are assigned if the dog touches or knocks down jumps, takes the obstacles out of sequence or misses an obstacle, goes over the course time or misses a contact zone. The dog within each height division that has the fastest time with the least number of faults wins. The complexity of the courses increases and the time allowed decreases at the higher levels of competition. There are four organizations that currently offer Agility competitions in North America: the AKC, the UKC, the North American Dog Agility Council (NADAC) and the United States Dog Agility Association (USDAA). The competitions offered by these groups differ from each other primarily in the height/jump requirements and number of faults allowed to qualify for a title. USDAA is generally considered to offer the most difficult courses, and NADAC the least difficult.

Many of the obstacles used in Agility competitions offered by the four organizations are similar. These include an A-frame consisting of two panels 3 to 4 feet wide and about 8 to 9 feet high, joined at the top and angled to be approximately 5 to 7 feet high; weave poles (poles about three feet high and twenty inches apart, through which the dog must weave); a dog walk about 8 to 12 feet long, 3 to 4 feet high in the center and approximately 12 inches wide, with ramps at each end; soft-sided ("collapsed") and rigid tunnels; a teeter-totter the dog must climb until it is just past the balance point to make it fall, then walk down the other side; a "pause table" on which the dog must jump, then wait in a down or sit position until released; a "tire" jump consisting of a tire or ring mounted in a frame, through which the dog must jump; and a wide variety of types of bar and panel jumps that the dog must clear without knocking over the top cross-piece.

Not only must the dog negotiate the equipment when asked; there are also "contact zones" on each of the major pieces of equipment that the dog must touch when climbing up and down. The equipment is designed to be appealing to the eye but also safe for the dogs, and the contact zones on the large obstacles help to ensure that the dogs will not injure themselves. In addition, the equipment is designed to ensure good traction in any weather, and the jumps have bars that are easily knocked down if the dog misjudges the height or falls.

Agility is different from Obedience in that each course in Agility competition is unique, whereas in Obedience the sequence and standards for each exercise always remain essentially the same. To draw a comparison with performance activities for horses, Obedience is similar to dressage and

The Agility Dog must be in excellent condition in order to avoid injury. Here, "Drummer" balances atop the A-Frame. *4U2C*

One of the most titled Westies in Agility is "Maggie," Townyridge Once Upon a Time, U.S. CD, CG, CGC, Can. CDX, Bermuda CD, Can. TD, AAD, AADC and FDX (Flyball Dog Excellent), owned by Jane McLaughlin of Toronto, Ontario. Maggie was number-one "Mini Dog" in Canadian Agility for 1992 and 1993, and the only Westie ever to compete in the USDAA Grand Prix Agility competition.

Agility is more like a combination of jumping events and flat races. Preparing to compete in Agility involves about a year of training for both you and your dog, and because there is a large amount of equipment involved, it is difficult to learn without joining or attending classes at a club or training center.

In Agility, the dog runs the course off-lead and in most cases does not wear a collar (to prevent injury to the dog should the collar become caught on the equipment). Because of this, your dog must respond to basic commands and follow your directions from a distance. This is one reason why most organizations require basic Obedience skills before they will allow you to train your dog in Agility. Most dogs, if introduced to the equipment properly, absolutely love Agility and participate enthusiastically. Food and praise are used to encourage a dog being trained in the use of the equipment, and negative reinforcement or corrections are seldom if ever used either in training or in competition.

One concern of which Westie owners should be aware when choosing which trials to enter is the required jump heights. Jump heights are set based on the height of your dog at the *shoulders*. USDAA has the highest required jump heights. If you have a large Westie that measures over 12 inches at the withers, he would be required to jump 18 inches in competition. Many people consider this too high for our short-legged terriers, and not worth the risk of injuring the dog. The other organizations have different criteria for jump heights, but generally the dog would not be required to jump more than his height at the shoulders.

Agility is one sport where it is very important that your dog be in good condition. Dogs that are older, are overweight or have physical problems are not good candidates for Agility training. More than with other dog sports, there is a risk, even with healthy, fit dogs, of injury. The best protection against injury is to train your dog carefully and gradually and to condition it with vigorous exercise such as long walks, swimming or running. In addition, you should not begin serious training in jumping and weaving until your dog has finished growing. Dogs may not compete in AKC trials until they are 12 months old (18 months old for USDAA and NADAC trials). While the dog is young, you can introduce jumping and the obstacles at lower heights and get the dog used to the equipment and commands needed for competition.

If you are serious about competing in Agility, it would be advisable to have your dog's hips and knees X-rayed at the age recommended by your vet. Because of increased interest in canine performance activities, there are now a greater number of veterinarians who are knowledgeable about conditioning and "sports" injuries in dogs, and there are also several excellent books on conditioning techniques for the "canine athlete."

WESTIE AGILITY TITLE HOLDERS

Agility is a fairly new sport, but already Westies are gaining titles from all four Agility organizations. All the possible titles from the four organizations that offer competitions will not be listed here, because the number alone would be confusing. In addition, we were not able to obtain information on Westies who have earned titles from organizations other than the AKC.

The first Westie to earn an AKC Agility title was Dawn's Fanci Clancy, NA, (Novice Agility, the first Agility title) owned by Patricia Sullivan. The first Westie to earn an AKC Open Agility title (second level title) is Doubletake's Texas Aspen, owned by Cynthia Macklin and Mary Cunningham; there are three Open Agility title holders as this book goes to press. The Westies who have earned AKC NA titles (Novice Agility Dog—the first-level title) since competition began in 1995 include the following dogs:

NOVICE AGILITY TITLES

Year	Dog's Name	Owner(s)
1995:	Dawn's Fanci Clancy	Patricia Sullivan
	Doubletake's Texas Aspen	M. Cunningham & C. Macklin
	Susie Q II	Joanne Unbehaun
	Maxwell Jamieson, CD	William & Diane Daubenmier
1996:	Hayastan's Kinetic Kyla	Jane McLaughlin
	Lady Katie Wynn	Joanne Unbehaun
	Princess Maggie Kate	Sheila Mehring
	County Clare's Sir Toby	Patricia Sullivan
	Kirkton's Conundrum, SE	Lynn Stonesifer & Allison Platt
	Molly	Jenny Kaemmerer
	Clanblair Piper O'Peter Pan	Mary B. Kuhlman

	Miss Maddy of Waverly	Fran Huxley
	Ch. Tiptop's Elementary My Dear, CD	Sherron Corner & Louis & Marjory Conway
	Crystal's Forecer in Blujeans, CD	Renee Tekotte
1997:	Miss Charlotte of Mpls	Susan & David Nelson
	Bella Vista's Flying Solo	Stephanie Capkovic
	Kirkton's Quicksilver Girl	Allison Platt
	Skaket's Guess Who, CD, TD, JE	Nancy Gauthier
	Patent Pending O'Peter Pan	John & Marcia Lozes
	Ch. Lonach Devil Demon, CD, TD	Nancy Gauthier
	Sassy Cassie Kae, CD	Karen Morris

OPEN AGILITY TITLES

1997:	Doubletake's Texas Aspen, NA	Cynthia Macklin & Mary Cunningham
	Lady Katie Wynn, NA	Joanne Unbehaun
	Kirkton Quicksilver Girl, TDX	Allison Platt

One Westie enthusiast who has done exceptionally well in Agility is Jane McLaughlin of Toronto, Ontario, Canada. Two of her dogs have earned several titles in Agility, including the only advanced USDAA Agility titles for a Westie in North America. Towynridge Once Upon a Time ("Maggie") qualified in first place in a USDAA Chicago regional trial in 1992, which earned her a free trip to the Pedigree Grand Prix national in Texas that same year, the first and only Westie ever to do so. Maggie was also the first-place AAC (Agility Association of Canada) mini-dog in Canada in both 1992 and 1993, the first Westie to earn an Agility title in the United States (note: USDAA Agility competitions preceded AKC competitions by several years) and the second in Canada. Maggie's full titles include the following: CD, Bermuda CD, Can. CDX, Can. TD, CG, AAD (USDAA Advanced Agility Dog title), AADC (Advanced Agility Dog—Canada) and FDX (Flyball Dog Excellent).

EARTHDOG TESTS

Earthdog tests (the term *terrier* comes from the Latin word *terra*, meaning earth) are among the most relaxed and enjoyable activities you can do with your Westie. The tests were first organized by the American Working Terrier Association, a group formed to promote hunting tests for small terriers and Dachshunds. Late in 1994, the AKC began holding earthdog tests as well, and this sport is rapidly growing in popularity.

The tests are meant to measure the dog's ability to hunt. The AKC states in its regulations: "The purpose of non-competitive earthdog tests is to offer breeders and owners of small Terriers and Dachshunds a standardized gauge to measure their dogs' natural abilities when exposed to a hunting situation. The noncompetitive program begins with a basic introduction to den work and quarry and progresses through gradual steps to require the dog to demonstrate that it is capable of being trained to follow game to ground and work its quarry."

"Going to ground" at an Earthdog test means that a dog enters and navigates the "artificial earth"—a man-made tunnel meant to simulate an animal's den. The tunnels are made from three 9-inch-wide boards fastened together to create a top and two sides, which is then buried in sections to create the various configurations of tunnels needed for the tests. At the end of the tunnel there is a cage with rats, which the dogs can see but not reach. The tunnel and the entrance to it are scented as an animal's natural lair would be. The dog is released near the entrance to the tunnel and must enter the tunnel, follow it to the end and then "work" the quarry (that is, scratch, bark or dig at the cage).

There are three levels of titles that can be pursued at AKC tests: Junior Earthdog (JE), Senior Earthdog (SE) and Master Earthdog (ME). There is also an Introduction to Quarry class, which is designed to introduce the dog and handler to going to ground. In this class dogs do not compete for a title; instead handlers and judges assist young or inexperienced dogs to enter the tunnel, follow it to the end and begin to work the quarry. Usually after a time or two in this class, and sometimes with a small amount of outside training, the dog will suddenly "get it," and after that very little training is needed.

The Junior tunnel is 30 feet long, with three right-angle turns in it; the handler must release the dog at the judge's direction with a single command from a point about ten feet from the den opening. The dog then has thirty seconds to enter the tunnel and reach the quarry. Once the dog reaches the quarry, it cannot leave the area until the end of the test. The dog has thirty seconds from the time it reaches the quarry to begin "working," and must work without stopping for sixty seconds. The handler must not give any further commands after releasing the dog. Once the test is completed, the judge will signal the handler to come and remove the dog from the tunnel through a trap door near the end. The dog must qualify at two tests under two different judges to obtain the JE title.

Earthdog tests are meant to evaluate a dog's hunting ability. Here, Ch. Benchmark Little Cloud, CG, CD ("Becky"), with owner Don Budge standing by, enters the "artificial earth" on command. *Ann Budge*

In the non-titling Introduction To Quarry class, the judge and handler may assist young or inexperienced dogs in "going to ground." Here the judge and the handler, Allison Platt, try to call Kirkton Kinetic Energy ("Zippy") through the tunnel, but Zippy decides to come back out the entrance! *Sue Ammerman*

Handler-owner   Lou Herczeg   releases   Ch. Hayastan Highland King, CD ("Corky"), at the tunnel entrance in a Master Earthdog test. In June 1997, Corky became the first Westie to earn an AKC Master Earthdog title. *Allison Platt*

In the Senior Earthdog test, the tunnel is also 30 feet long, but it has two additional elements: a false (unscented) entrance and a false den (with scent, but without any live animals). The dog is released at a point approximately 20 feet from the tunnel entrance, and the dog has ninety seconds to enter the tunnel and reach the quarry. The dog may come out the false entrance as long as it reenters, and may explore the false den as long as it gets to the quarry within the specified time. The dog then has fifteen seconds to begin working, and must work the quarry continuously for ninety seconds without leaving the area. At the end of ninety seconds, if the dog has qualified up to that point, the judge and steward remove the quarry from the tunnel and signal the handler to recall the dog from the entrance with voice or whistle. The dog can leave the den by any entrance and the handler must go and pick up the dog once it has emerged, all within ninety seconds of the judge's signal to recall the dog. A dog must qualify at three tests under at least two different judges to obtain the SE title.

In Master Earthdog, the tunnel is the same as for SE, except two obstacles are added: a constriction of the tunnel width from 9 inches down to 6 inches for a length of 18 inches, and a 6-inch PVC pipe placed crossways in the tunnel and meant to simulate a root that the dog must climb over. The dogs are hunted in pairs, which are drawn the morning of the test. A line of scent is laid from the tunnel entrance approximately twenty feet from the entrance. The judges, handlers and dogs walk naturally toward the den from a point approximately 100 feet away. The tunnel entrances are blocked, and the first dog who finds the den is allowed to work first, with the second dog staked nearby while the first dog works (the second dog works after the first dog is finished). The dog is released at the tunnel entrance and has ninety seconds to negotiate the tunnel and ninety seconds to work the quarry. During thirty seconds of the time the dog is working, the judge will strike the top of the working area with an implement meant to simulate the sound of digging to the quarry. The dog is then removed from the den by the handler at the judge's signal. The ME test is meant to be the most realistic test of a dog's ability to hunt in a pack and find the quarry as it would in the field. A dog must qualify at four tests under at least two different judges to obtain the ME title.

The best way to understand the tests is to go and observe one. Locations and dates for AKC Earthdog tests are listed in the back of the "Events" section of the *AKC Gazette*. These tests are great fun for the dogs, handlers and spectators, and they do not require much specialized knowledge to appreciate. At Conformation shows, exhibitors often tend to be keyed up to some extent. They spend hours preparing their dogs for the ring and often leave soon after judging, so they don't have much time to sit and talk or observe the judging. At Earthdog tests, on the other hand, most people spend the day even though their dogs are only in action for a few minutes. Very little preparation is necessary, so there is time to relax and enjoy your fellow exhibitors and your dogs. People dress informally, cheer each other on and have time between runs to "talk dogs."

Although little formal training and no special equipment is needed for Earthdog tests, especially with dogs who are naturally keen hunters, some people who really enjoy the sport often introduce their dogs to hunting before going to tests by constructing their own tunnels and burying them on their property. These tunnels become "playgrounds" for puppies and older dogs and make them confident about entering the tunnels at tests. Because the dogs do most of the work, this is also an excellent sport for handlers of all ages and levels of activity.

WESTIE EARTHDOG TITLE HOLDERS

The first Westie to attain its JE title was Wee Geordie McPeg, CDX, owned by Mary Kuhlman. After a little less than two years of AKC trials, there are already fifty JE Westies. The first SE Westie was Ch. Hayastan's Highland King, owned by Dawn Martin and Louis Herczeg, and as of October 1997 there are eleven SE Westies. The Earthdog titlists are as follows:

JUNIOR EARTHDOG TITLES

Year	Dog's Name	Owner(s)
1995:	Wee Geordie McPeg, CDX	Mary Kuhlman
	Ch. Czarcrest's Cameo	Mary & Reed Brooks
	Sioux Windsor of Digby	Karen Tangeman
	Ch. Rime's Impudence	Suzanne Stebbins
	Ch. Dawn's Kit N' Kaboodle, CD	Dawn Martin & Patricia Marks
	Ch. Dawn's Kop N' A Plea	Dawn Martin & Patricia Marks
	Dawn's Manhattan Project	Thomas & Amy Stahl Juzwik
	Ch. Dawn's Moment N' Time	Patricia Marks & Dawn Martin

	Ch. Dawn's Peaches N' Cream	Patricia Marks & Dawn Martin
	Ch. Hayastan Highland King, CD	Dawn Martin & Louis Herczeg
	Ch. Rime's Off to See The Wizard, TD	Sil & Anne Sanders
	Cassandra Curious Forbes	Christine Forbes
1995:	Ch. Forbes' MacDuff The Bold, CD	Christine Forbes
	Krison's Kipper	Nancy Sankus
	Ch. Skaket's Champagne, TD	J. Brown-Sackrison & J. Sackrison
	Skaket's Guess Who	Nancy Gauthier
	Ch. Skaket's Lord Toby Tweedmouth, CD, TD	Catherine Padyk
	Ch. Wee Mack's Kelsey of Kirkton, CDX, TD	Allison Platt
	Ch. B-Jay's Bright N' Breezy, TD	Patricia Berndt
	Camrick's Peaches Cream, CD, TD	Cheryl Gauthier & S. and Camarda
	Ch. Forbes Highlander Queen	Christine Forbes
	Kirkton's Conundrum	Lynn Stonesifer & Allison Platt
	Leman Clodie	Ginette Lemieux
	Ch. Skaket's Taffy, CD	Mitzi Beals
	Alexis of Daisy Valley	Stephanie Capkovic
	Ch. Sandalwood's Flash O'Brybern	M. & R. Brooks & Berna Gaul
1996:	Dawn's Hole N' One	Dawn Martin and Stephanie Capkovic
	Ch. Skaket's Kit Kat, CDX, TD	Nancy Gauthier

Ch. Skaket's Nigel Saunders	Crecia & Terry Closson
Ch. Skaket's Bakers Joy, CD, TD	Patricia Berndt
Ch. An-Van's Rough and Rowdy Rascal	Anne Van Walleghem
Happymac's Rhythm and Blues, TD	Roberta Mocabee & Renee Glover
Wee Darby Glencanna	Kimberly & Joseph Budiselich
Ch. Cederfell Milk-N-Honey	Angeline Austin
Ch. Dawn's Kick N' Up A Fuss	Dawn Martin & Patricia Marks
Ch. Den Marcs Ruby Tuesday	Marc & Denise Collins
Renie's Tina Two Colada	Renie Spingarn
Liberty's AcAlpin Spicer, CDX	John & Marcia Lozes
Ch. TipTop's Elementary My Dear, CD, NA	Sherron Corner & Louis & Marjorie Conway

1997:	McIntyre's Cailidh	Jane Filkins
	Chewbacca The Albino	William Koerner, Jr.
	Ch. Bella Vista's Avalamche Lily	Stephanie Capkovic
	Ch. Leman Daphne, CDX	Ginette Lemieux
	Bearland's Kelly the Clown	Arlene & Tom Tarter & R. & M. Brooks
	Dawn's Koz N Komotion	Dawn Martin & Patricia Marks
	Rime's Fantasy Fulfilled	Debra Duncan
	Glenmar's Rock Hunter	Judy & Brian Baird
	Kirkton Carolina on My Mind	Allison Platt

Kirkton Kinetic Energy	Allison Platt
Bella Vista's You the Man	Susan & Dennis Ammerman

SENIOR EARTHDOG TITLES

Year	Dog's Name	Owner(s)
1995:	Ch. Hayastan's Highland King, CD, JE	Dawn Martin & Lou Herczeg
1996:	Ch. Dawn's Kit N' Kaboodle, CD, JE	Dawn Martin & Patricia Marks
	Kirkton's Conundrum, JE	Lynn Stonesifer & Allison Platt
	Ch. Dawn's Kop N' A Plea, JE	Dawn Martin & Patricia Marks
	Dawn's Hole N' One, JE	Dawn Martin & Stephanie Capkovic
	Ch. An-Van's Rough and Rowdy Rascal, JE	Anne Van Wallegham
	Ch. Wee Mack's Kelsey of Kirkton, CDX, JE, TD	Allison Platt
1997:	Bella Vista's Indyan Summer	Stephanie Capkovic
	Krison's Klipper, CD, JE	Nancy Sankus
	Dawn's Kick'N Up a Fuss, JE	Dawn Martin & Patricia Marks
	Chewbacca the Albino, JE	William Koerner, Jr.
	Leman Clodie, UD, JE	Ginette Limeux

MASTER EARTHDOG TITLES

Year	Dog's Name	Owner(s)
1997:	Ch. Hayastan's Highland King, CD, SE	Lou Herczeg & Dawn Martin
	Ch. Dawn's Kit N' Kaboodle, CD, SE	Dawn Martin & Patricia Marks
	Ch. Dawn's Hole N' One, SE	Dawn Martin & Stephanie Capkovic

In June 1997, the first two Westie Master Earthdog titles were awarded. The first went to Ch. Hayastan's Highland King, CD, SE ("Corky"), owned by Lou Herczeg and Dawn Martin and handled by Herczeg. The second went to Ch. Dawn's Kit N' Kaboodle, CD, SE, owned by Dawn Martin and Patty Marks and handled by Martin, on the very next day. Boasting an impressive record in Earthdog tests, Corky was the first JE Westie on the East Coast and the first SE Westie nationally. Even more impressive is the fact that Corky had a spinal injury that threatened his ability to walk after he earned his first Master leg in the summer of 1996. That he not only recovered from surgery but went on to earn the first Master title for a Westie was an inspiration for all who witnessed it and epitomizes the spirit of our wonderful breed.

It is interesting to note that many Earthdog titlists are also Conformation champions and have titles in other dog sports as well. This is an excellent indication that our Westies have not lost the ability to hunt, for which they were originally selected and bred.

TRACKING

Tracking is definitely a sport at which Westies can do well, since they were bred to use their noses to hunt. Tracking is what our dogs often do when they are out for a walk. They detect the scents of various animals and people as they walk, and often they try to follow the ones that interest them. In tracking events, you train your dog to follow a scent you choose for it.

There are various ways in which the dog's natural ability to follow scent is utilized. Search and rescue work, bomb-sniffing and drug-detection work, Schutzhund Tracking and AKC Tracking are all examples of ways in which

In Tracking, the dog is trained to follow a scent chosen for it.
Here at the starting flag, handler Allison Platt indicates to
Sprite the beginning of the scent path, or track. *Sue Ammerman*

While tracking, the dog must follow the scent of a person who
walked along a charted course as much as five hours earlier
and indicate to the handler as many as four personal articles
(gloves, socks, wallets) left along the way. *Sue Ammerman*

dogs use their noses to assist (or entertain) their people. Although Westies might be useful and proficient in any of these venues, most people train their Westies to pass AKC tracking tests. The AKC offers titles for the successful completion of tracks of increasing length and difficulty. There are now three titles in AKC Tracking: TD (Tracking Dog), TDX (Tracking Dog Excellent) and, most recently, VST (Variable Surface Tracking). If a dog gets all three titles, the initials CT (Champion Tracker) may be used before its name.

A track in an AKC Tracking Test consists of a path through the outdoors chosen and marked with flags by two judges and a tracklayer the day before the test, then walked the day of the test by a tracklayer. The tracklayer removes the markers as they retrace their steps, leaving only one or two flags at the start to mark the beginning. The track is then aged a prescribed amount of time, and the dog and handler are brought to the start. The dog is placed in a nonrestrictive harness and on a 20-to-40-foot lead, and at the handler's command must follow the track from beginning to end, finding and indicating to the handler any articles left along the way. Articles are small personal items belonging to the tracklayer, such as a glove, wallet, tie or handkerchief. The handler must follow at a distance of at least 20 feet from the dog (10 feet in VST) and may talk to and encourage the dog, but must not do anything to indicate the direction of the track. There is no time limit as long as the dog continues to work. To gain each of the three AKC titles, the dog needs to qualify only once. Once you have submitted an entry, selection is by random draw among all the people who submit entries, so you are not assured a place.

A TD test is the only tracking test for which the dog must be *certified*. To be certified, the dog must be tested by an AKC judge on a track of equivalent length and level of difficulty to a regulation TD track. If the dog passes, the handler is issued three certification slips, which must be sent in with the entry form. A TD test consists of a track between 440 and 500 yards in length, with three to five turns, including right and left turns and more than two 90-degree turns. Each *leg* (the distance between two turns) must be at least fifty yards long, and the age of the track not less than thirty minutes and not more than two hours (most TD tracks are run at between thirty minutes and one hour). There is only one article on a TD track, at the end—either a glove or a wallet. For the TD, there are no *changes in cover,* as from short grass to tall grass or from fields to woods, and no *obstacles* to cross, such as streams, fences, or roads. The pass rate for all dogs taking the TD test is a little better than 50 percent. Most handlers with dogs who show aptitude for Tracking can be ready to compete for a TD title in from four to six months to a year if they work steadily (i.e., once or twice a week) during that time. Forty-six Westies have earned AKC Tracking titles.

A TDX test consists of a track of between 800 and 1,000 yards, aged three to five hours. It has five to seven turns, more than three of which are 90-degree turns, and includes both right and left turns. In addition to this, there are at least three obstacles, two sets of crosstracks and *four* articles.

In a TD test, the track is usually aged about thirty to forty minutes, and there are no changes in cover (e.g., from grass to
woods). Here, Ch. Skaket's Reese's Pieces, with owner-handler
Mitzi Gauthier, starts off toward the second flag on her successful TD attempt at the first WHWTCA TD/TDX test in October
1996. *Allison Platt*

In a Tracking test, the handler does not know where the track
goes and must rely on clear indications from the dog about when
the track changes direction. Here Sprite, after following this
TDX track along the edge of a field for about sixty yards, has
indicated clearly that the track turns into the woods to the left.
Sue Ammerman

Obstacles can include changes of cover, woods, gullies, streams, fences or lightly traveled roads. Crosstracks are two places along the track where two people walking together cross the main track at right angles. Crosstracks are always approximately half the age of the main track. The AKC rules state that the purpose of the TDX test is to is to "show unquestionably that the dog has the ability to discriminate scent and possesses the stamina, perseverance and courage to do so under a wide variety of conditions." The dog only needs to pass one time to earn a title, but TDX tests are very difficult to enter and difficult to pass. Often fifteen to twenty dogs will enter a test that offers two to six TDX tracks, and the pass rate is between fifteen and eighteen percent *of those that are chosen in the draw*. Those who pursue a TDX are usually very committed to the sport. Five Westies have earned TDX titles.

The newest Tracking title is the VST. It was introduced in 1995 and includes a track of 600 and 800 yards, aged between three and five hours. The main feature of this type of tracking is that 40 percent of the track is laid on *nonvegetated* surfaces such as concrete, asphalt, gravel or sand. Such surfaces hold very little scent, making this test extremely difficult. During the first year, twenty-seven dogs were entered in six tests and only one qualified (less than a 3 percent success rate).

Tracking is the one sport where positive reinforcement is not just recommended, but *required* to train the dog. Because a dog's sense of smell is thousands of times better than ours, we really have no idea how they track, and if they decide not to track, we cannot "show" them how. The dogs are the experts, so we can only encourage them to learn to enjoy it, trust them, follow behind and marvel at their skill. Perhaps because of this, Tracking is for many people the most engaging and fascinating of all the dog sports.

Tracking is often introduced to the dog with food, or by heavily scuffing the ground for a short distance to create a strong scent. At the end of the track, a glove, wallet or other personal article is placed by the tracklayer, often with food or a toy on it or in it. Beginning tracks are short—only twenty yards or so—and very *hot*, that is, laid and run within a few minutes. The dog is shown the food or the scuffed area at the start and is encouraged to explore. Very quickly, the dog will get the idea that if it follows the scent, it will find more food, an article at the end of the track with lots of food on it or in it and playtime. Soon the food along the path and the heavy scuffing can be lessened and the dog learns to follow the tracklayer's scent to find the article, where there is a reward. In stages, the dog is introduced to older tracks, turns and greater distances until it is ready to compete for its TD. If your Westie shows Tracking aptitude, you can then continue to train for the TDX and perhaps to become the first Westie VST and CT!

Tracking is an excellent sport for people who enjoy the outdoors and who are in reasonably good physical condition. Tracking events are held in all but the most severe weather, so warm and waterproof clothes are a requirement. Some people who have large dogs need to be able to run to keep up with them,

Participants in the first WHWTCA TD/TDX test. *From left, back row:* Mitzi Beals, judges Donna Thompson and Richard Zerbe, test organizer Allison Platt, Sil Sanders and Lynn Stonesifer. *Front row:* Test Chairman/Secretary Dawn Martin, Stephanie Capkovic, Nancy Gauthier, Anne Sanders, Rita Kline and Debbie Duncan. *Sue Ammerman*

but this is not usually a problem with Westies and their handlers. If you enjoy tracking and want to continue past your TD, however, you will find that advanced Tracking work requires both you and your dog to be very fit, since you may need to climb fences, ford shallow streams and move through woods, high grass and dense cover in all types of weather, both in training and in competition.

WESTIE TRACKING TITLE HOLDERS

In 1996, the WHWTCA held its first TD/TDX test on October 2, during the week before the national Specialty. This historic event was organized by Allison Platt; Chairman and Secretary was Dawn Martin. The trial was a great success, adding a new TD and a new TDX to the roster of Tracking-titled Westies. There were four TD tracks and two TDX tracks; three of the TD dogs qualified, as did one of the TDX dogs (two of the TDs already had their titles). The qualifiers at the first Westie tracking test were:

Ch. Skaket's Reese's Pieces (new TD), owner, Mitzi Beals

Ch. Wee Mack's Kelsey of Kirkton, CDX, TD, SE (qualified in TD), owner, Allison Platt

Beowulf O'Shaughnessy, CDX, TDX (qualified in TD), owner, Debra Duncan

Kent's Little Sass N Back, TDX (new TDX), owner, Rita Kline

As of October, 1997, there were forty-six Westies with TD titles and five with TDX titles. The Westies that have earned American TD and TDX titles are listed below. Under the AKC rules, if a dog earns a UD and a TD, it may bear the combined title UDT; and if it earns a UD and a TDX, it may bear the combined title UDTX.

TRACKING DOG TITLES

Year	Dog's Name	Owner(s)
1970:	Vimy Ridge Catriona, CDX	(unknown)
1977:	Windemere of Rosewood, CD	Vern & Mary Bell
1978:	Bob's Merry Mandy	Robert & Sharon Sipla
	Maxwelton's Hopscotch Lass, UD	Laraine & Karen Moffa
1982:	Nikki Jo O'Riagain, CDX	David & Lawana Nyman
	Rob Roy MacDuff II, UD	Maribeth McMahon
1983:	Ch. Rime's Gamble Ag'in, CD	Sil & Anne Sanders
1984:	Ch. Rime's Alicia Aquena, CDX	Sil & Anne Sanders
1986:	Camrick's Sailin To Beckfoot	Steve Camarda & Jan Daly
	Ch. Kintail Kiltie At Braemoor, CD	Rebecca & Robert Parsons
	Ch. Laird Doon Macduff of Helmsdale, CD	Vicki Beets
1987:	Camrick's Peaches and Cream	Steve Camarda & Cheryl Gauthier
	Kyle Cuillan O'Holyrood, CD, CG	Hilary Mercer
	Ch. Lord Derbyshire	Patricia Berndt
	Rime's Bonie Bridie, CD, CG	Frank & Lyn Hickey
	Ch. Skaket's Candy Man, CDX	Nancy Gauthier & Mitzi Beals
	Ch. Tacksman of That Ilk	Dorinda Dew

	West Highland Candida	Patricia Berndt
1989:	Pennygyll's Will He, CD	Elaine Brunner
1990:	Casper of McCamish, CD	Linda Spitzengel
1991:	Beowulf O'Shaughnessy, CDX, CG	Debra Duncan
	Ch. Rime's Off To See The Wizard, CG	Sil & Anne Sanders
	Ch. Rime's Quonquering Hero	Sil & Anne Sanders
1992:	Ch. B-Jay's Ms Bright N' Breezy, CG	Patricia Berndt
	Ch. Skaket's Lord Toby Tweedmouth, CD, CG	Catherine Padyk
	Skaket's Travis	Nancy Gauthier
1993:	Bonnie Guinivere of Ben-Mar	Sheryl Benson
	Carol's Scottish Pride, CDX	Carol Hoekstra
	Ch. Rime's Astral Aura	Sil & Anne Sanders
	Ch. Skaket's Kit Kat, CDX, CG	Nancy Gauthier & Mitzi Beals
1994:	Happymac's Rhythm N Blues	Roberta Mocabee & Renee Glover
	Lonach Devil Demon	Nancy Gauthier & C. Forbes
	Ch. Rime's Beguiling Belle	Sil & Anne Sanders
	Ch. Skaket's Baker's Joy, CD, JE, CG	Patricia Berndt
	Ch. Wee Mack's Kelsey of Kirkton, CDX, CG	Allison Platt
1995:	Kent's Little Sass N Back	Rita Kline
	Kirkton Quicksilver Girl	Allison Platt
	Rime's Absolutely Adorable	Sil & Anne Sanders
	Ch. Skaket's Champagne	Joy & John Sakrison
	Skaket's Guess Who, JE	Nancy Gauthier

1996:	Ch. Camrick's Pampered Pirate	Stephen Camarda
	Ch. Skaket's Reese's Pieces	Mitzi Beals
	Rime's Fantasy Fulfilled	Debra Duncan
1997:	Bella Vista's You The Man	Susan & Dennis Ammerman
	Rimes Game Goddess	Sil & Anne Sanders & Sandy Campbell
	Skaket's Tami of Krison's	Joy & John Sackrison

TDX TITLES

Year	Dog's Name	Owner(s)
1984:	Ch. Rime's Alicia Aquena, CDX, CG, TD	Sil & Anne Sanders
1991:	Ch. Rime's Quonquering Hero, UD, TD	Sil & Anne Sanders
1993:	Beowulf O'Shaughnessy, CDX, TD	Debra Duncan
1996:	Kent's Little Sass N Back, TD	Rita Kline
1997:	Kirkton's Quicksilver Girl, NA, TD	Allison Platt

FLYBALL

Flyball was invented in California in the late 1970s. According to Ian Hogg, Flyball home page administrator, "Legend has it that Herbert Wagner first showed it on the Johnny Carson Show. Soon afterwards dog trainers and dog clubs were making and using Flyball boxes. In the early 1980s the sport became so popular that the North American Flyball Association (NAFA) was formed." There are now associations and competitions for Flyball in North America, the United Kingdom, Europe and Australia.

Flyball is basically a relay race in which two teams (each with four dogs of any breed or combination of breeds) race each other and the clock to jump over four hurdles, retrieve a ball from the Flyball box and return over the hurdles to cross the finish line. The team whose dogs have the fastest times without errors wins the heat and goes on to compete against other teams, until the fastest team wins. The hurdles are 10 feet apart, the first jump is 6

In Flyball, when the start signal is given, each dog in the team of four must jump over four hurdles, push on the flyball box to eject and catch a tennis ball, turn, jump back over the four hurdles and cross the finish line as fast as possible. The Westies shown here are U-CD D'Artagnian's Tartan Lass, CDX, Can. CD, FD ("Dart"), and Ch. Kirkton Connecticut Yankee, FDX ("Duncan"), owned by Kimberly Lohr. *Allison Platt*

feet from the starting line and the Flyball box is 15 feet from the last hurdle. The Flyball box consists of a spring-loaded box that shoots a tennis ball out when the dog jumps on the surface. As soon as the first dog crosses the finish line, the second dog starts, and so on. Competitions are in tournament format, with either double elimination (best of three or five rounds) or round robin, and the first team to win three heats receives a point towards their standing in the tournament.

In addition to team competition, each dog competes for individual titles based on individual times. Flyball is rewarding because a reasonably fast dog can win a title in a single weekend. If you continue to compete, there are eight levels of titles. A point is gained for each run under thirty-two seconds. Five points are gained for each run under twenty-eight seconds (the fastest time recorded so far is 16.93 seconds). The titles and points needed to earn them are as follows:

Flyball Dog (FD)—20 points

Flyball Dog Excellent (FDX)—100 points

Flyball Dog Champion (FDCh)—500 points

Flyball Master (FM)—5,000 points

Flyball Master Excellent (FME)—10,000 points

Flyball Master Champion (FMCh)—15,000 points

ONYX (ONYX award)—20,000 points

Flyball Grand Champion (FDGCh)—30,000 points

The dogs who are best at Flyball are (1) fast; (2) competitive; and (3) crazy about tennis balls. Many of the fastest teams in the world are made up of Border Collies. However, one wrinkle makes the sport competitive for small dogs: The jumps for all four dogs on the team are set to the height of the smallest dog, with an 8-inch minimum height and a 16-inch maximum height. For many teams, this means that the lead dog will often be a small terrier or other competitive small breed (there are many Border Collie/Jack Russell Terrier teams).

Flyball is very exciting to watch. It is like watching horse racing at close range. The dogs get very keyed up about running, and one thing to be aware of is that Flyball practice and competition is *very noisy!* The dogs bark out of excitement when they are getting ready to run or when the are *not* running, because they want to. The handlers yell to speed up their dogs. This is definitely *not* the sport for you or your dog if either of you are sound-sensitive! If you watch the competitive dogs, you can tell that they *know* they are in a race with the dog on the other team: sometimes the lead dog will look over his shoulder to be sure his team is winning, and the second-place dog will try to speed up to catch his opponent.

To compete in Flyball with a Westie, your dog must like to chase tennis balls and not be bothered by the constant commotion that is a part of the sport. If you think your dog might like it but you need to know more, you can get instructions on how to build a Flyball box from NAFA or from the Flyball home page on the Internet. You can also play fetch with the dog and encourage it to bring the ball back to you. Since this is a new sport and still played on a small scale, you will need to find a team to practice with or form your own. Flyball groups are still a little hard to find, but if you contact NAFA you can learn the location of teams or clubs that offer Flyball or where you can go to see a Flyball tournament.

One thing to be aware of in Flyball is that the dogs often get so keyed up and competitive that they can be quarrelsome. You need to be alert, and you need a dog that is not easily intimidated. If you have a lively, brave, fast dog, this could be the perfect sport to expend all its excess energy.

Several Westies have obtained titles from NAFA. Unfortunately, NAFA does not keep records of the full names of dogs, just the call names. Six Westies have FD titles, the same six have earned FDX titles, and two dogs, "Molly," owned by Jenny Kaemmerer, and "Maggie" (Towynridge Once Upon a Time, CD, AAD, Can. CDX, TD), owned by Jane McLaughlin of Canada, are Flyball Dog Champions (FDCh).

THE VERSATILE WESTIE

In 1980, the WHWTCA introduced a trophy known as the Versatile Dog Award. To qualify, the owner must be a member of the club and the dog must have earned titles in three of four areas: Conformation championship, Tracking, Earthdog tests and Obedience or Agility. The list of winners is presented near the end of this section on performance activities, because these dogs represent the best the West Highland White Terrier has to offer: beauty, brains and heart in unlimited measure.

VERSATILE DOG AWARDS

Year	Dog's Name	Owner(s)
1978:	Ch. Skaket's Chunkies, UD, CG	Ernest & Nancy Gauthier
1980:	Windemere of Rosewood, CDX, TD, CG	Mary & Vern Bell
1982:	Ch. Rime's Alicia Aquena, CDX, TDX, CG	Sil & Anne Sanders

1983:	Ch. Rime's Gamble Ag'in, CDX, TD	Sil & Anne Sanders
	Ch. Politician O'Peter Pan, CD, CG	Tom & Barbara Barrie
1985:	Ch. Renie's Tina Colada, CD, CG	Renie Springarn
	Ch. Heritage Farms Jenny Jump Up, CD, CG	Marjadele Schiele
	Ch. Royal Scott's Lady Abigail, CD, CG	Dawn Martin
1986:	Ch. Laird Doon Macduff of Helmsdale, CD, TD	Vicki Beets
	Ch. Dawn's Up N Adam, CDX, CG	Dawn Martin
	Ch. Donnybrook's Trudy CD, CG	Shane & Scott Albee
1987:	Ch. Happymac's Dear Abby, CD, CG	Nancy Herman
	Rime's Bonnie Bridie, CD, TD, CG	Frank & Lyn Hickey
	Kyle Cuillan O' Holyrood, CDX, TD, CG	Hilary Mercer
	Ch. Firepath's Andsome Endeavor, CD, CG	Cathleen Blattler
	Ch. Skaket's Candy Man, UD, TD, CG	Nancy & Mitzi Gauthier
1988:	Ch. Lord Derbyshire, CD, TD	Patricia Berndt
	Ch. Skaket's Taffy, CD, CG	Mitzi & Nancy Gauthier
	Ch. Clydesdale's Mae Westie, CD, CG	Sandra & Adrian Radziwon
1989:	Ch. Olac Moonraider, CD, CG	William & Ann Theberge
	Ch. Rime's Cameron McLean, CD, CG	Kathleen Nelson
	Ch. Skaket's Katie, CD, CG	Mitzi Gauthier
	Ch. Rime's Quonquering Hero, CDX, TDX, CG	Sil & Anne Sanders
1990:	Ch. Dawn's Baby Goosenberry, CD, CG	Kathleen Latz

1990	Ch. MacCord's Bonny Cassandra, CD, CG	Janice Nanus
	Ch. Parsons Frasher of Pandwyck, CD, CG	Marleen Burford
1991:	Ch. Skaket's Kit Kat, CDX, TD, CG	Nancy Gauthier & Mitzi Beals
	Ch. Rime's Off To See The Wizard, TD, CG	Sil & Anne Sanders
	Ch. Wee Mack's Kelsey of Kirkton, CDX, TD, CG	Allison Platt
	Beowulf O'Shaughnessy, CDX, TDX, CG	Debra Duncan
1992:	Ch. Skaket's Lord Toby Tweedmouth, CD, TD, CG	Catherine Padyk
	Camrick's Peaches And Cream, CD, TD, CG	Cheryl Gauthier
1993:	Ch. Dawn's Sabella Vanilla, CD, CG	Stephanie Capkovic
	Ch. Skaket's Baker's Joy, CD, TD, CG	Patricia Berndt
	Ch. Paddyhill's White Chocolate, CDX, CG	Robert & Susan Masch
	Ch. Borgo's Princess Yoda of D and D, CD, CG	Deborah Borgo
1994:	Ch. Rose-N-Roy's Island Warrior, CD, CG	Thelma Johnston
	Ch. B-Jay's Ms Bright N' Breezy, TD, CG	Patricia Berndt
	Ch. Penelope O'Peter Pan, CD, CG	Thomas & Barbara Barrie
	Ch. Hayastan Highland King, CD, JE, CG	Louie Herczeg & Dawn Martin
	Ch. Dawn's Kit N' Kaboodle, CD, JE, CG	Dawn Martin & Patti Marks

1995:	Ch. Forbes' Macduff The Bold, CD, JE, CG	Christine Forbes
1996:	Ch. Sandalwood's Flash O'Brybern, CD, JE, CG	M. & R. Brooks & Berna Gaul
	Skaket's Guess Who, CD, TD, JE	Nancy Gauthier
1997:	Ch. TipTop's Elementary My Dear, CD, NA, JE	Sherron Corner & Marjorie Conway
	Ch. Cedarfell Milk-N-Honey, CD, JE	Angeline Austin
	Ch. Lonach Devill Demon, CD, TD	Nancy Gauthier

Starting in 1997, the rules for qualification for a Versatility title were changed slightly. To qualify, the dog must now have titles in three categories. One of the categories must be either Conformation or Earthdog, and the other qualifying categories include Agility, Tracking and/or Obedience. This rule change places Agility in a separate category from Obedience and recognizes that correct conformation and ability to hunt are both essential elements of breed type in West Highland Whites.

SOURCES OF INFORMATION

To obtain information and literature about any of the sports discussed in this chapter, including rules and regulations, as well as the names of clubs that offer classes and/or events for the activity in which you are interested, write to the individual organizations that sponsor the activities. A list of organizations and addresses is provided below. This information is usually available at no charge or for a nominal fee.

Another great source of information is the Internet. The home page addresses are provided for the organizations listed below if they are known. In addition to these sites, there are many other organizations and individuals who provide web sites with information on training, seminars and events offered in these activities. Some sites also provide book lists, reviews and answers to FAQs (computer-speak for Frequently Asked Questions) that are particularly helpful to newcomers. There are also Internet forums where people who train in these events have free-wheeling discussions about topics of interest. Because servers, listings and forums on the Internet change frequently, it is recommended that you use one of the web browsers to find information on the activities that interest you. For instance, a quick weekend afternoon search for information on Agility identified hundreds of web sites, forums and articles. Use key words such as "dog Agility" or "Tracking." Many of the sites provide services such as listings of upcoming shows and complete

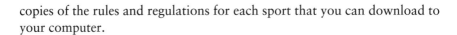

copies of the rules and regulations for each sport that you can download to your computer.

Organizations

American Kennel Club (AKC)
Mailing Address: 5580 Centerview Drive
Raleigh, NC 27606-3390
Phone: 919-233-9780 or fax 919-233-3627
Web Address: http://www.akc.org

Information on AKC rules, upcoming events and member clubs. Brochures about Obedience, Agility, Tracking and Earthdog Trials are one dollar each from the above address with SASE.

West Highland White Terrier Club of America (WHWTCA)
Mailing Address: Anne Sanders, Corresponding Secretary
33101 44th Avenue NW
Stanwood, WA 98292-7106
Phone: 360-629-3615 or 0-700-4WESTIE
Web Address: http://pages.prodigy.com/westie

General information about the Westie and how to reach local clubs, breeders, performance activities and rescue groups. Information is now being compiled for the home page about Westies in performance activities.

United Kennel Club (UKC)
Mailing Address: 100 East Kilgore Road
Kalamazoo, MI 49001-5598
Phone: 616-343-9020
Web Address: none yet, but one is being created

Information, member clubs, rules and registration forms for UKC Obedience and Agility events.

North American Dog Agility Council (NADAC)
Mailing Address: HCR 2, Box 277
St. Maries, ID 83861
Phone: 208-689-3803
Web Address: http://www.teleport.com/~jhaglund/index.html

Information, member clubs, rules and registration forms for NADAC Agility events. Rules are ten dollars, or twelve dollars including membership.

United States Dog Agility Association (USDAA)
Mailing Address: P.O. Box 850955
Richardson, TX 75085-0995
Phone: 214-231-9700
E-mail Address: info@usdaa.com
Web page address: http://www.usdaa.com

Information, member clubs, rules and registration forms for USDAA Agility events.

North American Flyball Association (NAFA)
Mailing Address: P.O. Box 8
Mount Hope, ON, L0R 1W0
Canada
Web Address: http://www.cs.umn.edu/~ianhogg/Flyball/Flyball.html

Information about Flyball, names of teams in your area, official rules, national and international standings.

RECOMMENDED READING

This is a very short list of recommended books and videos that the author has found to be helpful for those training terriers in general, and Westies in particular. Because many of these books and tapes are self-published, they can be difficult to find. One excellent source for most of these books and tapes is the Direct Book Service, phone 800-776-2665, or e-mail at dgctbook@ cascade.net.

The DBS web address and on-line catalog is at http://www. dogandcatbooks.com.

General Training and Conditioning Techniques

Benjamin, Carol Lea. Mother Knows Best: The Natural Way to Train Your Dog. Howell Book House, New York, NY. This book provides insight into the way dogs learn to help you train your dog more effectively.

Pryor, Karen. *Don't Shoot the Dog! The New Art of Teaching and Training.* Simon & Schuster, New York, NY. This is an approach to training that emphasizes positive reinforcement.

Cecil, Barbara, and Gerianne Darnell. *Competitive Obedience Training for the Small Dog.* T9E Publishing, Council Bluffs, IA (self-published). This book is useful because, although it addresses Obedience training only, it presents many excellent tips and tricks for training small dogs.

Clothier, Suzanne. *The Clothier Natural Jumping Method.* Flying Dog Press, Stanton, NJ. Tape also available. This book presents a very useful approach to training your dog to jump.

Clothier, Suzanne. *Your Athletic Dog.* Workbook and tape also available.

Zink, Chris. *Jumping from A to Z, Teaching Your Dog to Soar.* Canine Sports Productions, Lutherville, MD.

Agility

Simmons-Moake, Jane. Agility Training, Fun Sport For All Dogs. Howell Book House, New York, NY. This is regarded by most Agility enthusiasts as the best and most useful book on the sport for the novice.

Daniels, Julie. *Enjoying Dog Agility.* Doral Publishing, Wilsonville, OR.

Tracking

Ganz, Sandy, and Susan Boyd. Tracking From the Ground Up. Show-Me Publications, St. Louis, MO. Videotape, Tracking Fundamentals with Sandy Ganz, also available. Clearly written and illustrated, this is the best introduction to Tracking for the novice.

Johnson, Glen. *Tracking Dogs: Theory and Methods.* Arner Publications, Rome, NY. This 1977 book is a classic, and although many people find the proposed training schedules unrealistic, there is much to gain from reading the book.

Thompson, Donna, and Julie Hogan. *Practical Tracking for Practically Everyone.* Cross Junction, VA (self-published). This is a helpful manual with a practical approach to Tracking that recognizes that most people cannot train every day.

Flyball

Olson, Lonnie. Flyball, The Dog Sport for Everyone. This paperback was published in 1987 and the information in it is slightly out of date, but it was the first book on flyball and the only one available for many years.

Parkin, Jacqueline. *Flyball Training, Start to Finish.* Alpine Publications, Loveland, CO, 1996. This large-format paperback was just released and has not been reviewed, but since there is so little in print on the subject, it is worth mentioning.

Payne, Joan. *Flying High: The Complete Book of Flyball.* KDB Publishing Co., 1505 Kenilworth Place, Aurora, IL 60506. This book was published in 1996 and is more up-to-date than Morgan's book. Includes sections on skill development, problem solving, conditioning and equipment.

Also, consult the Flyball home page on the Internet for the address of the Flyball mailing list, as well as newsletters from NAFA and the British Flyball Association.

Earthdog Tests

Migliorini, Mario. Dig In! Earthdog Training Made Easy. Howell Book House, New York, NY. A 1997 publication, this book gives the rules for Eathdog tests, profiles the eligible breeds and tells how to prepare a dog for the tests. It also includes personal sidelights from the author's life with working terriers and some interesting historical background.

There is at least one other book about Earthdog tests at the time this book went to press. The rules for AKC Earthdog tests are available from the AKC address listed in this chapter, or on the AKC home page on the Internet. Until more information is available, the best way to learn about Earthdog tests is to attend one.

Most Westies are blessed with life long vigor and good health. There are, however, certain disorders known in the breed and the conscientious owners will become informed regarding these disorders for their dog's sake.

chapter 11

Westie Health
By Anne C. Sanders

While the Westie is generally a healthy, hearty dog, there are a few tips that will keep your Westie in the best possible shape. Preventative care is the first line of defense against accidents and illness. Regular observation and care will alert you to possible problems while they are still minor and treatable. Should your Westie become ill or simply grow infirm with advanced age, good veterinary care and careful nursing will help him recover quickly and/or live out his life as comfortably as possible.

PREVENTION

Prior to bringing your new Westie home, and throughout his life, you will need to look for and be alert to any possible danger and potential for accidents. It helps to view your home, yard and any other areas your Westie will frequent through its eyes. Look down low, on your dog's level, and imagine what sort of things might be oh so interesting for an active, inquisitive puppy to play with. Be particularly aware of electrical cords, poisonous plants and any other items that would be unsafe toys for a dog. Just like a toddler, a Westie is quick, he likes to put things in his mouth, and he loves to chew and dig!

Check out your fencing. A small puppy can escape through an extremely small hole. He is also capable of making a tiny hole bigger . . . after all, he is an earth dog. Swimming pools can be a death trap for any dog, and a small Westie may not be able to learn to climb the stairs. It is best that your Westie never be allowed access to a pool area—even if people are present. In addition, while some Westies have been taught to swim, chlorinated water is not healthy for their skin and coat. Jumping off of laps, chairs, retaining walls, etc., is another dangerous activity for a small dog. A rule of thumb is not to let your Westie jump off of anything it cannot jump onto. All jumping should be avoided until the dog is grown and sufficiently mature. Young bodies are not ready for the stress that jumping puts on the joints.

It is important to feed your Westie a well-balanced diet. A high-quality kibble will give him all the nutrients he needs to grow strong bones and a sturdy body. Be careful not to feed a food that is too high in protein (over 26 percent for dry food), as it seems to be too "hot" for a Westie and may contribute to skin problems. Sometimes additional oil is required to keep his skin healthy. Up to a teaspoon of corn oil per cup of kibble may be just what your dog needs. Your Westie's breeder will recommend appropriate foods and may provide a small supply of the food your Westie is currently eating. Most of the better foods are available through your local pet supply store or pet food dealer. While many people leave dry kibble available at all times (free feeding), it is best to feed your Westie measured meals at the same approximate time each day. It is easier to monitor your dog's eating habits, and you will notice any changes that may indicate that he is not feeling well.

While it is very tempting to give a Westie treats, it is important to keep his figure trim. An overweight dog is more susceptible to some illnesses, such as pancreatitis, and obesity influences adult onset diabetes and heart disease. Your dog should not be too thin either, but you should always be able to feel his ribs under a well-muscled body.

Dogs, like other mammals, are susceptible to a variety of internal parasites. They may or may not cause disease, but should be prevented and controlled in order to keep your Westie in peak health. A few of them are transmittable to humans and cats. You will need to consult your veterinarian for diagnosis, treatment and prevention. Roundworms (ascarids, hookworms, whipworms, threadworms, stomach worms, eyeworms and heartworms) are the most common of the internal parasites. Some of these are more prevalent in certain parts of the country, and your Westie's breeder and veterinarian can advise you which are common to your area. All except eyeworms and heartworms are diagnosed by fecal analysis and are safely treated with oral medications or injections. Heartworms now occur at some level throughout the United States. Since heartworm infestation can be a serious, even life-threatening problem, it is best to rely on preventative medication. Diarrhea that is not responsive to home treatment may indicate that your Westie has coccidia or giardia. Your veterinarian can diagnose and prescribe medication to treat these protozoans.

No chapter on health is without some words of advice on flea control. Many Westies, like many other dogs, are allergic to fleas. They are actually allergic to the flea saliva that is injected into their skin when the flea bites them. In addition, fleas are hosts to the immature tapeworm. When a dog eats a flea while chewing and scratching, it ingests the tapeworm, which takes up residence in the intestine. These are two powerful reasons to control fleas. Good flea control begins with the environment (your yard, house and especially the areas where your dog sleeps). It is important to understand that fleas must first bite the dog if medications given internally to kill fleas or inhibit their reproduction are to be effective. If your Westie is highly allergic, you may need to include additional flea control measures to avoid flea allergy dermatitis. Other external parasites to watch for are ticks, lice, mites and flies. Consult your breeder and/or veterinarian for the necessary and appropriate control of fleas and other external parasites.

And now the "E" word. Yes, just like you and me, our dogs need exercise for a healthy body and to relieve stress and tension. A well-exercised Westie will be less apt to develop behavior problems and will have a healthier heart and lungs too. Besides, unlike some of us, Westies usually *love* to go on walks or jogs, or to just chase a ball. Some Westies will exercise themselves while chasing a squirrel from the yard or playing with another canine companion. Others will spend the day as a couch potato, waiting for your return to join it in its favorite activities.

So, get out the leash and go for a stroll together. A Westie in excellent condition can easily walk one or two miles. Remember to start with short outings and build up to longer ones. Westies love to be with you and will really make a valiant effort to keep up, so you must be careful to not overdo. The carriage of a dog's tail is a good clue to his condition. If it is up and wagging happily when you start off, you may notice it start to droop as the dog tires. Just like you, he will not be able to go as far or as quickly if it is warmer than normal, and his feet may get burned on hot pavement or frozen on icy ground. Neither of you should be exercising after a big meal. Remember, you are your Westie's personal trainer, and he looks to you for encouragement as well as sensibility in its exercise program.

The last and simplest item of preventative care is your dog's annual veterinary examination and proper vaccinations. The breeder from whom you purchase your Westie and/or your veterinarian can advise you on the best vaccination schedule for the various diseases from which it must be protected. Immunization to canine distemper, hepatitis, adenovirus cough, parainfluenza, leptospirosis, parvovirus and rabies are considered mandatory by most professionals. Other vaccines are available for coronavirus, Lyme disease and bordetella (kennel cough). You may also want to consider preventative medication for heartworm, depending on where you live. Your Westie's breeder should provide you with a complete record of all vaccinations and wormings given along with recommendations for further treatments. There are various schedules that different breeders and veterinarians recommend. It is best to follow their advice, since recommended schedules and vaccines change over the years.

MAINTENANCE

It is helpful to be aware of your Westie's normal habits, because any change may indicate that he is not feeling up to par. Make mental notes on how much and how quickly your dog eats, how much water he consumes, his bathroom habits (frequency and quantity) and activity level. Any sudden change without obvious cause should raise a red flag.

Grooming is important to your Westie's health as well as appearance. Brushing stimulates circulation to the skin and improves skin and coat condition. Keeping nails and the hair between the pads trimmed makes for more comfortable and stronger feet. Weekly brushing of the teeth and gums will keep them healthy and aid in keeping the dog's breath pleasant.

Daily and weekly grooming routines also offer an opportunity to monitor your dog's health. By regularly examining your Westie, you will be able to note any problems or changes in his condition before they become serious. While grooming or petting your dog, you can quickly note his weight, the clarity of his eyes and the cleanliness of his ears. Check for any lumps, sores or foreign objects that may become imbedded in his skin, feet or ears. If this type of examination is begun when he is a puppy, your Westie will become accustomed to it and will even enjoy the added attention.

CARE

It is important to find a veterinarian whom you trust and with whom you have good communication. You can get referrals from your breeder and from friends who have small dogs. Responsible veterinarians will welcome your questions, give you a tour of their facilities and explain their services completely. Ask about after-hours and emergency care. Also, don't be afraid to ask for referrals to specialists if you think you might need further diagnoses and specialized services. Your local veterinarian treats several to many species, such as cats, birds, reptiles and exotics, and cannot be expected to be highly trained in all of the specialties any more that your own general practitioner. Just as your family doctor relies on specialists in a variety of disciplines, your family veterinarian should be willing to suggest specialists when your Westie could benefit from those services.

You should also invest in some tools for the care of your Westie at home. Buy a good book (see Bibliography for suggestions) that covers the basics of canine health care and first aid, and keep it handy. It will be a valuable help in conjunction with the advice and directions you receive from your veterinarian. You will also want to have a thermometer reserved for your dog. If you suspect an illness, take his temperature (following the instructions in the aforementioned book). A Westie's normal temperature is approximately 101.0 to 102.5 degrees Fahrenheit. By having this information when you call, your veterinarian and/or emergency clinic will be better able to advise you. Also, some dogs get "veterinary clinic fever," a false high temperature caused by excitement and stress. By taking his temperature at home, you can help the doctor provide a more accurate diagnosis for your Westie. Keep the phone number of your local or regional poison control hotline available for emergencies and some antiseptic soap and spray for treating superficial wounds.

Should your Westie become ill, you may need to provide home nursing care. If your Westie is accustomed to a crate and exercise pen, set them up as temporary quarters in a warm, draft-free area and keep the dog confined if necessary. It is very important to follow your veterinarian's instructions regarding the time and amount of medication to be given. Make sure you understand them completely (it helps to have it in writing) before you leave the office. Westies can be very clever about separating and discarding a pill from the "goodie" in which it is hidden. Therefore, it is helpful to learn how to give pills without the aid of treats, just in case. If your dog has been trained to let you examine its mouth, it is not difficult to put a pill in the back of the mouth, gently hold the muzzle closed and stroke its throat until it swallows. Then, don't forget to tell the dog quietly how good it was!

One more suggestion, if you are providing nursing care: Keep a log of your Westie's progress and the time and amount of all food and medication given. This is especially helpful if you are sharing the nursing duties with another family member. It is surprising how quickly we can forget whether or not the dog got its pills, especially when we are tired. Westies are usually appreciative of our love and care, so following through on necessary treatment should be relatively easy.

Suggested books for bibliography that are related to health:

The Well Dog Book, by Terri McGinnis, Random House, New York, NY.

Dog Owners Home Veterinary Handbook, by Delbert G. Carlson, DVM & James M. Giffen, MD, Howell Book House, New York, NY.

WESTIE DISEASES

Inherited diseases occur in all breeds of dogs, just as they do in people. The number of reported diseases in any given breed correlates highly with the popularity of that breed, because in order for a disease to be reported, the dog usually must be seen at a veterinary school clinic. There are more than 350 inherited diseases that occur in various pure breeds and mixed breeds, and approximately thirty-seven of them are reported to occur in Westies. This is about the average number for any breed. Westie lovers are lucky that most of these diseases occur early in life and do not have extremely high levels of frequency.

It is helpful to be aware of the diseases that are known to occur in a particular breed, because it helps breeders and veterinarians come to a quicker diagnosis and proceed with the necessary treatment. While the list may appear long and scary, it is important to remember most Westies are not affected by serious illness. In fact, some of the genetic anomalies are not detrimental to the health, happiness and longevity of the Westie. A large percentage of people are near-sighted, but we do not consider them to be ill or defective. Similarly, a Westie with an undershot bite is perfectly healthy, although it may not be a candidate for show ring honors. In general, the serious diseases do not occur in great numbers in Westies. All of the skin diseases combined are the breed's greatest problem.

CHOOSING A HEALTHY COMPANION

You should be aware that the West Highland White, like any other breed, is subject to certain diseases or anomalies. When you interview breeders and look at puppies, don't be afraid to ask questions about the health of their dogs and those they have produced in the past. Ask them what diseases they screen their stock for. Do they do test matings to identify carriers? Do they keep records on their litters and follow them throughout their lifetimes? You may ask about health guarantees, but once a puppy is taken home, most owners are reluctant to part with the dog should it become ill. Therefore, it is probably more important to ask the breeder about his or her policy regarding the treatment costs, should your puppy develop one of the inherited diseases known to exist in the breed.

Some anomalies, such as bad bites and missing teeth, are basically cosmetic in nature. If you acquired your Westie as a pet and do not intend to use it for breeding, they are of no consequence. Other anomalies do not cause any pain or suffering and are corrected with a simple surgical procedure. For instance, an inguinal hernia is usually not serious and can be surgically repaired when the puppy is neutered, or a retained testicle can be removed during neutering. There are no residual effects. You may need to decide if you will be willing to provide care and love for a dog that needs short-term or long-term care. Craniomandibular osteopathy (CMO) is a disease that requires short-term treatment, as described below. Legg-Calvé-Perthes may require surgery and rehabilitation. It may also cause the dog to develop arthritis later in life. Skin problems can be the most difficult to treat and often recur every year or may require continuous treatment for the life of the dog.

Should your Westie contract a serious disease at any time in its life, the breeder will want to know. It is very important to cooperate with your veterinarian and breeder to insure an accurate diagnosis. By incorporating this information into his or her breeding records, a breeder can then try to reduce the possibility of producing additional dogs with the same problem. Emotions can become charged when a beloved pet becomes ill or a champion brood bitch produces a genetic fault, but by working together, veterinarians, breeders and pet owners can provide the best outcome for the affected dog and the future of the breed. Every pet owner can help the breed by registering genetic health information with the appropriate open registry. The information then becomes available to all breeders to use when they are breeding dogs related to yours.

MOST COMMON DISEASES

A complete list of genetic diseases as reported in the veterinary literature appears at the end of this chapter. The following are some of the most common and more serious anomalies.

Atopic dermatitis (synonyms: canine atopic dermatitis, canine inhalant dermatitis, allergic inhalant dermatitis) is the inherited ability to form reaginic antibodies against environmental allergens and to express clinical allergic signs to these allergens. Additional signs are reversed sneezing, discoloration of the coat, bilateral conjunctivitis, erythema (reddening), papules and alopecia (hair loss). Typical allergens are dander; pollens of grasses, weeds and trees; house dust; and molds. In approximately 75 percent of cases, the disease appears in individuals between 1 and 3 years of age, and in a few cases may occur before twelve months of age. Antihistamines are effective in a small percentage of cases, and progress is being made in improving the effectiveness of hyposensitization injections. The common treatment is corticosteroids. The prognosis is variable, depending on the specific allergen(s) and sensitivity of the animal. The disease is clearly inherited, but the exact mode of inheritance has not been determined.

Cleft palate is a condition in which the palate (roof of the mouth), which separates nasal and oral cavities, is not completely closed. The cleft palate of the type seen in Westies is formed when the two bony plates of the hard palate fail to fuse normally in the fetus. This disorder is present at birth. Prognosis is poor, and puppies born with cleft palates are usually euthanized shortly after birth. Breeding studies in Westies have shown that the trait is polygenic (requiring more than one gene to cause the trait to appear).

Copper toxicosis (CT) in Westies is due to an error in copper metabolism that allows copper to accumulate in the liver, resulting in cirrhosis of the liver; it can be fatal if not treated. The disease is usually well advanced before the first clinical signs (symptoms) are observed. Early in the disease, the dog may have elevated alanine aminotransferase (ALAT) and alkaline phosphatase (AP) levels. As copper continues to accumulate, the dog may show weight loss, listlessness, anorexia, vomiting, abdominal pain and sometimes jaundice. Onset of clinical signs varies greatly, but they usually occur in dogs four years of age or older. Dogs diagnosed with CT can be treated with zinc therapy or Cupramine. Both medications require veterinary supervision. The prognosis of treated animals is good. The mode of inheritance has not been determined for Westies.

Craniomandibular osteopathy (CMO) is a noncancerous growth of bone on the lower jaw bone or over the angle of the mandible and tympanic bulla.

The bony growth can occasionally occur on other parts of the cranium, and the radius and ulna may also be involved. Early in the disease there is an in-flammatory component. The disease is most often recognized between the ages of 4 and 7 months, but it can occur as early as 3 to 4 weeks and, rarely, as late as 9 to 10 months. The puppy usually expresses pain around the jaw, mouth or skull. Definitive diagnosis is made by radiograph. The treatment of choice is corticosteroids or other anti-inflammatories, which may need to be continued until the puppy is 10 to 14 months old. Low dosage and rela-tively short-term usage make the treatment safe. The prognosis for recovery is excellent in all but the most serious cases. The disease is inherited as a simple autosomal recessive trait. (Autosomal recessive means that it can occur in either sex, and both parents of an affected animal carry the gene for the dis-ease.)

Epidermal dysplasia (synonym: armadillo syndrome) is a disorder that begins with reddening and itching of the skin, especially on the feet, the legs and the ventral parts of the body. With time the dog's skin becomes thick-ened, black, greasy and malodorous, which has led to the eponym "Arma-dillo Westie Syndrome." Armadillo syndrome appears at a few weeks to a few months of age. Treatment of the symptoms has varying levels of success and requires dedication of the owner. Euthanasia is recommended in the majority of cases. The mode of inheritance has not been determined.

Globoid cell leukodystrophy (synonym: Krabbe's disease) is a degenera-tive disease of the white matter of the brain and spinal cord. It is the result of a genetic deficiency of an enzyme that is involved in the breakdown of cer-tain fats in the brain and spinal cord. Clinical signs begin as early as four weeks of age and nearly always before five to six months. Lack of coordina-tion, weakness, stumbling, loss of control of the hindquarters and tail trem-ors may be observed. Signs progress rapidly; there is no treatment, and the disease is invariably fatal. The disease is autosomal recessive. There is a DNA test that identifies affected and carrier animals.

Hip dysplasia (HD) is a widespread degenerative disease of the hip joint. It involves the improper fit of the head of the femur into the hip joint socket of the pelvis. Due to the size and weight of Westies, it seldom requires treat-ment. It is inherited as a polygenic trait.

Inguinal hernia is a disorder in which the abdominal organs, omentum or fat protrude through the inguinal ring, forming a skin-covered sac in the groin. It can be bilateral or unilateral. It may be self-correcting, but if it per-sists and is severe enough, it may be corrected by surgery. Inguinal hernias usually develop before 12 weeks of age. The mode of inheritance has not been determined.

Juvenile cataracts is any opacity of the ocular lens or its capsule that has an early onset. These cataracts develop in animals less than 6 months old. There is no treatment, and blindness is the outcome. The mode of inherit-ance has not been positively determined, but it is thought to be autosomal recessive.

Keratoconjunctivitis sicca (KCS) (synonym: xerophthalmia, dry eye) is an acute or chronic inflammatory disease of both the conjunctiva and cornea resulting from decreased tear production. Affected animals may have almost continuous squinting, with intense reddening and inflammation. The disease appears between 4 weeks and 12 years of age. Cyclosporine is the treatment of choice, and new veterinary drugs are available that are quite effective. Results are variable, and treatment may be required for life. The mode of inheritance has not been determined.

Legg-CalvP-Perthes (synonyms: Legg-Perthes, osteochondritis deformans juvenilis, avascular necrosis, coxa plana) is a noninflammatory avascular necrosis of the femoral neck and head that usually occurs in small breeds of dogs. The first sign of the disease may be irritability, which progresses to a chronic hind limb lameness of apparent sudden onset. The age of onset is typically 3 to 11 months. Diagnosis is made by radiograph. While very mild cases may not be noticed, severe cases require surgery, which is generally successful. However, some arthritis may develop as a result. Breeding studies in West Highland Whites and Poodles have shown the mode of inheritance to be complex and probably polygenic.

Luxated patella (synonyms: slipped patella, slipped kneecap, slipped stifle) is a disorder in which the patella slips out of the trochlear groove, usually to the inside of the leg. The disease usually occurs at 4 to 5 months of age. Restriction of activity may mediate the problem, but surgery is often required. With treatment, the prognosis for a complete recovery is good. The mode of inheritance has not been determined for Westies.

Pulmonary fibrosis (synonym: Westie lung disease) produces radiographic changes in the lungs. The blood gases are abnormal, showing hypoxia, or lack of oxygen to the tissues. This disease is seen in some middle-aged to older Westies but does not seem to be a problem in other breeds. Clinical signs are troubled, rapid breathing and in some dogs, an unexplained cough. The cause is unknown. Treatment, such as bronchial dilators, can comfort the dog. Affected dogs can live for months or years, depending upon the severity of the disease. At this time, there is not enough information available to determine whether this is a disease or a normal part of the aging process in terriers. While there is evidence of familial cases, whether the disease is genetic and, if so, the mode of inheritance is not known.

Seborrhea (synonyms: idiopathic seborrhea, dirty puppy disease) is characterized by scaly, oily patches adhering to the skin. Lesions may be most severe on elbows, hocks and ears. Typically local lesions are hairless, scaly patches with dark centers surrounded by a reddened area and flaking keratin rim. They generally occur on the trunk and chest. The primary type usually occurs in very young puppies. However, some cases develop after one year of age. Secondary non-inherited forms can occur anytime but are usually seen in adults. Treatments are varied, as is their success. Dedication and persistence by the owner may result in reasonable control. The mode of inheritance has not been determined.

WHAT BREEDERS CAN DO

First, breeders need to be aware of all of the various diseases that occur in the West Highland White. They also need to keep accurate records on their dogs and all of the puppies their bitches and stud dogs produce. Depending on the tests available and the mode of inheritance of the trait or disease, different strategies can be followed to reduce the incidence of disease while improving the type and structure of the puppies produced.

It is extremely important to have accurate diagnoses of any and all anomalies. For example, it is critical that the veterinarian, breeder and owner know the difference between hip dysplasia and Legg-Perthes. They are two distinct diseases, and the breeder cannot possibly reduce the incidence of Legg-Perthes if he or she is told a dog produced hip dysplasia. It is also extremely important that a disease not be labeled genetic if the neurological signs are caused by a poison rather than an inherited enzyme deficiency. By developing good communication with puppy buyers and by insisting on accurate diagnoses from the attending veterinarian, the serious breeder will be able to maintain accurate records on his or her stock.

Breeders should screen their breeding stock for the various diseases that affect their breeds. Many breeders of the large breeds routinely have their dogs' hips radiographed, and other breeders have their dogs' eyes examined for genetic defects. Westies can be radiographed to screen for hip dysplasia, Legg-Perthes and luxated patella. There is a DNA blood test that can identify carriers of globoid cell leukodystrophy. Eyes can be examined for PRA. Test matings can be done to identify carriers of CMO. All of these tests cost money, but serious breeders who do screen their stock can be more confident of their puppies' health and the fact that they will enhance the value of their stock.

Record keeping is another very important task that can help Westie breeders improve the health of the breed. Open registries are an important tool that the Westie breeder can use to record and retrieve genetic health information. By knowing which dogs produce and, more importantly, which dogs do not produce a specific disease, a breeder can breed healthier puppies. Open registries will allow breeders to keep valuable animals in the breeding pool even though they carry one or more genes for disease "A," because it allows the breeder to learn about dogs that do not carry genes for disease "A." The American Kennel Club is providing funding assistance for the Institute for Genetic Disease Control (GDC), a multiple-breed open registry, and is encouraging breeders to share health information openly. The GDC cooperates with national breed clubs to provide an open registry service for various genetic diseases so that breeders can work together to improve the health of their respective breeds.

Diseases Occurring in West Highland White Terriers
(as reported in the Veterinary literature)

Excerpted, with permission, from Inherited Diseases of Terriers, by George A. Padgett, DVM

System

Disease   Mode of Inheritance
Brief Description

Eye Diseases

Cataract   Recessive, Polygenic
Lens opacity, which obscures vision and may cause blindness

Keratoconjunctivitis sicca (KCS, dry eye)   Unknown
Inadequate tear production causing irritation of the conjunctiva and cornea

Lens Luxation Recessive   Unknown
Dislocation of the lens from its normal site behind the cornea (partial or complete)

Microphthalmia   Unknown
An anomaly in development causing the eyeball to be abnormally small

Progressive Retinal Atrophy (PRA)   Recessive, Unknown
Degeneration of the retinal vision cells which progresses to blindness

Neurologic Diseases

Deafness   Dominant, Recessive, Unknown
Inability to hear; may be unilateral or bilateral

Epilepsy   Unknown
Seizures commonly called fits; they recur generally closer together

Globoid cell leukodystrophy (GCL, Krabbe's) Recessive
Collection of fatty material in brain cells due to lack of an enzyme, leads to ataxia, usually fatal

Hydrocephalus   Polygenic
Accumulation of fluid in the brain causing severe pressure and degeneration of the brain

Scotty cramp   Recessive
Muscle cramps triggered by excitement or exercise; you may see a rabbit-like, hopping gait

White Shaker dog syndrome   Unknown (may by viral)
Generalized tremor, usually of the whole dog which worsens with excitement, may see nystagmus and seizures

Hard Tissue Diseases

Cleft Lip/Cleft Palate   Polygenic
A fissure in the roof of the mouth and upper lip, may be present together or separately

Craniomandibular osteopathy (CMO)   Recessive
Abnormal growth of bone on the lower jaw, on the back angle of the lower jaw, on the head, or on the extremities, any or all sites

Crooked tails   Recessive?
Abnormal bend or crook in the tail

Hemivertebra   Recessive
Abnormal formation of the body of the vertebra, can cause posterior ataxia and paralysis

Hip dysplasia   Polygenic
Abnormal formation of the hip socket, causes rear limb lameness

Legg-Calvé -Perthes Polygenic
Aseptic necrosis of the head and neck of the femur, causes rear leg lameness

Overshot bite   Polygenic?
Upper jaw extends beyond lower jaw

Patellar luxation (slipping stifle)   Recessive, Polygenic
Poor development of the structures holding the patella (knee cap) in place, usually medial (inward) in small breeds

Undershot bite   Polygenic?
Lower jaw extends beyond the upper jaw

Respiratory & Alimentary Diseases

Copper toxicosis (CT)   Unknown
Abnormal deposition or accumulation of copper in the liver, causes cirrhosis; may be relatively mild or severe enough to cause death

Portosystemic shunt (extrahepatic)   Polygenic, Unknown
Born with extra vessels, which allows blood to bypass the liver

Pulmonary fibrosis (Westie lung disease)   Unknown
Seen in middle-aged to older Westies, the disease is indicated by troubled, rapid breathing, and sometimes a dry cough.

Behavioral Diseases

Aggressiveness (excessive)   Unknown
Excessively assertive or forceful with other dogs or people, may attack or bite without reasonable provocation

Blood, Heart & Immune Diseases

Pyruvate Kinase deficiency (PK)   Recessive
Absence or low levels of an enzyme (pyruvate kinase) essential for the production of red blood cells; causes anemia

Subaortic stenosis (SAS)   Polygenic
Narrowing at the base of the aorta by a fibrous band, causes murmurs, weakness and sudden death

Selective IgA deficiency   Unknown
Lack of IgA immunoproteins, which defend against infections allowing repeated lesions to occur in the skin and lungs

Dermatologic, Endocrine, & Muscle Diseases

Atopic dermatitis   Unknown
Roughened, itchy, oozing skin caused by immune reactions to various allergens such as fleas or pollen

Icthyosis   Unknown
Scaly, thickened, roughened skin; also called alligator skin

Inguinal hernia   Recessive?, Unknown
Out pouching of skin in the area of the inguinal ring, which may contain viscera; a scrotal hernia is a type of inguinal hernia; Very common disorders in dogs and probably occur in most, if not all, breeds

Seborrhea (dirty puppy disease)   Unknown
Weepy, greasy skin due to excessive production of sebum, dirt sticks to it

Seborrhea (greasy skin, adults)   Unknown
Weepy, greasy skin due to excessive production of sebum; May be the same disease as the puppy seborrhea, but occurring later

Umbilical hernia   Recessive?
Out pouching of skin over the "belly button"; may contain abdominal viscera, may regress spontaneously; Very common disorders in dogs and probably occur in most, if not all, breeds

Diabetes mellitus (adult onset)   Unknown
Excessive sugar in the blood and urine due to a lack of insulin

Hypothyroidism   Recessive
(autoimmune thyroiditis, lymphocytic thyroiditis, Hashimoto's disease)
Destruction of the thyroid gland due to an attack from the animal's own immune system causes rough, scaly skin; hair loss; weight gain

Myotonia (dystrophic myopathy)   Unknown
Muscles continue to contract after voluntary movement ceases causing a stiff gait

Reproductive & Urinary Diseases

Cryptorchidism   Recessive?, Unknown
Absence of testicles in the scrotum due to retention in the abdomen or inguinal region, may be one or both sided or may slide in and out of the scrotum; Very common and probably occurs in most, if not all, breeds

Ectopic ureters   Unknown
The ureters do not properly attach to the bladder causing urine dribbling

chapter 12

The Ageless Westie

The official Standard of the West Highland White Terrier calls for a *hardy looking terrier*. The first-time owner often asks, after a few months of ownership, when his or her puppy will cease being a puppy and become an adult; the long-time owner, with a twinkle in his eye, responds with "Oh, give him about fifteen years." It is not unusual to see a Westie in his teens frolicking with the spirit of an adolescent and, when the owner of an older Highlander decides to purchase a puppy so that, upon the occurrence of the inevitable, there is another Westie in the household, they often find that the older "puppy" has had years added to his life.

Determining the oldest of the breed is difficult—while there is a report of a dog who lived to 25 years of age, no one appears to be able to identify that dog. There are many who are known to have been part of their families for more than two happy decades.

The following are among the older dogs whose accomplishments can be substantiated:

Ch. Shirley Bliss of Belmertle, a bitch, finished her championship at the age of 10 in 1949. Born June 20, 1939, she was by Ch. Charan Minstrel out of Allana Phyllis, bred by Mr. and Mrs. George H. Shears of Hutchinson, Kansas, and owned by Dr. Douglas A. Tyler of Texas.

Am., Can. Ch. Poolmist Philoralia of Valucis, by Poolmist Pauchtie out of Olac Moongirl, was whelped on November 7, 1980, and imported from Scotland by handler Denis Springer in the spring of 1989. In September 1990 he was Winners Dog and Best of Winners at the WHWTC of Greater New York Specialty show, thereby making him the oldest Westie to win the points at a Specialty show; the next weekend, at the WHWTCA Specialty with the Montgomery County Kennel Club, he won the Veteran Dog class and made the cut in Best of Breed competition for his owner, Sandy Davis of Lanarkstone

Am., Can. Ch. Poolmist Philoralia of Valucis, owned by Sandy Davis and shown by Denis Springer, truly demonstrated the qualities of a laster. In addition to making some impressive wins, "the General" left behind a number of quality offspring.

Ch. Biljonblue Belle of Katydid, owned by Nancy Guilfoil and bred by Sylvia Kearsey and Biljonblue Kennels, was noteworthy in the show ring and in the heart of her devoted owner.

Westies. "The General" finished his American title on January 13, 1991, and his Canadian title a few months later.

Ch. Highland Mercury finished his championship in 1953 at the age of 8, six years after his full-litter brother Ch. Highland Ursa Major had completed his title. Born on August 26, 1945, he was bred in Canada by Rosamond Billett; his sire was Can. Ch. Belmertle Aldrich and his dam, Edgerstoune Star Dust. He was owned by Dorothy Pubols of Colorado.

Ch. Briarpatch Raggamuffin, born on September 5, 1972, was Best of Breed from the Veteran Bitch class at the WHWTCA annual Specialty on October 7, 1979, under breeder-judge Dorothea Daniell-Jenkins and handled by her breeder-owner, Barbara Goss. Incidentally, her sire, Ch. Rudh're Glendenning, born May 3, 1971, was shown in the Veteran Dog class the same day. Among the bitches present in the Veterans class that day was Sylvia Kearsey's Pillerton Pickle, born June 15, 1961; there were no dry eyes watching that 18-year-old exhibit her own no small amount of self-esteem that day.

Ch. Glenfinnan's Something Dandy, born October 28, 1982, won the breed from the Veteran Dog class at the annual specialty show of the WHWTCA on October 6, 1991, under breeder-judge William Ferrara. Shown through a successful career by handler Mark George, "Nicky" was on this day handled by his co-owner, James Boso. Nicky, sired by Ch. Whitebriar Jeronimo out of Ch. Craigty's Something Special, was entered in the Veteran Dog class for the 1997 Roving but died unexpectedly ten days before the show, on February 26, 1997.

Ch. Skaket's Candy Man, CD, born on April 5, 1979, won the breed at the 1981 annual Specialty show of the WHWTCA and went on to a Group fourth at Montgomery County KC. "Buster," now sporting the CDX, TD and CG titles, returned to the same show with his breeder-owner-handler, Nancy Gauthier, on October 9, 1988, for breeder-judge Neoma Eberhardt, who gave him his second WHWTCA Best of Breed from the Veteran Dog Class. He then went on to a Montgomery Group second. Not one to rest on his laurels, Buster won his Utility Degree in October 1992 at the age of 12½.

Ch. Monsieur Aus Der Flerlage, born on November 17, 1962, won the breed from the Veteran Dog Class at the WHWTCA Roving Specialty Show on June 3, 1972, under breeder-judge Barbara W. Keenan; he went on to win Group second at the all-breed Fox River Valley show of which that Roving was a part. "Bobby" was owner-handled to this win, as to his other achievements, by Bergit Coady.

Ch. Olac Moondrift, an import bred by Derek Tattersall and owned by Pat Darby, won the Veteran Dog class at the 1984 Roving Specialty show of the WHWTCA and went on to capture the breed under breeder-judge Patricia Storey. By Ch. Backmuir Noble James out of Miranda Moon of Olac, he was whelped January 25, 1977. He went on to obtain his Canadian title after this victory.

Ch. Holyrood's Hootman O'Shelly Bay, by Ch. Glenfinnan's Something Dandy out of Ch. Holyrood's Ms. Mayhem, won the Breed from the Veteran Dog Class at the 1997 WHWTCA Roving Specialty show, thereby retiring the Eng. Ch. Pillerton Peterman Memorial Trophy offered for three wins for a dog under the same ownership. "Manley," born November 28, 1987, already had two legs on the trophy by virtue of having won at the Roving Specialties of 1990 and 1991. His owners, James H. and Elizabeth J. Boso, in 1991 retired both the Tom Drexler Memorial Challenge Trophy and the Clifford Hallmark Memorial Challenge Trophy offered at the Annual Specialty show of the WHWTCA, with two of the legs on those trophies also coming courtesy of Manley. All three of his Roving wins came under Westie breeders Robert Shreve, Mary Torbet and James Eberhardt.

Ch. Elfinbrook Simon, a multiple Best in Show and Specialty winner, came out of retirement one month short of his tenth birthday to win another Specialty Best at the 1968 West Highland White Terrier Club of California Specialty under Derek Rayne, handled by his owner, Barbara Keenan.

Ch. Biljonblue's Belle of Katydid, born on December 26, 1981, won the Veteran Bitch class at both the Roving and National Specialty shows of the WHWTCA in 1990. Bred by Sylvia Kearsey and Biljonblue Kennels, Kristy was owned by Nancy Guilfoil.

Ch. Ashgate Alistair of Trewen, born on December 19, 1986, a multiple all-breed Best in Show winner, was Best Veteran in Show at the Chester Valley Kennel Club all-breed show in May 1994. Co-owned by Martha Black and Angeline F. Austin, "Alistair" succumbed to cancer in June 1997.

Ch. Principals MacGyver, born October 19, 1986, a multiple all-breed Best in Show winner in 1990, was awarded Best Veteran in Sweepstakes at the WHWTCA annual specialty on October 7, 1995, while a daughter born November 16, 1994, was awarded Best Puppy in Sweepstakes at the same event.

Ch. Whitebriar Jollimont, born April 20, 1981, was awarded Best Veteran in Sweepstakes at the first Veteran Sweepstakes competition of the WHWTCA on October 3, 1992, at the age of 11½; in the five years this event has been recognized, "Monty" is thus far the most senior of the winners of this popular competition.

Ch. Heritage Farms Jenny Jump Up, born on April 18, 1973, did not enter the show ring until she had already whelped eighteen puppies; after getting her championship in one month, she went on to become a multiple Best in Show winner. At age 10 she got her Companion Dog degree, and at the age of 13 she won her Certificate of Gameness.

Am., Ber., Can. Ch. Forbes' MacDuff the Bold CD, JE, CG, whelped January 28, 1985, won the Veteran Terrier Group at the all-breed Hochelaga Kennel Club show on May 18, 1996, for his owner, Christine Forbes. "Mickey's" first title was the CG, earned when he was 3; he later went into the conformation ring and was 5½ when he got his championship. He earned his Companion Dog title at the age of 10 and his Junior Earthdog title when 10½; at the age of 12, he was training in tracking. A housemate, Cassie, earned her JE title at the age of 11.

Ch. Punch O'Peter Pan, CG, born April 4, 1969, was the oldest Westie (and quite possibly the oldest dog of any breed) to earn a Certificate of Gameness from the American Working Terrier Association, doing so at a trial in Georgia at 13 years, seven months and two days of age in November 1982. His breeder-owners were Thomas H. and Barbara Barrie.

Wee Geordie MacPeg, CDX, JE, CG, born on June 30 1982, was the first West Highland White Terrier to earn a Junior Earthdog title, doing so on January 22, 1995 at the age of 13½, handled by owner Mary Kuhlman.

Ch. Cedarfell Milk-N-Honey, owned by Mrs. A. Fleming (Angeline) Austin, and **Ch. Dawn's Peaches and Cream,** owned by Patti Marks and Dawn Martin, each got their Junior Earthdog titles at the age of 10. Just a month after celebrating birthday 11, Peaches won the WHWTCA's Veteran Sweepstakes competition on October 5, 1996.

Ch. Penelope O'Peter Pan, CD, CG, born July 23, 1984, got her Companion Dog title at the age of 10 for proud owners Thomas and Barbara Barrie.

Whether in the Conformation or Obedience ring, whether pursuing the breed's original purpose or curled up in front of a roaring fire or on an adoring owner's lap, the West Highland White Terrier is, indeed, ageless.

Ch. Snowbank Same O'l Shenanigan, owned by Daphne Gentry—everyone owns one special dog.

Parting Thoughts

This volume has addressed at length the achievements of those West Highland White Terriers that have done this and won that. You have heard about the first Westie to come to the United States, the first Westie to win an all-breed Best in Show, the Westies who have produced the most champions, the Westies who have won the most Specialty shows and all-breed Bests and the Westies who have excelled in the various areas of performance events.

But, for you, the reader, the most important West Highland White Terrier in the world is the one who has won your heart. And so I end with the Westie who initiated me into this wonderful, and sometimes wacky, world of Westies: Ch. Snowbank Same Ol' Shenanigan. Whelped by Martha and Cliff Replogle on May 23, 1974, by Ch. Laird Brig-A-Doon MacDuff out of Snowbanks Whispering Wind, Shane entered my life on October 6, 1974. Not my first Westie—that was Highlands Buttermilk Skye (1972–1976)—Shane was my first show dog and my first champion. He produced only one champion, but Ch. Snowbank Song of Killundine produced four champions, including a multiple Best in Show winner. Shane and I shared laughter and tears, ice-cream cones and fried chicken for almost sixteen happy years. When he crossed the Rainbow Bridge on August 6, 1990, Shane left my home but never my heart.

Int., Am., Norw., Dan., Nordic, Dutch, Swed. Ch. Oaklund's Max Mekker, a Norwegian import owned by Penny-Belle Scorer, getting into some good reading. *Richard Mason*

Bibliography

This bibliography of Westie literature was compiled by Daphne Gentry, with the assistance of Anne Sanders, Lois Drexler, Wayne Kompare and Dianne Conway. A bibliography of recommended reading is appended to the chapters on training and health.

Ackerman, Lowell, DVM. *Dr. Ackerman's Book of West Highland White Terriers*. Neptune City, NJ: T.F.H. Publications, Inc., 1997 (96 pages, illustrated, hardcover).

Bolle-Kleinbub, Ingrid. *West Highland White Terriers*. Hauppauge, NY: Barron's Educational Series, 1994 (64 pages, index, illustrated, paper, translated from German).

Buckley, Holland. *The West Highland White Terrier, A Monograph*. London: Link House, 1911 (48 pages, illustrated, hardcover).

This, the first book devoted solely to the breed, is quite rare.

Cartledge, Joe, and Liz Cartledge, editors. *The Complete Illustrated West Highland White Terrier*. London: Ebury Press, 1973 (136 pages, index, illustrated, hardcover).

Cleland, Sheila. *Pet Owner's Guide to the West Highland White Terrier*. New York: Ringpress Books Limited, 1995 (80 pages, illustrated, hardcover).

Dennis, D. Mary, and Catherine Owen. *The West Highland White Terrier*. 7th ed. London: Popular Dogs Publishing Co., Ltd., 1986 (204 pages, index, illustrated, hardcover).

The first edition was published under Mrs. Dennis' name in 1967 and subsequent editions appeared in 1970, 1973, 1976, 1979 and 1982. This most recent edition was published with an additional chapter and revisions by Ms. Owen.

Dennis, George B. *A Photographic History of the West Highland White Terrier Club of England.*

Diana, Donatella. *Il West Highland White Terrier.* Milan, 1993 (204 pages, index, illustrated, paper, in Italian).

Faherty, Ruth. *Westies from Head to Tail.* Loveland, CO: Alpine Publications, Inc., 1981 (220 pages, index, illustrated, hardcover).

Flamang, Inga. *West Highland White Terrier.* Kosmos Hundebibliothek, Dusseldorf, 1995 (140 pages, illustrated, hardcover, in German).

Hands, Barbara. *All About the West Highland White Terrier.* London: Pelham Books, Ltd., 1987 (160 pages, index, illustrated, hardcover).

————*A Westie Sketchbook.* Preston, England: Bernard Kaymar Ltd, 1986 (unpaged, illustrations, hardcover).

————*The West Highland White Terrier.* Edinburgh: John Bartholomew & Son, Ltd., 1977 (96 pages, index, illustrated, paper).

Hasslegren, Birgitta. *WESTIE!* NYA förlaget, 1984 (72 pages, illustrated, hardcover, in Swedish).

Johns, Rowland, editor. *Our Friend, The West Highland White Terrier.* London: Methuen & Co., Ltd., 1935 (86 pages, illustrated, hardcover).

This was the second book devoted to the breed.

Martin, Dawn. *A New Owner's Guide to West Highland White Terriers.* Neptune City, NJ: T.F.H. Publications, Inc., 1996 (160 pages, index, illustrated, hardcover).

Marvin, John Tasker. *The Complete West Highland White Terrier.* New York: Howell Book House, Inc., 1961 (256 pages, illustrated, hardcover).

This, the first book devoted to the breed published in the United States, is divided into two parts. The first, contained in 126 pages and written by Mr. Marvin, has ten chapters on the breed; the second part, written by Milo G. Denlinger and revised by A.C. Merrick, is on more general topics of concern to the dog owner.

————*The Complete West Highland White Terrier.* 2nd ed. New York: Howell Book House, Inc., 1967 (288 pages, illustrated, hardcover).

Again, this edition is divided into two sections, with the first part on the breed and written by Mr. Marvin taking up 160 pages; the second part is called "General Care and Training of Your Dog" and is co-authored by Elsworth Howell, Milo G. Denlinger and A.C. Merrick.

————*The Complete West Highland White Terrier.* 3rd ed. New York: Howell Book House, 1971 (256 pages, illustrated, hardcover).

The general care information has been eliminated from this edition and a trimming section added.

————*The Complete West Highland White Terrier.* 4th ed. New York: Howell Book House, 1977 (256 pages, illustrated, hardcover).

McCandlish, W.L., and B.W. Powlett. *The Scottish Terrier and (A Chapter on the) West Highland White Terrier.* Manchester: Our Dogs Publishing Co., Ltd., 1909 (80 pages, illustrated, paper).

Nicholas, Anna Katherine. *The Book of the West Highland White Terrier.* Neptune City, NJ: T.F.H. Publications, 1993 (222 pages, index, illustrated, hardcover).

Pacey, May. *West Highland White Terriers.* London: W. & G. Foyle, Ltd., 1963, reprinted in 1971 (90 pages, index, illustrated, hardcover).

Schneider, Earl, ed. *Know Your West Highland White Terrier.* New York: The Pet Library, Ltd., n.d. (64 pages, illustrated, hardcover).

Sherman, Mrs. Florence. *How To Raise and Train A West Highland White Terrier.* Neptune, NJ: T.F.H. Publications, Inc., 1982 (96 pages, illustrated, paper).

Tattersall, Derek. *Westies Today.* New York: Howell Book House, 1992 (160 pages, illustrated, hardcover).

Wallace, Martin S. *Guide to Owning A West Highland White Terrier.* Neptune, NJ: T.F.H. Publications, 1995 (64 pages, illustrated, paper).

Weil, Martin. *West Highland White Terriers.* Neptune, NJ: T.F.H. Publications, 1984 pages, illustrated, hardcover).

Weiss, Seymour. *An Owner's Guide to a Happy Healthy Pet: The West Highland White Terrier.* New York: Howell Book House, 1996 (160 pages, illustrated, hardcover).

West Highland White Terrier Club of America. *Illustration & Clarification of the West Highland White Terrier Standard.* n.p., n.d. reprint 1997 (28 pages, illustrated, paper).

Wright, Roger. *West Highland White Terrier: An Owner's Companion*. Ramsbury, Wiltshire, UK: Crowood Press, 1992 (256 pages, index, illustrated, hardcover).

A SELECT BIBLIOGRAPHY OF JUVENILE LITERATURE

Where Is My Puppy? Derrydale Books, 1994 (10 pages, illustrated, hard paper cover).

Adler, C.S. *With Westie and the Tin Man*. New York: Macmillan Publishing, 1985 (194 pages, hardcover).

Aldin, Cecil C.W. *Mac*. London: Humphrey-Milford, 1972 (97 pages, illustrated, hardcover).

———*Gyp's Hour of Bliss*. London: Collins Clear Type Press, (192 pages, illustrated).

———*Rough and Tumble*. London: Humphrey-Milford, 1910. (24 pages, illustrated).

———*Jock and Some Others*. New York: E.P Dutton, 1912, (Unpaged, illustrated).

Becker, Patricia Ann. *My Friend Judy*. n.p.: Harcourt Brace & Company, n.d. (12 pages, illustrated by Deborah Borgo, paper).

Cameron, Katharine. *Iain the Happy Puppy*. Edinburgh: The Morah Press, 1934. (88 pages, illustrated, hardcover).

Chase, Catherine. *Duncan McTavish in Switzerland*. New York: Dandelion Press, 1978 (28 pages, illustrated, paper).

Cline, Paul, and Judythe Sieck. *Ginger's Moon*. Medlicott Press, 1990 (30 pages, illustrated, hardcover).

De La Roche, Mazo. *Portrait of a Dog*. Boston: Little, Brown, and Company, 1930 (200 pages, illustrated, hardcover).

Gini (Virginia E. Daniels). *Meet MacGregor*. Tacoma, WA: Mercury Press, 1975 (100 pages, illustrated, paper).

Gray, Lucile M. *Tammy's Tales*. New York: Vantage Press, 1969 (38 pages, illustrated, hardcover).

Hilton, Nette. *Prince Lachlan*. New York: Orchard Books, 1989 (30 pages, illustrated, hardcover).

Johnson, Margaret S., and Helen Lossing. *Runaway Puppy*. New York: Harcourt Brace and Company, 1942 (88 pages, illustrated, hardcover).

Little, Jean. *Mine for Keeps*. Boston: Little, Brown and Company, 1962 (186 pages, illustrated, hardcover).

———*Spring Begins in March*. Boston: Little, Brown and Company, 1966 (156 pages, hardcover).

Meredith, Elizabeth Gray. *A Terrier's Tale*. Boston: Houghton Mifflin Company, 1920 (48 pages, illustrated, hardcover).

Merrill, Flora. *Kippy of the Cavendish*. New York: Robert M. McBride & Company, 1934 (288 pages, illustrated, hardcover).

Potter, Beatrix. *The Fairy Caravan*. Philadelphia: F. Warne & Company, 1929 (191 pages, illustrated, hardcover).

Quigg, Jane. *Jenny Jones and Skid*. New York: Oxford University Press, 1947 (100 pages, illustrated, hardcover).

Turner, Marjorie. *Gallant and Dopey*. London: Raphael Tuck & Sons, Ltd., n.d. (unpaged, illustrated, hardcover).

Wells, Rosemary. *Lucy Comes to Stay*. Dial Books for Young Readers, 1994 (24 pages, illustrated by Mark Graham, hardcover).

———*McDuff and the Baby*. Hyperion Books for Children, 1997 (24 pages, illustrated by Susan Jeffers, hardcover).

———*McDuff Comes Home*. Hyperion Books for Children, 1997 (24 pages, illustrated by Susan Jeffers, hardcover).

———*McDuff Moves In*. Hyperion Books for Children, 1997 (24 pages, illustrated by Susan Jeffers, hardcover).

Wolman, Judith. *Duncan McTavish in Paris*. New York: Dandelion Press, 1979 (30 pages, illustrated, paper).

Zeplin, Zeno. *Clowns to the Rescue*. Nel-Mar Publishing, 1993 (48 pages, illustrated, hardcover).

Zeplin, Zeno. *Popcorn Is Missing!* Nel-Mar Publishing, 1990 (36pages, illustrated, hardcover).

POETRY

Strong, Patience. *Thumper: The Musings of a West Highland White Terrier.* London: Frederick Muller, 1984 (56 pages, illustrated, hardcover).

YEARBOOKS OF THE WEST HIGHLAND WHITE TERRIER CLUB OF AMERICA

1950. John T. Marvin, editor.

1952–1953. John T. Marvin, editor (52 pages).

1955–1956. John T. Marvin, editor (66 pages).

1909–1959. *The Golden Anniversary Edition.* John T. Marvin, editor (68 pages).

1961–1962. John T. Marvin, editor (82 pages).

1962–1966. John T. Marvin, editor (118 pages).

1966–1969. John T. Marvin, editor (166 pages).

1970–1975. Barbara Keenan, Edward Keenan, Don Frederick, editors (204 pages).

1976–1981. Seymour Weiss and Bernard Rosenthal, editors (274 pages).

1981–1985. Wayne Kompare, editor (280 pages).

1985–1990. Joan Graber, editor (346 pages).

1990–1995. Anne Pyle and Joan Graber, editors (492 pages).

Index